VERTICAL PLEASURE

Vertical Pleasure

the secret life of a tax man

Mick Fowler

CORONET BOOKS
Hodder and Stoughton

Copyright © 1995 by Mick Fowler

Maps drawn by Martin Collins.

The right of Mick Fowler to be identified as the Author of
the Work has been asserted by him in accordance with the
Copyright, Designs and Patents Act 1988.

First published in Great Britain in 1995 by Hodder & Stoughton
First published in paperback in 1996 by Hodder & Stoughton
A division of Hodder Headline PLC

A Coronet paperback

10 9 8 7 6 5 4 3 2 1

ISBN 0 340 66006 6

Printed and bound in Great Britain by
Cox & Wyman Ltd, Reading, Berkshire

Hodder and Stoughton
A division of Hodder Headline PLC
338 Euston Road
London NW1 3BH

To George for starting me off,
all those with whom I have had so many great days climbing,
and, in particular, to Nicki, Tess and Alec
who have had to put up with my irrepressible urge to go climbing

CONTENTS

ILLUSTRATIONS

Education with George: Idwal Slabs, Skew Ghyl
Sea cliffs of the South-West: puking fulmar, Henna
Southern chalk: Great White Fright, Dover
Winter weekends: London escapees, Cryogenics, Cold Hole
Taulliraju: Chris Watts on day three
Spantik: the approach from Nagar
Sea stacks, *Deflowerer*, Skeleton Ridge, A'Chailleach
Cerro Kishtwar: approach, day two
Some travelling companions: author, Sustad, Saunders, Watts,
  Morrison

MAPS

1

Education with George

Poor Ian was never really a climber; in fact he was never really an outdoor enthusiast at all. My grandmother always assured me (much to my irritation) that he had 'fine limbs' but this alone seemed not to be a qualification for enjoying a life grappling with the joys of nature. Personally I felt he had rather fat limbs and, being a somewhat precocious child, never tired of saying so. I had however been close friends with Ian since nursery days. He was a ginger tousle-haired child with a mischievous sense of humour reminiscent of William in Richmal Crompton's books. Although we ended up at different schools our friendship continued in the holidays and our early adventures tended to be planned together. As those consisted of exploring the local sewage system or cycling at night (without lights) up the M1, George, my father, felt that perhaps a rather more hygienic and less dangerous pastime was called for.

He had always had an interest in the outdoors, but living in the rather rundown North London suburb of Harlesden with no car had been a major handicap which consigned escape to the hills to his annual holidays from the printers where he worked. Finances were also a problem. Pre-war expeditions to the Alps tended to be on a 'one-off' basis and trips further afield were definitely out.

Ironically, as was the case with many British servicemen, it was the 1939–45 war which was to give him the opportunity to visit other parts of the world and to develop his love of exploration, other cultures and, most importantly for me, mountain environments. In retrospect he was perhaps rather fortunate to have survived the war and in fact seems to have had rather a good time. Despite volunteering for front-line duties at various intervals, his most memorably unpleasant experience was digging up an old toilet area with his bare hands whilst trying to fashion a pillow out of North African sand dune many miles away from the nearest water supply. This left a marked impression (and odour) and distinctly spoiled his war until a combination of poor eyesight in one eye and good fortune saw him being posted to South Africa where the Drakensberg mountains provided unlimited recreational possibilities in what appeared to be unlimited recreation time. A subsequent stint in Ceylon (now Sri Lanka) and then northern India gave him a more varied diet of outdoor pleasure and a distant first sight of Everest.

The bug had bitten, so to speak, but it was to be thirty-five years before he would see the Himalayan giants again. Marriage to my mother immediately after the war was followed by much hill-walking in Britain and, the highlight of this era, a guided walk up the Allalinhorn (4027m) near Zermatt. My arrival in 1956 put a brake on such extravagances. Then my mother's sudden illness and tragic death in 1959, followed almost immediately by my father's redundancy from a supposedly secure job, were hardly events likely to result in a surge in recreational activity.

My grandmother moved in, ostensibly to replace my mother as best she could, and gradually George's enthusiasms came to the fore once more. Along with Arthur and Tony, a couple of friends of his from the printing trade, he used to pay intermittent visits to the sandstone outcrops around Tunbridge Wells, with me continually pestering him to include the eight-year-old Fowler body in such activities. Initially he was reluctant, but as our childhood games became increasingly dangerous the time came when it was clearly safer for us to be engrossed in vertical excitement under the parental wing rather than being left to our own devices.

There was, however, one final obstacle to the start of my climbing career – my father's Reliant Supervan Mark III. I could never understand why he insisted on being the proud owner of one of these vehicles and took delight in emphasising the camaraderie involved in waving to fellow Reliant three-wheeler owners. This vehicle was the overriding embarrassment of my schooldays and I would spend hours dreaming up schemes to avoid being seen anywhere in it. Those few friends who knew of the vehicle's existence referred to it disparagingly as 'the Spazwagon', a name which I always felt to be eminently suitable.

It was a sort of putrid blue colour – Aztec blue was, I believe, the exact tone. Having no interior lining, it was possible to see the ribs and veins of the fibreglass and get the feeling of being truly at one with the road, or exposed to the elements, depending on one's interpretation. Almost overriding the fibreglass factor was the lack of a fourth wheel. My father assured me that this was a good point in that it saved money by allowing him to tax the vehicle as a motorbike and drive it on a motorbike licence. Personally I tended to notice more its unnerving habit of lurching round corners.

Altogether I felt it was a rather inauspicious vehicle in which to start my climbing career. Thus there was nothing else for it but to start climbing either on my own or with someone from the small circle of friends who already knew of the Spazwagon's existence.

Ian expressed the most interest and was duly persuaded to join me. It is true to say that he did not really possess a rock-climber's physique. I was soon to discover that having 'fine limbs' compared to my 'thin scrawny ones' (my grandmother again) did not seem to be an advantage when grappling in the depths of narrow slimy rock chimneys in the sandstone outcrops just south of London. The choice of my first climbing experience was in the hands of my father and so I suppose he can be held responsible for Ian not exactly taking to the sport in a very enthusiastic or effective manner

High Rocks, two miles west of Tunbridge Wells, was the scene of these early exploits. It is the highest of the sandstone outcrops and one which was ultimately to become my favourite. Lying in the private grounds of the High Rocks Inn, a fee is charged for climbing, and this combined with its northerly, slow-drying aspect made it one of the least frequented of south-east England's sandstone outcrops. In the mid-1960s it was known primarily for its horrifically undergraded chimney climbs and two isolated buttresses. George and his friends were just about soloing at the standard necessary to get a rope to the top of the two isolated rock towers – the Isolated Buttress and Hut Boulder. Leading was (and still is) very much frowned upon and the usual thing was to solo to the top and rig up a rope around either a tree or, in the case of Hut Boulder, a cemented-in iron ring. After considerable grovelling, one of the adults would stand victorious on top and having arranged the rope down a climb, would then abseil down to the ground and in the true spirit of High Rocks retreat to the tea hut for refreshments. The ropes would hang forlornly, inviting action of some kind. As swings they were ideal and soon we boys were on the receiving end of some serious verbal abuse whilst adults tried in vain to untangle our swing ropes. Our efforts did indeed create an impressive tangle. Solving the problem from below was often out of the question and on one memorable occasion I remember Arthur shaking his way tenuously back to the top whilst Ian and I kept a low profile and sneaked away to explore the other excitement on offer. For a youngster, the dark passages of High Rocks seem to exert an irresistible pull. The endless possibilities for squirming through semi-dark narrow slits, hiding round the innumerable corners and wallowing in the sand, dirt and rare mosses gave me many happy childhood memories.

On this particular occasion we ended up at the east end of the rocks beneath a notably repulsive cleft called Boa Constrictor Chimney. The name is perhaps apt: a slimy two-foot-wide fissure runs thirty feet back into the cliff face. Being heavily shaded it is seldom dry. Today I see that it receives little attention from intrepid climbers. In the 'sixties things were different; the days of designer Lycra were many years away. One's success, or otherwise, as a climber seemed to be gauged by the general scruffiness of one's equipment and the cultivation of a dishevelled 'hard man' look. Boa Constrictor Chimney was ideal for giving clothes that well-worn look and bringing a colour to the face which generally conveyed the impression that one had been well exercised. To be well exercised and dirty was deemed to be 'good'.

Anyway, having abandoned the adults and their tangle of ropes on the Isolated Buttress, it was at the foot of this chimney that we were eventually tracked down by a rather annoyed father who had spent the last hour or so nosing around the depths of the passages failing to appreciate the joys of youthful exploration or find his son.

Ian had banana sandwiches for lunch, caringly prepared by Mrs Roffe who could not have been expected to foresee what her poor son would be put through. For some unfathomable reason, Boa Constrictor was one of George's favourite climbs at High Rocks. He presumably felt that finding us at the foot of the route indicated that we wished to climb it; or perhaps it was a desire to inflict some perverse sort of punishment that led him to rig up a top rope on this greasy horrorshow. Either way the end result was unfortunate for Ian. As well as being greasy the chimney is initially overhanging on both sides and a tremendous effort is required to struggle up to a horizontal break which provides the first respite at fifteen feet. Ian's fine limbs appeared to slip easily over the slime and despite much furious activity little progress was evident. On a more positive note, dirt and grazes were liberally spread all over his knees and elbows as the 'hard man' look was becoming apparent. Ian seemed unable to appreciate this. Grovelling and grunting noises were interspersed with occasional pleas of 'Let me down!' which, of course, no one else was able or willing to hear.

The episode gradually drew to a slithering climax as, with a despairing gushing sound, the contents of Ian's stomach were ejected on to the already slimy walls of the chimney. Half-digested banana and High Rocks slime appeared to be a combination notably lacking in friction, and upward progress was promptly reversed into a friction-free slide back to the ground. Boa Constrictor was not attempted again that day.

Mrs Roffe was perhaps used to her son being impregnated with banana-flavoured vomit but she had not met the penetrating quality of High Rocks slime. George was quizzed about how to wash it out and Ian did not come climbing again!

George, though, persevered. Having lost my mother when I was three, he was rather lumbered with me and, not put off by Ian's rapid exit from the climbing scene, moved on to such exploits as hauling a small and frightened Fowler Junior up a wide variety of modestly graded but memorably exciting climbs.

Away from the South-East, Scotland appeared to be his favourite area. A combination of slow roads and the Spazwagon factor inevitably meant that two precious days were necessary for the journey from London to the Highlands. The journeys were punctuated by my father's renderings of 'Oh I'll take the high road and you'll take the low road and I'll be in Scotland afore ye', whilst I sat looking generally bored and wondering how the Spazwagon could possibly hope to get there before anyone. Being of that tiresomely inquisitive and questioning age, I was quick to observe that the wording of this famous ditty seemed not to stand up to scrutiny.

It was blatantly obvious that the A74 (the low road) provided the quickest way to Scotland and it seemed ludicrous to me that we should be wasting time fumbling about in the Scottish border towns instead of getting on to the real road and pressing down on the accelerator pedal. George, however, was not to be persuaded and the trips north were inevitably made up of a series of traffic jams in Hawick, Selkirk, Jedburgh and so on as he blasted his tuneful rendition through open windows and I hid below window level so as to avoid seeing the reflection of myself in the Spazwagon in the plate glass of the shop windows as we passed by.

Although I did not realise it at the time, this bonny country was also where my future climbing partner Victor Saunders was at that very moment suffering even greater embarrassment than mine. Royal sycophants may consider he should have felt honoured but somehow Victor never seems to have felt very proud at being chastised by Prince Charles for cycling across the forecourt at Gordonstoun School. Needless to say, such thoughts have inspired me through many a distressing moment on later occasions.

Overall though, the Spazwagon did us well; it successfully made many trips to Scotland, shielding us from both rain and midges. George had a marked enthusiasm for hill-walking with a touch of 'scrambling' thrown in. This could mean we tackled anything from walking up Ben Nevis in summer to desperate grappling with ice-encrusted sections of the Skye Ridge in spring.

I particularly recall the one occasion when I ever saw him genuinely 'gripped'. The date must have been back in the mid-'sixties. The Spazwagon had safely managed the 630 miles to Skye in two days and had with ingenuity negotiated the two plank bridges of the single-track road to arrive at the Glenbrittle campsite in the heart of the Cuillin Hills. Years later it was a drive that we would manage regularly for the weekend, but twenty-five years ago I regarded it as something of an exploratory expedition. George was engrossed in a long-standing project to drag me along the Cuillin Ridge missing out the most difficult bits. Such a project is not an easy one to define, as the definition of a 'difficult bit' is open to considerable interpretation. Obstacles such as the Bhasteir Tooth and the Thearlaich Dubh Gap were classed as 'too difficult', whereas by the mid-1960s the long side of the Inaccessible Pinnacle (moderate grade) was clearly classed as worth a try. Rigged up with a traditional waist belay, I was duly positioned at a stance at the foot of the difficulties from where I could witness my father's every move and theoretically be ready and prepared to halt any death-defying plummets. It had never really sunk home before that a leader fall was anything other than an inconceivably remote possibility. On this occasion though, a steady shaking from above revealed that all was not well. The appearance of a large crowd of over-interested walkers did not ease the situation.

'Are you all right? Traverse left a bit. I think you've passed the crux.'

George seemed not to respond positively to this series of helpful interjections. The rope continued to transmit uncomfortable sensations whilst a judderingly hesitant descent interspersed with loud whispers of 'watch me', 'take in' and other less repeatable comments enthralled the avid onlookers. A final semi-controlled leap saw him arrive rapidly back at the belay ledge to a round of appreciative murmurs from below.

Such exposure to the masses seemed not to be George's idea of fun and climbing visits to frequented areas became few and far between. Instead I found myself experiencing a forced introduction to climbs like Bentley Beetham's routes in Borrowdale. Bentley Beetham was active in the Lake District, and Borrowdale in particular, for forty years from the 1920s through to the 1950s. A schoolteacher from Barnard Castle, he delighted in the exploration of new crags and is credited with the discovery of Shepherds Crag in Borrowdale. Though a talented climber, he was unusual in that he also relished the prospect of unearthing easy routes from beneath copious quantities of vegetation and stringing together a series of pitches connected by vegetated walking. He wrote prolifically and some of the route descriptions in his 1953 Borrowdale guide, which formed George's Bible at the time, are the antithesis of today's crisp blow-by-blow accounts which leave so little room for uncertainty. Here is his description of North Buttress at Shepherds Crag:

North Buttress – about 150 feet – Very Severe.
On the only known ascent of this fine challenge the climber spent ten hours a virtual prisoner on the crag. The route followed, if it could be plotted, would look like maniacal hieroglyphics, but eventually he crawled out at the top – an ascent had been made but no route found!

No one was credited with that first ascent and it is hardly surprising that on numerous trips to Shepherds Crag in the early 'seventies I never saw anyone on it.

A lot of Beetham's routes were never really popular. George, however, seemed to find the easier ones ideal introductory routes, 'away from the crowds' as he put it.

Troutdale Introductory sticks in my memory. Current guide books have long since given up trying to describe its tortuous path up Black Crag, Borrowdale via a series of short rock steps and challenging vegetation. Every Easter without fail would find us grappling up the steeply vegetated hillside, referring hopefully to the guide book in an unsuccessful attempt to pinpoint our location. Occasionally climbers would appear on steep clean pieces of rock to one side or the other. Their confused looks said it all. I became adept at avoiding eye contact and stared inanely at the vegetation. George meanwhile cursed the guide book, which insisted on describing everything in relation to the vegetation (hardly surprising), and valiantly fought his way upwards.

We used to stay at the Langstrath Hotel in the picturesque village of Stonethwaite where George would enthral the Easter clientele of old ladies with tales of our daring deeds. Several of the Easter guests at the hotel were there every year and lived in Keswick, just a few miles down the road. The fact that they could enjoy a holiday so close to home was inconceivable to me. Their average age must have been in the region of eighty and their understanding of the urge that led to my father dragging a wiry twelve-year-old up steep areas of vegetation appeared limited. He always went to great lengths to emphasise the safety precautions taken, which, to the best of my memory, consisted of a length of old hawser-laid rope, some very heavy steel karabiners and ancient hawser prusik loops which he had once carried around on glacial walks in the Alps. Accidents were somehow averted on the steep bits but, as always seems to be the case, our closest shave was whilst descending relatively easy ground on a zigzag track down Stanger Ghyll above Stonethwaite.

I had a marked enthusiasm for cairn-building at this time and would grace even the most obscure Lakeland trails with remarkably ornate and fragile specimens which, much to my concern, dismally failed to weather the slightest breeze and would frequently completely disappear from one Easter to the next. On this occasion I was meticulously adding the finishing touches to a particularly fine example of delicate Fowler stonework when a shout from above revealed that all was not well. The next moment George's stumbling body clipped my back and we were both rolling down towards a steep rocky gully. Panicstricken clawing at the steep grass and rocks just about had the desired effect after forty feet or so and a rather battered father and son compared an impressive array of bumps and grazes. If nothing else I was duly impressed that such a potentially disastrous predicament could arise on such a boring straightforward walking path.

George, of course, having concluded that there were no serious injuries, was becoming increasingly concerned about the ear bashing that he was likely to endure from the OAP contingent back at the hotel. His fears proved to be well founded. Advancing years bring out the worst in some people. It struck me that their views on most things were likely to equate to my own view of 'exceedingly tedious and boring behaviour'. I vowed to ensure that a certain amount of irresponsibility and excitement was injected into my life. George fought his corner well but could see it was a losing battle.

It was shortly after this that the emphasis changed and steep vegetated scrambles were replaced with horrendously long walks over the fells which George was subtle enough to describe as 'Alpine training'; complete with 5 a.m. starts and a rucksack full of fitness-enhancing rocks.

George's very limited experience of the Alps consisted of walking up the Allalinhorn – a straightforward 4000-metre peak in the Zermatt region – with my mother and a guide some time in the early 1950s, and a rather more adventurous incident with friends a few years later. This involved an attempt to climb a sharp rock pinnacle called the Aiguille de la Tsa above Arolla in the Swiss Alps. The result was the sort of epic-laden outing essential to any mountaineer's pub repertoire. The details are rather hazy, but it seems that on leaving Arolla the intrepid trio's approach to the Bertol Hut, where the usual route up the mountain starts, was not the pleasant walk that the guide book described. A classic three-way disagreement amongst the team resulted in not only the wrong path, but also the wrong valley being followed. Remarkably it took several hours before it was realised that very few other people frequented this particular valley and the serious ice slopes they were now contouring in the evening light appeared not to be the *voie normale* to the hut in question. An enforced bivouac followed by several roped pitches to traverse an intervening ridge completed probably the first two-day approach to the hut. Worse was to come. Having braved a misty Alpine start, a slight technical error with regard to navigation resulted in a lengthy session of wandering around on the flat glacier, followed by an adrenalin-pumping descent into the Val d'Herens on the other side of the mountain. This was doubly unfortunate as not only had the mountain failed to reveal itself, but much of their sleeping gear had been left at the Bertol Hut. This of course necessitated another walk up from their base at Arolla which, if nothing else, enabled them to see exactly where they had gone wrong the first time.

Equipped with such dubious credentials, George made the realistic decision to book us both on a two-week course with the Austrian Alpine Club. This introduced a rather nervous thirteen-year-old Fowler to the questionable pleasures of Alpine starts but it was not until the following year that we were to venture out on our own and discover what it was really all about. George's desire to succeed where he had failed twenty years earlier surfaced, with the result that the summer of 1970 saw us admiring the scene of his team's route-finding talents back in 1950, whilst successfully following the clearly marked path up from Arolla to the Bertol Hut.

I had never seen anything like it before. The hut perched on a huge pinnacle at the edge of the glacier and was gained only by a series of precarious ladders and rope handrails. 'Hut' of course is a relative term; the building slept over a hundred people and had a resident warden who tried his best to operate some sort of restaurant service single handed. Dropping down on to the snow slopes below was a fifty-metres-long one-metre-diameter tube which supposedly funnelled effluent down into a wide crevasse in the glacier. An extensive brown stain demonstrated that this was not always the case. Settling down in the hut seemed not dissimilar to being one of an enormous swarm of flies homing in on a solitary turd. Bodies scuttled around as part of a seething mass whilst excrement fumes wafted intermitently up from the glacier below. Meals were theoretically conducted in three sittings whilst many, including ourselves, chose to fend for themselves outside on the walkways.

Sleeping was an experience not to be missed. I believe the hut was holding something like three times its supposed capacity and I ended up squeezed between the wall and George who was, in turn, forced heavily against me by an enormous Frenchman who had somehow mastered the art of sleeping in such circumstances and emitted a constant reverberating snore. The whole place was filled with nasal grumblings while the forced insomniacs could occasionally be heard muttering amongst themselves. Worse was to come. Presumably it was the rich salami consumed earlier on the hut balcony that was having a distressing effect on a body more used to a strictly English diet along the chops, peas and potatoes line. Lying awake in the fetid atmosphere caused by a serious excess of body heat, I lay in fear of the moment that I would have to find a torch, climb over the sleeping bodies on the communal mattresses and search for the upper end of the awesome defecating tube. My stomach churned mercilessly, I felt distinctly unwell. The moment had come. Searching furiously for a torch, I realised too late that an attack of diarrhoea was upon me.

In such situations fourteen-year-old boys tend to seek the advice and support of their parents. George had somehow managed to dose off and had joined the band of snorers, so was understandably displeased to be woken up and faced with an inconvenient and odorous predicament which threatened to lose him not only his hard-won sleeping position but also the chance to do any climbing the next day. Nevertheless, parental duty called and together we stumbled awkwardly over restless bodies towards the fresh air of the outside toilet balcony. Stomach disorders seemed popular that night and the length of the queue guaranteed further mishaps. It was a rather sorry-looking and still slightly smelly young Fowler who spent the rest of the night perched on a bench on the hut balcony, while George spent most of the remaining hours climbing over bodies in an effort to regroup all our scattered belongings, most of which it seemed had found their way underneath our less than slim French sleeping companion. My Mars bar in particular suffered badly from this experience.

At 4.30 a.m. on the dot the first alarms sprang into life and the hive stirred into activity again. Remarkably, I felt rather better and battled valiantly to secure a realistic-sized piece of bread and jam to go with the half bar of Kendal mint cake which George assured me would soon see me 'bursting with energy'. This might have been something of an overstatement but it was true that once clear of the hut things went much more smoothly and a reasonable walk across glaciers, followed by some fine pitches on good rock, saw my first Alpine peak conquered. In retrospect I can only recall two emotions: the elation of standing on top and the embarrassment of my little 'incident' in the hut. The Bertol Hut is of course now much bigger and more modern, but my aversion to staying in organised mountain accommodation has remained with me to this day.

Summer Alpine trips continued, albeit reluctantly on occasions as the disco scene began to exert its pull, and many of the major 4000-metre peaks succumbed to our efforts. What we lacked in competence and good equipment we certainly made up for in enthusiasm. Standing on top of the Dent Blanche it was with an undoubted sense of pride and satisfaction that I was able to look around and mentally 'tick off' those mountains that we had climbed: the Rothorn, Bishorn, Dom, Monte Rosa, Lagginhorn, Strahlhorn . . . all 4000-metre peaks which succumbed to our efforts, and with the enthusiasm of youth outpacing ability, I began to have my own objectives. Doubtless, I became a complete pain to George who deeply wanted to do the routes that I nagged him to take me on but knew we were not up to them. This did not stop me learning in hope the guide-book descriptions to the Teufelsgrat Ridge on the Täschhorn, the Zmutt Ridge on the Matterhorn and many more.

George was now in his late fifties and so, back home, was less keen on weekly visits to the south-eastern sandstone. But for me a typical weekend involved a Saturday job at Wembley's Woolworth's *en route* for too much drink with Ian (who had by now foresworn climbing), ending with the relentless pounding of the North London Saturday night disco scene, then up in a still hungover state at 5 a.m. on Sunday morning to catch the 6 a.m. Tube from Stonebridge Park to get to Harrison's Rocks by 10 a.m. Standing in the dark on a deserted station platform after only five hours' sleep never struck me as a very good way to start the day but at the age of sixteen/seventeen with no alternative forms of transport there was no other choice. Sundays are always the height of British Rail's track maintenance programme with the result that the journey time varied tremendously and the numerous stops and starts played havoc with the rather delicate 'morning after' feeling. Groombridge station, a few miles west of Tunbridge Wells, marked the end of suffering and the beginning of the climbing experience.

In those days Terry's Festerhaunt provided an ideal meeting place. In the 1960s and early '70s. Terry Tullis was one of the leading lights of the South-East climbing scene and had soloed many of the hardest routes at Harrison's. A rotivator blade broke and embedded itself in his leg, curtailing his difficult climbing, but he retained his enthusiasm and love of the area, set up the Festerhaunt café and climbing shop and even today is still very closely associated with activities at the Rocks. Julie, his wife, was also an enthusiastic climber and it always struck me that there seemed to be a battle of consciences going on over whether they should be serving customers or out there climbing. Julie, of course, was to become increasingly keen on mountaineering and became a well-known Himalayan climber before her tragic death in 1986 on K2 after having achieved the first British ascent of the mountain.

The Festerhaunt in the 1970s was the undisputed social centre of climbing in the South-East. It opened at 10.00 a.m. on Sunday mornings and most activists of the day could be found there between 10 and 11 a.m. drinking endless cups of tea, consuming endless slices of cake and generally building up to a strenuous day on the crag or (for the less energetic) transferring direct to a pleasant lunchtime in one of the numerous excellent pubs in the area.

Climbing on the sandstone outcrops of Kent and Sussex has always attracted a select band of talented devotees, few of whom show very much interest in making their mark elsewhere. The climbs are short, averaging only ten metres or so, and the quality of the rock varies enormously. The best climbs though are classics of their kind and remain firmly engrained on the minds of even the most widely travelled of climbers. Weathering of the soft rock has created formations varying from fingery walls of overhanging honeycomb to horrorshows with little to hang on to but rounded edges covered in ballbearing-like grains of sand. The whole area is well cut by vertical faults which give appealing climbing lines. Because of the softness of the rock and the shortness of the climbs, leading routes has never been popular and 'top roping' is the norm. In essence the area could be regarded as a sort of outdoor climbing wall.

Arriving on the dot of 10 a.m. every Sunday, I soon began to recognise the locals. Trevor Panther I remember as a classical and talented sandstone climber. Rarely showing interest in visiting anywhere other than Harrison's Rocks, he had at that time been a regular Sunday visitor for something like ten years. His bare-foot style of climbing was as unique as it was effective. Frequently the Panther toes could be spotted straining in some sharp-edged pockets whilst his immensely strong frame hauled him up the hardest route. I could not help but inspect my own weedy arms and wonder if I was getting involved in the right sport for me. Panther was a schoolteacher who introduced many teenagers to the joys of rock-climbing and wrote at least two guide books exclusively covering Harrison's Rocks. These were unconventional in format and extended the grading system in various ways which never caught on but, in conjunction with the 'official' Climbers' Club guide to the area, they provided unlimited inspiration for the likes of me. Every week I would meticulously comb the pages to choose objectives for the forthcoming Sunday.

Initially I would set up my top rope (an ancient hawser-laid rope borrowed from George) and beg other passing climbers to belay me, but gradually I became aware of another youth about my age who was clearly doing much the same thing. He had long hair, I short (verging on a crew cut); he wore jeans and a scruffy jacket, I wore my retired 'stay pressed' disco trousers and an ageing crombie overcoat – and, horror of horrors, he was clearly a South London boy whereas I was Wembley (behind the stadium) born and bred. Such differences seem major in teenage years, but dissolve more rapidly in a common cause. A climbing partnership which has lasted over twenty years was about to begin.

Like me, Mike Morrison was at the mercy of British Rail and would suffer similar early starts and hangover-ridden journeys from Thornton Heath. In terms of technical ability, we were much the same, but I was completely taken aback by his irrepressible urge to climb virtually from dawn to dusk. I had learned the guide books more thoroughly than he had, but in terms of footage of rock covered per day, I had clearly a long way to catch up. We soon proved to be compatible climbing partners; my crombie became a shared 'toe rag' (essential for cleaning boot soles) and the traditional North/South London divide became a matter for wide-ranging discussion rather than division. After a few Sundays we were fast completing all the routes at Harrison's Rocks that we were capable of doing and began to make plans to visit farther afield. High Rocks loomed prominently in the guide books, but was not so easily accessible by train. Frustratingly the railway runs virtually beneath the crag and there once was a High Rocks station. By the early 1970s though Groombridge was the nearest stop which meant that it was possible to catch a fleeting glimpse of the crags before being carried five miles further down the line.

Mike was reluctant to waste valuable climbing time walking the five miles to the rocks and five miles back at the end of the day. I too was not exactly over-enamoured at the prospect either, and as a result our exclusive association with Harrison's Rocks was extended by several Sundays as we contemplated ways of overcoming this problem, and sized up who might be persuaded to give us a lift.

It was during this period that we both became aware of another lad, much our age, who could be seen regularly poring over the guide book and meticulously tackling classic lines. He was a lightly built, dark-haired chap with a childlike face who shared the early train from Mike's home station of Thornton Heath and the two soon fell into conversation. Jon Stevenson was, we discovered, every bit as keen as we were, and usually in as poor an initial state, due in his case to the Saturday night Croydon disco scene. It proved more difficult than we had envisaged to cadge lifts to High Rocks from Harrison's Rocks devotees who could see little reason to move on. But persistent badgering sometimes paid dividends and the other outcrops gradually got put on the itinerary.

At High Rocks I was amazed at the difficulty of the routes I had managed to struggle up eight or nine years previously. Boa Constrictor Chimney in particular seemed to require an inordinate amount of effort. Its converging greasy walls were a race against failing energy which, when combined with a well-timed comment about poor Ian's banana sandwich, regularly resulted in talented climbers slithering helplessly back down to the ground.

Its modest grade of 4b (on a scale of 1–6) was typical of the harsh grading at High Rocks and the chimney climbs in particular. Many tended to shun the outcrop but as we struggled manfully our standards improved and we began to appreciate the quality of the more difficult climbs and even developed an affection for the north-facing outlook and the numerous slimy, energy-absorbing chimneys. Visits to other outcrops followed and soon we were a regular threesome at such overgrown and esoteric gems as Eridge Green Rocks, Happy Valley Rocks and Under Rockes.

Lack of our own transport continued to be a problem to us, but as we had now passed the age of seventeen the prospect of car ownership became a distinct possibility. Perhaps because I was a few months older than the other two and had saved some money from my paper round and Saturday job at Woolworth's, I was the first to apply myself to passing the driving test.

George was supportive in this aim, but for some reason which I have never fathomed felt that I should first pass a test on his 50cc moped. This was to provoke embarrassment on a par with the Spazwagon experience. I do not recall whether helmets were essential in 1972–3 but I shall always remember the fine specimen with a peak and leather ear-flaps that I was forced to wear. It was far too large and tended to swivel around on my head, causing the ear-flaps to obscure all vision at distressingly critical moments. But at least it eased George's conscience.

The top speed of the NSU 'Quickly', as it was called, was in the region of 30 mph. My christening it the 'Fartalong Slowly' did not go down well. Neither did my efforts to pass the test on it. Taking driving seriously on such a machine was difficult and practice sessions with George would result in frayed tempers, whilst those on my own were more geared to testing the moped to its limits rather than concentrating on the finer points of the Highway Code.

After failing my first attempt, a second moped test was duly booked but, much to my surprise, with only three weeks to go, George yielded to my continual pestering and it was arranged that the test should be taken in a car instead. This boosted my interest no end, but aside from a few lessons with the instructor (who spent most of the time trying to sell me pornographic material) it meant occasional sessions with George in the trusty Spazwagon which amounted to much argument, limited tuition and a rather inexperienced and hesitant young Fowler facing the joys of a driving test. I expected to fail.

Usually things go horribly wrong in such situations but on the day in question the instructor's Mini seemed remarkably obedient. It reversed round corners with ease, gear-changed smoothly, indicated at all times and generally behaved as if under the control of an experienced and competent driver. I knew the area around Harrow Test Centre well and became increasingly nervous as I realised that we were heading back for the Test Centre with a possible pass under my belt. I could hardly believe the end result. Officially, I was competent to drive. Six months later I had invested £200 and was the proud owner of a battered blue minivan – the first of thirteen to follow.

Mobility at last. The horizons broadened overnight.

2

Laying the Foundations

I got my driving experience driving fourteen miles a day between George's house in Wembley and Harrow Council where I had drifted into a job when I gave up on being a trainee quantity surveyor. This latter had involved four evenings a week at college, an effort that I decided was disproportionate to my enthusiasm for quantity surveying. Working for Harrow Council required no commitment and nurtured no enthusiasm, but it funded the disco scene and put petrol in the van, and by Christmas I had ten drives to work under my belt and felt ready for a week in North Wales with Mike and Jon.

The tedious 65 mph grinds (my top speed) up the M1 and M6 on a Friday came to be enlivened by vigorous arguments about the routes we should be aiming for on arrival and ferocious quiz sessions based on our devouring of the climbing guides. As a result of these I am still able to quote the order of difficulty of the Extremely Severe climbs listed in the back of the 1970 Crew/Harris guide to Tremadoc, a particularly useless talent which has attracted much derision at parties over the years. A stop at Hollies transport café near the junction of the M6 and A5 became the key to Friday night manoeuvres and a focal point for many carloads of climbers travelling to Wales from London and the South Midlands. What the regular lorry-driver clientele made of our flowery arm movements as we sought to impress each other with climbing tales can only be imagined. But a resilient team of serving ladies coped with us all. The Hollies was and still is an interesting microculture. Before visiting this fine establishment I would never have considered a transport café as a venue for a romantic evening out. But one frequently sees couples enjoying just that at the Hollies.

Beyond Hollies the A5 is, of course, now much improved but in those days the winding road responded to those who knew it well and, with rapidly increasing confidence behind the wheel, it was possible to make up some of the time lost to faster vehicles on the motorway. Even so it was still five to six hours' driving from Wembley to Llanberis. Rarely did we arrive before midnight. Mike Morrison would take a lift up with Bob Gookey of the Croydon Club and meet us at Humphrey's Barn. His stories of driving with Bob went a long way towards restoring my battered driving ego. It seemed that on one occasion Bob had missed the M6 turn-off from the M1 and simply reversed his ancient Ford back down the hard shoulder until he could start off again in the fast lane of the M6. On another occasion he had a brush with a crash barrier and careered across the M1 towards a concrete bridge strut. A fine piece of corrective steering saw the front end preserved but the back of the van swung round hard into the strut. In the back two newcomers were snoozing contentedly in their sleeping-bags until the force of the impact burst the back doors open and two cocooned bodies spewed forth to bump uncomfortably along the hard shoulder.

Humphrey's Barn in the Llanberis Pass was a favourite North Wales haunt in the early 1970s. It was not quite as basic as it sounds, containing twenty or so bunkbeds arranged around the walls, and boasting rudimentary washing facilities. Certainly on a wet and windy winter weekend it was distinctly more comfortable than the traditional Llanberis Pass campsites. Like most establishments, the barn has fallen in and out of favour over the years but at Christmas 1974 when we first went there it was definitely the 'in' place to be – so much so that overcrowding was a serious problem. I knew very few of the people there when we arrived but a healthy scene of after-pub banter and robust debate over who would get the beds as opposed to the floor guaranteed that my circle of climbing friends had enlarged considerably by the end of the week.

My climbing experience was in for a bit of enlarging too as I thrashed wildly on the greasy Tremadoc rock, endeavouring to convert southern sandstone 5c top-roping competence to North Wales 5c on the sharp end of the rope. I discovered that the key to success was keeping cool and moving quickly between resting spots. Sandstone standards were certainly higher and it was more the mental difficulties associated with leading that had to be overcome rather than the technical difficulty of making the moves. Mike, Jon and I were of much the same standard and fell in naturally as a compatible climbing team. The solid, well-protected classics of Tremadoc were suited to our abilities and despite the generally appalling weather we climbed virtually nonstop, whooping with delight up such classics as Plum, Meschach, Stromboli and Tensor.

The social life was equally new and exciting – from the Tremadoc café to the much revered Padarn pub scene in Llanberis. The latter was the Mecca of all visiting 'hard men' at this time. The Croydon Club team that Mike and Jon were loosely associated with preferred the rather more sedate atmosphere of the Vaynol Arms at Nant Peris, but for us three the Padarn exerted an irresistible attraction. It certainly was not a comfortable or in any way salubrious bar but it could not be denied that it was incredibly popular. In fact reaching the bar itself was something of an achievement and involved literally forcing oneself through a heaving throng of bodies. Beer spilled liberally in these jostlings and murky puddles would form in slight depressions in the undulating floor. A particularly deep puddle tended to form close to the toilet door which made a visit very challenging indeed. Not only was there a paddling manoeuvre which tended to focus eyes on the ground, but as an objective danger the dartboard was, for some reason that I never really understood, just next to the gents'. Unwary toilet-goers leaving with eyes to the ground stood a real risk of wavering into the path of inebriated but intense darts players who seriously resented the inconvenience of a body interfering with the flight path of their finest shot and would verbally open fire at any distraction regardless of where their darts ended up.

As with any pub, though, it was the people that made it great. It had been the traditional drinking spot for the likes of Joe Brown and Don Whillans, and the much revered Mr Brown enjoyed the privilege of his own glass behind the bar and a more or less reserved bar stool away from the major puddles. Joe Brown was a complete hero to the three of us who had avidly read his book *The Hard Years* and soaked up the aura surrounding the man and his climbs. Even now, twenty years later, his reputation has stood the test of time and one can see that he and one or two other members of the Rock and Ice Club boosted standards and laid the foundations of modern hard rock-climbing in Britain. Brown was undoubtedly the most prolific and his complete domination of the North Wales and Peak District scenes from the late 1940s to the early 1960s (not to mention his important routes in the 'seventies and 'eighties) was unprecedented and will probably never be seen again.

News travelled more slowly in those days. The glossy climbing magazines that we are now used to were still some years away and news about Brown's climbs was passed on by word of mouth with suitable embellishment. Tremedous reputations were built up and his routes were approached with a marked degree of trepidation even in the 1970s. His classic lines were to inspire future generations: Dangler, the Rasp and Valkyrie in the Peak; Cenotaph Corner, Cemetery Gates and Hangover in the Llanberis Pass; Shrike, Vember and the Mostest on Clogwyn Du'r Arddu (Snowdon); the Mousetrap, Red Wall and Dinosaur on the sea cliffs at Gogarth (Anglesey) – all were magnificent routes up stunningly obvious lines that just called out to be climbed. All three of us were hooked. A world full of Brown routes was out there awaiting our attention.

Sleeping three in the back of a minivan was cosy but at least went some of the way towards overcoming the inadequacies of our sleeping-bags purchased at ridiculously low prices from Woolworths and blatantly unable to cope with our requirements.

Breakfast in Llanberis was a problem in the early 1970s. Al Harris, a climber who had moved to North Wales to join the 'scene' (and was perhaps best known for his driving and partying escapades), ran a café for a couple of years but by 1975 when our regular visits started this had closed down and nothing had really taken its place. Such problems though could not be allowed to impede the young and keen. Mike somehow became responsible for breakfast, which was eaten in the van and invariably consisted of, for some odd reason, a couple of tins of mandarin oranges between us, along with a loaf of bread, all washed down by liberal quantities of stream water. Mike Morrison in particular seemed to thrive on this diet and, being an irrepressibly early starter, was prone to fling open the back door of the van at first light and let forth with exuberant ditties about the joys of the morning. So startled sheep and 6 a.m. starts from the van were the norm – a state of affairs which particularly distressed Jon who was not renowned for his early-morning enthusiasm, but could not deny it guaranteed maximum climbing hours. Gradually, we saw our standards edge upwards. Firstly we concentrated on ticking off as many routes as possible, rather than on technical difficulty, but as we gained confidence our attention turned to those Brown classics that had always seemed to be rather beyond our abilities.

Hangover on Clogwyn y Grochan in the Llanberis Pass was one of our early successes. At one point the route leaves the relative security of a groove and climbs an open face to a resting place; 5b technically, but sufficiently above protection to make ears tingle with the flow of adrenalin once one has overcome uncertainty and made the decision to go go go. Other routes followed as our confidence grew. Clogwyn Du'r Arddu became a favourite of mine, and varying the leads we gradually worked through the Brown classics with ascents of Vember, Shrike, Diglyph and the Mostest. The latter in particular sticks in my mind, as a Morrison-inspired early start saw us reaching the top at 8 a.m. just as the second party on a very busy summer day arrived at the crag. Vector at Tremadoc seemed a particular milestone that year, probably due to my having spent most of the Christmas trip six months before staring in awe at its intricate path weaving in and out of the overhangs of Vector Buttress.

Elated at our success, we felt literally ready for anything. What a mistake; little did I realise that the more clinical approach to climbing that took root in the early 1970s was paying dividends in the form of a huge leap in the technical difficulty and audacity. Unknown to me, British rock-climbing was undergoing a revolution. A year before our Christmas week, Pete Livesey made the first ascent of the Right Wall of Cenotaph Corner in the Llanberis Pass. This forty-metre vertical and slightly overhanging wall had been stared at in awe but never seriously attempted. A few antiquated bolts had appeared in the first few metres, but Livesey's approach was much more meticulous and heralded the start of a new way of tackling some of the most impressive unclimbed pieces of rock in Britain.

The exact technique varied from climber to climber but all followed the same basic approach. Starting from the top, an abseil inspection would familiarise the climber with the likely problems, allow clearance of any loose rock and vegetation, make sure that protection was reasonable and generally see whether or not the objective was feasible. Particularly hard sections could be practised whilst hanging off the abseil rope, and curiously unnatural-looking holds were to prompt serious debate about the ethics of some protagonists. Nevertheless the end results were spectacularly impressive and whilst we were struggling up the likes of Vector, described in our guide books as 'amongst the hardest in Wales', I was blissfully unaware of the surge in standards that was leaving us light years behind.

I was to be brought seriously down to earth before my ego had had a chance to grow out of control. Zukator on the cliffs near the café at Tremadoc had been first climbed by Pete Crew and Al Harris in 1964. It was reputed to be very hard and had recently been free-climbed by Pete Livesey. I had gloriously little experience of very hard technical climbing away from top-roped routes on southern sandstone. In fact the odd point of aid was not frowned upon as it is today and many climbers at the time, myself included, would often use some aid when they could perhaps have free-climbed if they had tried hard enough. On Zukator, though, I had heard that the real challenge was to climb the top pitch free. With this style of ascent stuck in my mind, I duly applied myself to a leaning, gently overhanging groove which appeared distressingly devoid of holds. Progress ground to an embarrassing halt. Never before had I come up against anything like this outside top-rope problems. I had never yet fallen off leading but here the difficulty was such that if I committed myself and failed to reach the security of the next protection peg, a nasty fall seemed inevitable. Naïvely I had imagined that our success on routes such as Vector meant that we were up there amongst the pace setters. Seldom has my self-esteem been dealt such a quick and crushing blow.

Initially I lacked confidence to launch up the groove; then when I had managed to clip the peg (by various jiggery-pokery), it became clear that my technical ability was woefully inadequate. Eventually I ended up standing in a sling on a very insecure rusty peg which promptly came out and resulted in a nastily twisted ankle as my foot became entangled during the fall. Bystanders watched with interest as I squirmed about ignominiously. Had I been a dog, my tail would have curled up so far between my legs that it would have tickled my tummy. Interestingly though, and perhaps it says a lot about styles of ascent and attitudes at the time, I climbed back up to my highpoint, used a couple of nuts for aid and completed the route in line with the guide book's aid recommendation, ticked it off and ultimately left the scene, having no great desire to return and try to complete the pitch free. It took ten years before changing attitudes, not least of all my own, convinced me that I had not really climbed it properly and that I should return to the fray. Such is the march of progress.

Frequent visits to the Padarn naturally had the effect of broadening our circle of friends and we were soon bumping into like-minded climbers from other parts of the country who enthused about crags which meant very little to me at the time. The likes of Leigh McGinley and Tom Jones from Merseyside emphasising the pleasures of their local outcrops and Phil Thomas and Andy Sharp enthusing about the joys of Avon, Cheddar and the South-West, gradually forced a realisation that there was more to rock-climbing in Britain than just North Wales and southern sandstone.

3

Branching Out

The real inspiration for branching out from North Wales came from
Geraldine Abrey who was later to become Geraldine Taylor and
one of Britain's leading female rock-climbers. In the mid-1970s she
was teaching in Ashburton, Devon and renting a room in Newton
Abbot from Peter Biven, who had done much to develop climbing
on the sea cliffs in the South-West. Personally I had always steered
clear of sea cliffs, not because of fear of loose rock or birds, but
simply because I had been brought up walking up hillsides to the
foot of a rock climb. To me the idea of abseiling *down* to the
foot of a climb was alien and I had dismissed sea-cliff-climbing as
a sideline to the real issue of climbing mountain crags. (Somehow I
had conveniently convinced myself that Tremadoc should fall into
the mountain crag category as the sea could not be seen or heard
from it and it involved at least a fifty-metre uphill walk from the
road!) In those days Geraldine was not the superfit rock-climbing
star that she was to become, but she was a keen and enthusiastic
advocate of outdoor activity for children at her school. This involved
her taking minibus-loads of screaming brats up to North Wales and
doing her best, along with another long-suffering teacher, to deliver
them back to their parents safe and sound on Sunday evening. So
my first climbing romance began amidst the beer puddles and flying
darts of the public bar of the Padarn and I have to admit it was more
the attraction of seeing Gerry than the inspiration of rock-climbing
in Devon (where are the mountains in Devon?) which led me to
persuade Jon and Mike that we should broaden our horizons and
spend some weekends based in Newton Abbot.

Biven rarely seemed to be around and we generally had the house
to ourselves. On that first weekend, though, he was there and I
remember the three of us being rather in awe of his reputation,
but keen to quiz him about his exploits. He was a big but kind

and gentle man who was forgiving of our complete ignorance of anywhere outside southern sandstone and North Wales. His name had attracted my attention in the first-ascents lists of numerous guide books but to me his exploits stuck in my mind for two reasons.

Firstly, I knew him for the climbing world's stories about his climbing with Trevor Peck. Peck was a rich businessman, complete with Rolls-Royce, who would habitually drive as close to the crag as he possibly could, frequently enjoying the assistance of local farm workers who naturally assumed that this well-heeled gentleman driving his Rolls across the fields could only be the landowner intent on a spot of estate surveillance. The image somehow stuck in my mind as immensely amusing and always recurred when, as was to become increasingly frequent, I found an *in situ* Peck stainless-steel peg, peg manufacture being one of Peck's sideline interests. Secondly, Biven's name conjured up sea-cliff exploits thanks to both guide-book historical records and, more vividly, because of the wonderfully inspiring photographs of him in John Cleare's book *Sea Cliff Climbing in Britain*, where he was featured climbing String of Pearls at Bosigran in Cornwall and tyrolean-traversing across the Blue Grotto on the Magical Mystery Tour sea-level traverse at Berry Head in South Devon.

He told us about the other climbers from his area, like the ever active Pat Littlejohn, and the thatcher/climber Keith Darbyshire, with a reputation for putting up a series of character-building climbs on the shale cliffs of the north coast. Biven spoke with infectious enthusiasm about his own climbs in locations varying from serious sea cliffs to abrasive Dartmoor tors and wooded limestone outcrops. It did not seem to worry him where the climbing was. If it was challenging and adventurous it clearly interested him, I could not help but feel that perhaps I was in danger of being rather narrowminded in concentrating on Welsh mountain crags and southern sandstone to the virtual exclusion of all else.

Biven had suggested that the old Redoubt Cliff at Berry Head might be a good one for us to visit, and a crack line called Moonraker an excellent first route. If this went well he thought that a harder climb called Dreadnought across the lip of a cave should keep us occupied. In retrospect I suppose our bull-shitting must have given him the impression that we were an awful lot better than we were. It was only several years later I heard that his two friends Frank Cannings and Pat Littlejohn who had first climbed Dreadnought in

1969 very nearly fell into the sea when their belay, twenty-five metres up on the lip of the cave, partially ripped and left them both hanging from one rather dubious peg. Perhaps Biven failed to mention this in case he put us off. I now know that he certainly directed us to the best and most exciting, but also the most intimidating cliff in South Devon.

On my first Devon weekend Gerry was committed to taking schoolchildren out on to Dartmoor on the Saturday but had arranged for someone called Stuart from Exeter University to take her place. I felt rather cheated by this turn of events, but was nevertheless grateful that we had someone with us who at least knew where the cliff was.

The Old Redoubt at Berry Head is near Brixham. I had been pessimistic whilst having breakfast in a Brixham café, simply not being able to accept that this bustling holiday town might have a cliff less than five miles away which compared with (as Biven put it) the best in Wales. I wondered vaguely whether I could keep a relationship going with Gerry based solely on weekends in Wales. But on arriving at the seventy-metre limestone cliff centred on a huge sea cave, even I had to admit that there did appear to be a fair amount of excitement on offer.

True to form, Mike was bubbling with enthusiasm as he feasted his eyes on the soaring crack lines of Moonraker and Goddess of Gloom and was the first to disappear into the murk at the back of the cave. Stuart had been here once before and assured us that the traverse round the cave to reach the routes was relatively easy. What he failed to mention was that the previous occasion had been in midsummer and at low tide. Shouts at the back of the cave were the first indication that all was not well. Closer inspection revealed Mr Morrison hanging batlike above deep water from a horizontal flake.

It was not immediately obvious how he had got into this position but it seemed certain that he would not be able to stay there much longer. A traverse line did continue in an intermittent fashion towards Moonraker but several sections, not least the one he was on, looked particularly challenging. Even the renowned Morrison high spirits were in danger of subsiding.

'Where now?' he squawked.

Stuart hopped around and made uncomfortable noises about the traverse 'not being possible today' whilst Mike, in response to cajoling from Jon and me, headed ever onwards and made a series of impressive lunges to gain a resting place fractionally out of the reach of the waves. This merely exacerbated the problem. With the tide coming in, Stuart flatly refused to contemplate the traverse, whilst Mike did his best to convince us that the way on was easy and if we too committed ourselves we could reach the bottom of the route and climb on up to escape the clutches of the sea.

From our vantage point on the other side of the cave negative comments flowed freely, and as Mike's situation worsened, I began to feel that there clearly was something in this sea-cliff-climbing business after all. Looking up I had to admit that the rock did not seem as solid as the mountain crags that I was used to, but it did not appear outrageously loose either, and it could not be denied that I found the sense of adventure and commitment combined with the appealingly obvious lines very attractive. Jon, too, was getting inspired and between us there was more a sense of hilarity and growing enthusiasm about the cliff in general rather than concern at Mike's predicament.

Faced with refusals from everyone else present and a rapidly worsening tidal situation, poor Mike was left with the options of either continuing and soloing up an eighty-metre route on a cliff that was new to him or returning the way he had come. Understandably he was soon hanging from the horizontal flake again hurling a steady stream of abuse at his companions as he fought his way back to a point where he could step into shallow water rather than plummet gracefully into the depths. Having regrouped, Stuart's advice was sought as to the next course of action. He recalled that some of his friends had abseiled in from the clifftop and the guide book also suggested this as a possible option if the traverse in proved unrealistic.

A scaffolding-type pole on top gave the impression that numerous parties adopted this line of approach but I now know that it once supported a 'No Climbing' sign erected by the local council who seem to be particularly sensitive about climbing on the Old Redoubt. There are of course reasons for this. One involves pressure from the RSPB which has since led to the remarkable spectacle of a huge closed-circuit TV camera mounted on the cliff to monitor the move- ments of any climber on Moonraker. An adjacent sign threatening a £1000 fine if caught climbing in the nesting season serves to reinforce the message. Another reason is because the crowded summer tourist boats from Brixham have an unnerving habit of nosing into the cave right beneath climbers grappling *in extremis* with occasional areas of loose rock. But on this occasion we were blissfully ignorant of the political problems or the unpopularity of the abseil approach. I was getting rather restless and set off first.

The reasons for this unpopularity soon became clear. It was September and the nesting season had just ended, but a pungent smell of guano still hung in the air and the odd straggling young bird still clung to the whitened ledges, plucking up the courage to take off for the first time. The rock seemed more loose than I was used to but far from unpleasant. The situation was excellent – full of atmospheric audacity with the huge cave below me on the right, waves beating against the cliff and the air echoing with the sound of calling gulls. Looking down I could see that the rope did not reach sea level but from my current position it was difficult to say whether it was one metre or twenty metres short. I had never abseiled down a sea cliff before and proceeded with both caution and interest.

A curious bird, species unknown, stuck its head out of a perfect nesting hole and peered at me quizzically, I wondered whether it would allow me to use the very fine incut edge of the hole as a handhold. Probably not, I concluded, as it had a tantrum when I moved into the range within which it clearly felt uncomfortable. Having studied the guide book on the drive down (and of course tested each other on its contents), I was well aware of the other routes on the crag and traced their respective paths up the parallel crack systems of the Moonraker wall and in between the beetling overhangs on the wall above the cave. Dreadnought looked particularly fine, wending its way up improbable ground in a bold and exciting fashion with nothing below but deep water.

Almost too late, I realised that the end of the rope was approaching and I was hanging three metres clear of the rock. I do not know how long Stuart's rope was but it was a good fifteen metres short of sea level. I hung forlornly, rotating gently, contemplating my predicament. George had forced me to undergo prusiking exercises up the most gruesome of High Rocks chimneys (under the guise of practising crevasse rescue) and though I did have some nuts on rope which would have enabled me to escape I had no desire to waste yet more time. Swinging into the rock, though, was remarkably difficult from a static position. Shouts from above were muffled by the sound of the waves but they sounded more annoyed than concerned. Jon,

I knew, would be mellow about the lack of climbing activity, but I could imagine a frantic Morrison distraught at the delay in him getting his weekend climbing 'fix'. Frantically I bounced up and down in an effort to start a swinging momentum. Eventually, I managed to dig my fingernails into a guano-covered ledge, pull into the rock and manoeuvre myself on to a ledge which as luck would have it turned out to be the end of the first pitch of Moonraker. Somehow the approaches to sea-cliff climbs, which I had always regarded as insignificant compared to mountain crags, were taking on a new light.

The top two pitches gave fine climbing and all three of us had to admit that there was some rather fine action to be had away from our usual haunts – and on sea cliffs at that. It did, however, bother me that we had not done the first pitch – the crux of the climb and one which, when combined with the atmospheric sea-level traverse approach, seemed likely to provide the highlight of the route.

Remarkably, my relationship with Gerry blossomed and, with a whole new area to explore, Mike and Jon were easily persuaded to spend more and more weekends in Devon. George, of course, being a traditional climber found it difficult to accept that Devon offered any good rock-climbing; he assumed that I was merely going for the female element and studiously dished out the usual paternal warnings.

For my part, I was determined to get back to our unfinished business with the first pitch of Moonraker and the traverse around the cave. We had somehow squeezed four into the minivan and I ended up climbing with Mike Hunt, another keen enthusiast from the Croydon Club, with whom Mike Morrison had done a few climbs. One of the rumours about him was that he had climbed an HVS in the Avon Gorge with a rope around his neck! As Mike and I descended the tricky wall down to the platform at the start of the traverse, it became clear that we had badly misjudged the tides and were in for another attempt at the high-level traverse. After our previous effort Biven had assured us that Mike Morrison had passed the hardest section and that the whole of the upper-level traverse was above VS standard. After an hour or so of taking it in turns to get frightened on overhanging greasy rock five metres above a boiling sea, I could only conclude that neither of us was capable of soloing 'Very Severe'. With the tide well in now, an awkward section was necessary to cross a steep wall and regain the platform. Having wobbled my way across I paused to wait for Mike Hunt who was beginning to look distinctly cold and unhappy after an unexpectedly large wave had caught him unawares at the back of the cave.

At first, I thought it was hilarious when he lost contact with the rock altogether and laughed mercilessly at the floundering body struggling to regain contact. A panicstricken thrashing suddenly convinced me that all was not well. Initially I thought that perhaps he could not swim and discarded my camera in order to prepare for an heroic rescue mission.

Fortunately for me though, before I launched myself gracefully into the water he was swept out on to a wave-washed rock about three metres clear of the platform. He seemed to have swallowed a lot of water and rolled around like an ungainly walrus trying to stand up. For the first time it struck me that something more serious might be wrong. There was no doubt about it – one shoulder was distinctly lower than the other, but then I had not exactly studied his physique closely and thought this might possibly be the norm.

Mike was extremely controlled about the whole affair: 'I've dislocated my shoulder,' he spluttered.

It seemed that this deformity was not his usual physical state after all.

'Don't worry.' It was all I could think to say and seemed a pitifully inappropriate comment, especially coming from a very poor swimmer in whom the injured had absolutely no option but to have complete faith.

Top priority was clearly to get him back to the relative safety of the platform. Tying him on to a rope and physically pulling him across seemed the best option and with this in mind I threw a rope end at the increasingly sorry-looking figure, Mike decided my suggestion that he tie on round the waist was dangerous. He had worked as a life guard at one point and felt that a waist tie would make him unstable in the water and could turn him upside down. A wrist tie was, he assured me, much safer. This may well be the case, but while one-handed bowline knots around the waist are reasonably easy to tie, the same cannot be said for similar knots around the wrist. It looked distressingly clear that I was going to have to get wet as well. On the other hand it seemed mildly ridiculous for us both to end up on the wave-washed rock unless there really was no alternative. Mike though was increasingly insistent and, trusting in his apparent expertise in water-based rescues (and keen for some progress in one direction or another), I acceded to his wishes. Having secured one end of the rope on the platform, I succeeded in floundering out to admire his predicament from close quarters. It was certainly an impressive dislocation and one which looked as if it would be a lot less painful if it could be popped back into place. There was a lull in the waves, and even Mike had to agree that a Fowler on-the-spot operation could ease matters considerably.

'Ready?'

'Yes.'

Having placed my left wrist under his armpit I pushed his elbow hard against his body and lifted at the same time. Aside from Mike emitting a curious squeaking noise and looking very faint, there was no discernible change. A second attempt had similar results and prompted an admission that my doctoring abilities clearly fell short of the standard required. There was little choice left but to cajole him into the water, across to the ledge and up a short tricky wall to the clifftop car park. In line with his preference, the wrist of his good arm was securely tied to the rope (my suggestion that his injured arm should be tied and pulled in an effort to click the joint back in place went down very badly) and I returned hand over hand along the rope which I had fixed to the platform.

Mike stood there rather forlornly. He was looking a little less happy with the wrist tie (or perhaps with the situation in general) now that action was imminent.

'Go for it!' I shouted over the noise of the sea.

The waves reverberating round the cave muffled any audible reply. I pulled hard as he stepped forward into the three-metre-wide stretch of deep water. Perhaps my handling of the rope was not as he had intended or perhaps he himself had misjudged something. Whatever was wrong, the end result was that as I was pulling his good arm, he was unable to use his bad arm to keep himself above water and he half sank beneath the waves with only one arm poking straight out the water, looking somewhat like a stricken submarine. By pulling furiously, I managed to sort of glide him across to the metre-high wall forming the edge of the platform where the swell scraped him mercilessly up and down against the rocks, whilst I wondered whether my efforts to get him out would result in the dislocation of his good wrist. It was a particularly soggy and uninspired version of the formerly exuberant Mr Hunt who finally lay gasping at my feet on the platform beneath the awkward wall and traverse leading to safety.

For those with full control of their limbs it was little more than a tricky scramble to escape. For Mike, with one shoulder dislocated and the other wrist looking increasingly red and swollen, the prospect was daunting. Because it was a traverse and had large overhangs above, I was unable to give any direct assistance and could do little but place as many pieces of gear as possible and fix a back rope to make sure he did not swing too far if he fell off. Poor Mike looked distinctly nonplussed at his predicament. It was October and with the chilling effect of the sea taking its toll, he sat miserably on the ledge, teeth chattering insistently as he contemplated the situation. Lending him my very baggy sweater, as knitted by my auntie and *extremely* stretchy when wet did nothing to improve the slightly ridiculous atmosphere surrounding the whole incident.

Gerry had arranged to come to the cliff as soon as she had finished work but a quick dash to the top revealed no sign of her and the look of disappointment on Mike's face when I returned was immediately obvious. Clearly he did not relish the prospect of having no one but me to rely on. Understandable as this was, things went relatively smoothly and a selection of precariously placed nuts with slings attached enabled our combined efforts to see him end up safe but cold and wet in the clifftop car park, where a friendly couple of pensioners sitting in their car to admire the view took pity on us and invited the dripping duo to share their Thermos on the back seat of an immaculately maintained Austin 1100 while we waited for Gerry. Our plight must have made a great yarn to tell around the Torbay rest-home circuit. They even had two muddy stains on their unblemished cloth upholstery to lend credence to their story.

When Gerry arrived Mike was organised into hospital where he spent a lot of time stripped to his offensively fluorescent yellow underpants being wheeled around the premises before a doctor twisted and thumped the arm in what looked to be exactly the same way as I had, but with such distinctly improved results that by the evening, in Biven's dry clothing, Mike was able to manage a complete round of the seven Chudleigh pubs (a favourite pastime of Exeter University climbers) and was pronounced recovered. He was not very keen to return to the joys of Berry Head, however, and it was to be a few months before Mike Morrison and I completed the traverse and Moonraker's first pitch – albeit in a boringly epic-free style.

Biven had also enthused about the North Devon and North Cornwall coasts. Here the cliffs are generally of a more recent sedimentary rock and are larger, more serious and more atmospheric than those in South Devon, with huge exploratory north-facing routes and wildly intimidating unclimbed cliffs rising to 200 metres – the highest sea cliffs in England. The same two names that Biven had mentioned kept coming to the fore: Pat Littlejohn, who climbed extensively all over the country, and Keith Darbyshire. Darbyshire had been killed whilst soloing on a South Cornwall sea cliff in 1975 and in 1976 local climbers were still in a state of shock to have lost one of their most adventurous and popular enthusiasts. His style of climbing seemed similar to my own and it has always been a cause of sadness that I was never able to meet the man and share a beer or two whilst discussing the sometimes esoteric pleasures of the shale coast.

He also drove the climber's obligatory scruffy minivan and, so the tale goes one day collided with a herd of cows in a Cornish lane. One poor animal ended up sprawled across the bonnet, with the windscreen shattered and the creature's flailing legs inches away from Darbyshire's face as he struggled to release himself from the belt and escape the driving seat. He was however too late; in its panic, the cow pivoted round and ejected enormous quantities of dung straight through the remains of the windscreen. The repaired van – not to mention everything therein, I would imagine – had a distinctively farmyard aroma for some time thereafter.

Darbyshire was known to us not only for his driving escapades. His exploits on the culm coast and the huge Cornish shale cliffs were legendary, as were stories about the more technically difficult challenge, generally led by Pat Littlejohn, during their tremendously fruitful partnership. Climbs like Eroica, Darkinbad and Il Duce have now gained classic status but it was those in the former category that particularly interested me. North Devon and Cornwall present the climber with a huge variety of challenges, varying from loose rock and vegetation to the mental demands of long serious climbs directly above the sea or rarely frequented beaches. Some short climbs had been made prior to the 1970s but only Tom Patey's magnificent Wreckers Slab at Cornakey Cliff near Hartland Point could begin to compare in terms of length and that was well short of the technical difficulty and seriousness inherent in the climbs that Darbyshire was interested in. His tragic death actually occurred before he was able to complete what he would doubtless have regarded as his real *tour de force* routes, but his success on routes like Sexton at Blackchurch (near Clovelly) and probings on huge cliffs like Henna and Bukator gave sure signs as to the sort of objectives he had in mind.

Our probings from Newton Abbot were rather timid due to our initial unfamiliarity with the rock. None of the shale routes were popular in those days and loose rock abounded. On the culm coast, broadly from Clovelly to Bude, it tended to peel away in sharp-edged slivers whereas south of Bude (say from Bude to Tintagel) the geology was less consistent and it was more difficult to judge the stability of both the crag and the individual hold. We felt very new to the game and tended to concentrate on culm cliffs such as Blackchurch which gave excellent climbing and were slightly off vertical, thus allowing one to stand in balance and contemplate the way ahead before becoming committed to a series of moves. The classic Littlejohn and/or Darbyshire routes of this era gave magnificent climbing – never too difficult technically but always worrying enough to keep the adrenalin flowing and the satisfaction levels high. One or two though were distinctly too hard for us. I remember jibbering our way up the Littlejohn/Darbyshire test piece Savage God, hammering a nut into a crack in sheer terror and subsequently reading Littlejohn's comments in an article (many years before I met him) chastising those 'operating out of their depth' and 'cluttering up classic lines with hammered nuts'. I kept quiet and beavered away in obscurity at easier lines.

Confidence was gradually growing though and by 1976 I felt brave enough to try my first new route at the now familiar crag of Blackchurch. In retrospect, I could not have chosen a worse line. Climbing on sight away from the established lines here tends to be a rather loose and frightening experience. Even so the choice of a wide crack obviously full of teetering blocks was a particularly curious one. I suppose we decided to give it a go simply because it was very obvious, relatively clean and not recorded in our rather scanty guide book. Also a crack line just to one side – Loose Women – had proved a fine climb. I over-optimistically felt that this line might reveal the same surprising quality. The crack was only obvious for the first twelve metres or so; thereafter the line rapidly degenerated into very steep vegetated ground. We were not to know that the norm at Blackchurch is to abseil down and clear off the majority of the loose rock and vegetation before attempting a new line.

If nothing else the route had an 'unclimbed' feel: the blocks gave the impression of being dangerously insecure and made hair-raising noises as they settled into the crack when my weight came on to them. Although technically of a reasonable standard, I arrived at the stance completely drained. Mike Morrison was looking distinctly relieved too – he had been belayed right in the line of fire. Further insecure climbing on disintegrating grass-covered slabs took us to the top of the crag and rather muted celebration – it was difficult to be too elated when the quality of the climbing had been so poor. In fact the whole affair left me feeling mildly deflated. Perhaps all the worthwhile lines in Britain had been climbed already and I had been born too late! This feeling was compounded when I was told that the route had in fact already been climbed by Ed Hart who was at that time making a name for himself repeating many of Littlejohn's finest creations in the South-West and had presumably had a few hours off to climb the truly awful line of Prayer Mat, as it became known.

Ed Hart's interest in Littlejohn's routes and Biven's complimentary comments about him, not to mention the impressive regularity of his name in first-ascent lists, led us to find out a bit more about the man whose reputation in the South-West was approaching the heroic status that Joe Brown managed to achieve in North Wales and the Peak. One of Littlejohn's earliest in his phenomenal list of new routes was Moonraker, climbed in 1967. He was only sixteen at the time and has managed to remain at the cutting edge of British rock-climbing ever since, clocking up literally hundreds of major first ascents in the South-West, Pembroke, North Wales and elsewhere. In the early 1970s he was based in the South-West and it was then that he teamed up with Keith Darbyshire. Darbyshire was by no means as technically talented as Littlejohn, but he was clearly a forceful and supportive companion with an insatiable appetite for excitement and adventure. Over the five years from 1971 to 1975 they were responsible for raising standards of technical difficulty and seriousness along the whole north coast of Devon and Cornwall. In 1976 when Darbyshire was still sorely missed and with Littlejohn having left the area for South Wales, the Littlejohn/Darbyshire lines were still seldom attempted, and spoken of with bated breath. Gerry's friends knew no one who had personally climbed them and from magazine reports and the grapevine in general it seemed that the three we were really interested in – America at Carn Gowla, Darkinbad the Brightdayler at Pentire Head and Il Duce at Tintagel – had only been repeated by Ed Hart. No one in our little group knew him either and the rumours and reputations grew accordingly.

Il Duce was the one we decided to aim for. Situated on the stunningly impressive seaward face of Tintagel island on the North Cornwall coast it was yet another crag that had no noteworthy climbing on it until Littlejohn and Darbyshire addressed the problem in 1972. Although a sea cliff, its position is such that it is impossible to see anyone climbing on it from a clifftop position; also the main section overhangs the sea which, being the North Atlantic, is rarely calm and makes for extreme excitement in the event of a forced retreat. Rumours abounded about the difficulties and remote situation but the only concrete facts we had been able to glean were that there was a rather dramatic overhanging crack at one point and that Darbyshire had taken a truly monstrous swing whilst seconding – after which he had only managed to regain the rock by means of a long prusik up from an airborne but wave-washed position. Adrenalin had, we understood, flowed freely.

4

Testing the Nerves

As with all big routes, we enjoyed a protracted build-up to a proper attempt. For a start it was a long way from Newton Abbot to Tintagel and visits to this part of the country tended to be full weekend affairs with a liberal intake of the North Cornwall disco scene on a Saturday night followed by nights in a varied selection of commendably comfortable barns which farmers seemed to have kindly lined with hay for us. Everything in the village of Tintagel is named after King Arthur. Breakfast in King Arthur's Café, followed by ice-cream in King Arthur's Ice-Cream Parlour and a walk down King Arthur's Path leads to the point where King Arthur's Castle is visible on what is almost an offshore island. A bridge connects the mainland to the steep steps leading up to the remains of the castle and – horror of horrors – a toll booth with a ticket collector guarding the way. This was a surprise as our approach description did not mention anything like this at all. We retreated in disarray. Perhaps we were in the wrong place. There was a very impressive cliff on the west side on the mainland peninsula leading out to the bridge, and after a quick conference we decided to slip round the back of the toll booth and head for this. Precarious moments followed (which again seemed worryingly adrift from the guide book's helpful words) before we were able to peer hopefully across a steep wall into an impressive groove line. The key feature of Il Duce was supposed to be a major groove line so at least something fitted. We could not see the overhanging chimney that we had heard so much about but then it would, we convinced ourselves, have been over-optimistic to expect to see every feature from the bottom.

The first pitch appeared distressingly challenging, gently over-hanging with what looked like very fragile pieces of ironstone projecting from the wall of smooth dusty white rock. Each of us in turn tried to push the other into the lead. Usually such situations are resolved by the keenest eventually stepping forward and getting on with it. Here it was different. Jon gazed contentedly down the coastline, soaking up the North Cornwall atmosphere, whilst Mike showed definite signs of enthusiasm – but for seconding only. Meanwhile I tried to convince myself that I could do it, but baulked each time at the continuously steep ground, the fragility of the rock and the complete lack of protection. Every now and then, Gerry could be seen on the clifftop shouting encouragement and wondering what was going on.

Ultimately it was clear that there was a distinct lack of moral fibre in the team. Jon was first to suggest a King Arthur's cream tea, but the support this idea received guaranteed that our first visit to a Littlejohn 'megaroute' was not to be a resounding success. It did though allow us to make a thorough reconnaissance of not only the tea shops and pubs in Tintagel, but also the stunning sea cliffs of the area. Lye Rock, Willa Park and Long Island a mile or two north of Tintagel particularly attracted our attention. There did not appear to be any routes here, but then after our experience on Prayer Mat, I for one was still feeling pretty negative about new routes and was sure that there must be a good reason why such impressive chunks of rock had been left alone. How wrong I was, but it was to be some years before my eyes were opened up to the pleasures so close at hand.

Perhaps the most positive discovery that day was the realisation that Il Duce was not on the wall that had defeated us so conclusively. In fact closer perusal of the literature showed it to be clearly described as lying on the north-west face of Tintagel island itself. We all had a strong aversion to paying to have a closer look, so a happy Sunday morning was spent stealthily approaching the island without attracting the attention of the admission-fee collector. At low tide we discovered it was possible to sneak across the exposed beach beneath the bridge and, by dint of walking through a sea-carved passage, reach the island at a point that was not visible from the toll booth. We were feeling very pleased with ourselves as the four of us scrambled up steep grass to gain the gate through the old castle walls, and were picking our way through the historical remains, when a horribly efficient-looking official headed purposefully towards us, pointing firmly at the rope across the top of Mike's rucksack.

'What is that?'
'A rope.'

Further questioning revealed that yes, we were climbers, and no, we did not have tickets because we 'had not noticed' the ticket booth. Both of these points went down very badly; climbing it seemed was not encouraged on the headland (but neither was it banned) and wandering through the remains of King Arthur's Castle without having paid was clearly regarded as a particularly heinous crime. Gloomily we paid our entrance fees, and sat around waiting for someone else to distract his attention from us and accentuate his undoubted ulcer problems. It took a long time, but eventually he lost interest and wandered over to harass some other visitors who were dripping ice-cream on to the castle walls. With unhindered movement restored, it took only one more false start before we located the descent ramp and were at last able to peer along the first pitch – a traverse line between overhangs leading away out of sight around a corner. It looked atmospheric, committing and likely to live up to its reputation. For us it would certainly require a full day's effort. We retreated to spend a week chewing over the prospects, involving an especially friendly 'goodbye' to the 'Guardian' of King Arthur.

He was on duty again the following weekend but we were prepared, tickets in hand and ropes concealed inside our rucksacks. This was a big moment for us; George's phone bill had gone up considerably during the week as Littlejohn's routes and Il Duce in particular were discussed to exhaustion. And here we were at last. If nothing else it looked more amenable than the scene of our erroneous reconnaissance the previous weekend. It was however, a horizontal traverse and therefore equally exciting for both leader and second. Jon somehow headed off in the lead – we would argue about who would go last later. The reported grade of 5a immediately felt tough. Jon, though, was going well. It was more the apparent difficulty of the moves that he was making rather than any hesitation on his part that had us worried. He seemed to be getting close to the stance when the rope suddenly went tight and he could no longer be seen. Initially we found this rather funny – at least Mike and I did – Jon could not be seen and the roar of the breakers below meant that he could not be heard either. The minutes ticked by as Mike, who was belaying, held the rope and waited for something to happen. Gradually the funny side of the situation began to fade. What was happening? Was Jon in the water? Or was he hanging in mid-air unable for some reason to climb the rope? Either way after ten minutes or so it was decided that Jon should be tied off and Mike should belay me along the traverse to the point where I could see what the problem was. At the back of our minds was the prospect of the extreme embarrassment involved in seeking assistance through King Arthur's Guardian. Jon's safety never really crossed our minds – it was taken for granted.

The traverse was difficult. Greasy rock, accentuated by occasional fine spray from the waves booming into the cliff fifteen metres below, made for maximum insecurity and called for extreme caution. The tight rope leading horizontally out to Jon disappeared over the sharp edge of a groove about twelve metres from the stance. In between, a shallow groove cutting through the traverse made the rope stand clear of the rock and form an extra obstacle to be negotiated *en route*. Time passed quickly but Jon must have been dangling for a good twenty minutes before I was able to peer over the edge of the groove and come face to face with a rather bedraggled Mr Stevenson prusiking up the rope. A tiny edge he was pulling on had snapped off and he had fallen six metres down an overhanging groove. Though still six metres above sea level, he was easily reached by the bigger waves breaking against the cliff and had to endure several soakings whilst searching for some suitable prusik loops. Most of our equipment was on thick tape slings and nuts on wire or thick rope. Neither is ideal for prusiking on 9 mm rope, and he had slipped back a couple of times before finding the successful combination for upward progress. We now indulged in a frantic scrabble along the remaining (fortunately easier) section of the traverse with Jon tied on to two ropes and me on to the other end of one of them. The rope, of course, ran out at the least opportune moment with both of us slithering about on an excitingly frictionless slab. Mike was out of earshot but his intuitive understanding of the situation saved the day as he rearranged belays and miraculously produced enough slack to enable both Jon and me to reach the stance. Mike, true to form, seconded the pitch and dismantled the knitting in minutes but, even so, more than two hours had passed climbing one pitch which was reputedly easy compared to what was to follow.

Delays were not over though; the sunny morning had faded into a rather cold and windy day. Jon, soaked through from his brush with the Atlantic, was by now shivering violently and suggesting that he would rather return along the traverse than risk the embarrassment of dying from exposure on the Cornish Riviera. And so the whole frightening process was reversed, this time with Jon placing lots of protection on the first half and none on the second so that I could traverse back to the halfway point and return to Mike without us losing any gear. Life was getting very complex and time-consuming – but eventually Mike and I addressed the problem of pitch 2. One point in our favour was that the sun had now pierced the clouds again and done a remarkable job at getting rid of the truly horrible greasy veneer which had massively increased our feeling of insecurity.

The famous chimney was now visible above us. We sympathised with Keith Darbyshire, who must have been dangling at least five metres away from the rock when he parted company whilst seconding this pitch on the first ascent. I could see the problem. An aid peg, necessary to gain the chimney (since done away with), looked to be the last piece of protection for some way. It also was not in place, which presented a whole new range of problems in that neither of us had ever placed an aid peg before. Mike, bristling with frustration at the previous delays, surged up the crack and smacked a peg hard into a rather blind crack. Unfortunately, our pegs had been reclaimed from a variety of Welsh mountain crags and Devon sea cliffs. They were past their prime. The fine specimen of a thin knife-blade peg that he had selected crumpled like a concertina as he struggled to hammer it home. The crack overhung and with strength fading fast he was soon back at the belay. The peg looked distressingly insecure but fortunately there were some protection nuts just below it and gingerly, we suspended first Mike's weight and then both of us together. The peg bent alarmingly but held. We did not have a clue how strong it might be, so it was decided that, as the lightest, I should have the pleasure of trusting my weight to this crumpled, rusty piece of steel.

The crack itself was not exactly easy, but soon a rather worried version of my former self was inspecting the bending piece of ironmongery from close quarters. It is surprising how clearly one's mind can focus on such an all-important item. The image of a bending rust-flaked peg is photographically etched in my memory right down to the detail of a particularly crucial-looking rust flake parting company just as I stretched up for a series of holds leading to the base of the chimney. But it held – and I gained height as a result. Now I effectively hung with my body wedged in the chimney. This was not like the familiar Boa Constrictor Chimney at High Rocks: it was more a wide crack between the wall and a huge overhang

above me. It was, however, wide enough for me to squeeze up
inside and jam hips, shoulders and any other convenient part of
the anatomy across at various points. The penalty of a mistake
was a bit more serious than a High Rocks slither to the ground.
Here a slip would result in one dropping clear into space. At this
moment I was glad to have a thin scrawny body. At school Gillian,
my childhood sweetheart, had laughed at it but here it was in
its element. Squirming on through constrictions unsuited to most
mortals, I arrived at a magnificent little rock ledge at the foot of a
long prominent groove line.

Mike, despite being of more normal dimensions, succeeded in his
usual sickening trick of seconding the pitch in half the time it had
taken me to lead it and we both peered hopefully at the ground
ahead. Although clearly difficult, it was more conventional in its
defences. Also we were well away from the clutches of the sea now
and the sun was warming the route nicely. It was hard, but possible
and with our fair share of adrenalin flow we continued over a small
roof, a huge flake and finally up a section of fascinatingly weathered
horizontally striated rock which gave way on to grass and the top.
The elation was tremendous. Never before had we succeeded on a
route like this. The fact that it had been touch and go for much of the
lower section simply added to the sense of achievement. The light
was fading fast as we danced amongst the ancient ruins, clambered
over the locked gate (quite challenging in itself), on down the path,
over the bridge, past the empty toll booth and back to Jon, Gerry
and an exceptionally fine night in King Arthur's pubs.

Between the three of us our climbing preferences were perhaps
becoming clear by now. Mike was just keen to go climbing; he
did not care where he went so long as he could pull on hand
holds and stand on (sometimes non-existent!) footholds over and
over again. If it was serious or intimidating he was happy; if it was
safe but technically difficult he was happy too. Effectively, wherever
he was in the world, he was an effervescing bundle of energy keen to
tackle any climb. Inactivity was and still is the only thing that could
depress the man's energy levels.

Jon was more mellow and less hyperactive in his approach to the
sport. He enjoyed the whole climbing environment. Perhaps there
was a slight preference towards more solid rock, but he was never
visibly upset by not getting to the top of routes like Il Duce. Being

a very relaxed communicator he tended to be our trio's ears and mouthpiece in the climbing scene, finding out what the general view was about everything from Cornish climbing ethics to the latest new route in North Wales.

I suppose I lay somewhere in between the two, I did not have the unquenchable thirst for nonstop activity of Mike, but I certainly went out of my way to find inspiring objectives which then became milestones which simply *had* to be climbed. Certainly I was different from Jon in this respect and could not sit back comfortably if for some reason the weekend's objective could not be achieved. Failures simply had to be returned to the following weekend. I was particularly taken by the adventurous challenge in the South-West and it was this and of course the proximity to Gerry's place in Newton Abbot that led me to Dawlish and one of Keith Darbyshire's finest creations.

The Parson is a sea stack that leans against the sandy conglomerate cliffs just to the west of the South Devon town of Dawlish. It is clearly visible from trains on the main South-West rail line and had also attracted my eye every time we drove along the coastal road hereabouts. It was many months after I had first spotted it that I discovered Darbyshire had climbed it by a route which was much respected both for the loose and serious nature of the climbing as well as for its approach through 500 metres of mainline railway tunnel. This unconventional activity is necessary because steep cliffs drop into deep water on either side of the stack and an abseil is out of the question owing to the fiercely protected privacy of the clifftop gardens. But the tunnel gives access to a tidal strip which at dead low tide enables one to reach the base of the Parson without getting wet. There is, however, something very worrying about the tunnel. It is on a bend. This means that it is not possible to see right the way through or even see if a train is approaching. This is particularly worrying on such a fast stretch of frequently used line.

The approach end of the tunnel is just above a pleasant beach, much used in the summer. I felt we were attracting some particularly penetrating and questioning stares. It has to be admitted that the average sunbathing beach family has difficulty understanding the urge that makes apparently sane men don harnesses, helmets and head torches, adorn themselves with ropes and ironmongery and disappear jangling into a railway tunnel on a nice sunny day. I suppose the boringly sensible amongst us would have checked the rail timetables but British Rail's reliability record seemed to negate such extreme behaviour and, having heard that Darbyshire himself had escaped injury upon meeting a train, we trusted that we too could avoid being squelched between train and tunnel wall. In fact it was not quite as bad as I had feared, the gap between the rails and the sidewall being wide enough to allow some leeway. It was, however, a particularly character-building experience walking into a tunnel, not being able to see out of the far end and only having someone else's word as to the length. Things could have been worse. Although the tunnel is curved it is possible to see the light at the far end before losing sight of one's entrance.

It took two attempts before I was to succeed on the Parson, the first being thwarted by our incompetent assessment of the tides which necessitated a return trip through the tunnel. As a result of this it was on my traverse of the tunnel that I met a train. Unusually, neither Mike nor Jon were present. I was climbing with a group of South-West climbers, one of whom, Steve Bell, not only went on to make a name for himself as a very fine rock-climber, but in 1993 became one of the first mountaineers to guide clients to the summit of Everest. There was no hint of the future prowess of any members of the team as the four of us lay down in a line hard into the corner between the oily stones and the sooty wall. The train rushed past fairly fast – at least it sounded that way. I just kept my nose into the corner and hoped that the driver had not spotted us in his lights. Nothing happened and in the absence of any British Rail body-searching teams I shall assume that we got away with it.

The descent from the embankment at the far end on to the beach was actually rather challenging. A frighteningly rusted ladder ended at a point six metres above the rocky foreshore from where an even more dubious piece of knotted rope dangled down from the last rung for a further three metres. The alternative to using the rope was some rather tricky wall-climbing on very greasy rock with a nasty landing below. Much whimpering was in evidence but at length the soot- and oil-stained team were on the beach ready for the final leg of the approach. At least the tide was out on this occasion. As we had discovered to our cost on my previous visit, anything other than dead low tide means either a serious swim or a return through the tunnel. Even at dead low tide the Parson itself is protected by a deep channel about two metres wide. The run-up is very limited indeed but the route looked sufficiently inspiring for Steve and me to make risk-packed jumps, both bruising our heels somewhat but successfully reaching the base of the stack. The other two were less certain but rescue appeared in the form of a father-and-son team floating around in an inflatable dinghy. Intrigued by what was going on, they rowed into the gap and were kind enough to allow access by clambering over the boat – which appeared to be only just up to the task and to us looked distinctly unsafe for rowing around in. No doubt they were thinking much the same about our activities.

The climb itself was just as I had hoped: not too difficult technically, but with a unique and adventurous feel. Large pebbles protruding from a very coarse crumbly red sandstone often provided the only holds and, although it was only thirty metres long, it had what I imagined to be the hallmark of Keith Darbyshire quality stamped all over it: uncertainty, adventure, excitement and, perhaps more than anything else, unique memorability. It is still clearly imprinted on my mind today – over fifteen years later. The top pitch was the crux and particularly exciting with awkward 5a climbing protected only by a large nut wedged between two projecting pebbles of dubious security. The top, too, provided anxious moments – a bald dome devoid of any natural belay possibilities. It was the first of many times that a drive-in ice-screw has come to my rescue. Increasingly shunned in British ice-climbing circles these fine pieces of hardware come into their own on crumbly rock of this type.

The description that we had spoke optimistically of jumping across to the clifftop and escaping through private grounds. Perhaps the summit had changed or maybe I was feeling particularly wimpish. Either way with the top sloping down very steeply, a gap of a metre, and the other side sloping up very steeply, a jump was out of the question and a delicate slither down (protected by the ice-screw hammered hard into the top) was followed by some tricky moves to gain the private grounds. These certainly appeared to be very private. I had hoped for an overgrown expanse through which a discreet getaway could be made, but what faced us was a series of immaculately cared-for gardens complete with orchard and vegetable patch and no obvious way out. The four of us wandered hopefully in the general direction of the car. At last, just as it became clear that escape was imminent, an impressively irate shout from a gardener 100 metres distant powered our sprint to the road.

The Parson contained almost all the features that I have come to prefer in rock-climbing. Respectable technical difficulty, exciting approach, unusual climbing, no queues and a memorable adventure. I made a mental note to search for such features in future objectives.

In fact the regular trips to Devon and Cornwall were about to end, Gerry's teaching job had come to an end and her unemployment, combined with my desire to leave my increasingly dissatisfying job at Harrow Council (and London in general) prompted a move to the Peak District. Both Mike and Jon were also keen and, with Sheffield fast becoming the technical rock-climbing centre of England, it is perhaps not so surprising that we were drawn to this climber's Mecca, despite the fact that we had only spent two or three extremely enjoyable weekends climbing there. It was however to change the course of things for the next year or so.

5

Hail to Shale

November 1976. Stoney Middleton. Every movement made the tent fabric shower ice crystals. The tent itself was not exactly large and with Gerry and me lying side by side with duvet jackets supplementing our seriously inadequate boy-scout Polywarm sleeping-bags, it was just about impossible to move without touching the sides. Jon was arguably better off in the back of the minivan but then he had all our gear piled around him in an impressively restrictive manner. Money was running out and Peggy, the landlady of the Moon Inn in Stoney Middleton, had asked us not to frequent the place unless we were prepared to drink more. As the pub was invariably empty midweek, I felt this a trifle harsh. Although it had to be admitted that the profit on half a pint each in exchange for an evening's warmth and comfort did leave us the takers rather than losers in the transaction.

Finding somewhere to live in Sheffield was not proving to be as easy as I had expected. Mike Morrison sat on the fence for a while, but ultimately decided to stick with Thornton Heath for a bit longer, whilst Gerry, Jon and I persevered. The problem seemed to be the university and polytechnic which prompted a huge influx into the town in September. Climbers choosing to arrive in October were on to a loser. Initially we did not regard this as a problem. The weather was fine, and having relatively little experience of Peak District climbing, the three of us enthusiastically set about tackling the classics of the area. Standards seemed harsh and my ego was in for a further bashing, but the knack of gritstone climbing grew, and by November, when the first winter frosts began to bite in earnest, our standards had improved to respectable levels and the occasional new route was being attempted.

Living accommodation, though, was still non-existent. Passionate romance huddled in a frosty tent may be fine for the odd weekend, but as a semi-permanent predicament, the situation left much to be desired. Furthermore, personal discomfort aside, George, whom I had remained close to, was making increasingly unenthusiastic noises about the prospect of his son becoming a longterm tent dweller in a quarry-ridden Peaks District dale. The situation was saved by a Polish secondhand car salesman on the Abbeydale Road who, having acquired the use of a showroom with a large unwanted flat above, was prepared to rent this many-roomed monster at an affordable price. It was in due course packed full of like-minded individuals and was to become the scene of some memorable parties which soon soured our initially good landlord-tenant relationship.

The number of climbers in the Peak District was even then tremendously high compared to the amount of unclimbed rock available. Nevertheless, for those so inclined, there were still gaps between existing lines to be plugged and even the occasional bona fide classic new line – although invariably of a very high standard. Competition was intense and perhaps because of this feelings ran high and there was a distinct mistrust of outsiders. In retrospect I can see that our initial fumbling incompetence on classic lines prejudiced feelings against us when, just a few months later, we were claiming substantial first ascents. At the time, though, a phrase attributed to Pete Livesey seemed admirably to sum up the fiercely competitive environment. 'These days,' he said, 'the crags are reverberating with the sound of "Intense Young Men".' He was talking about a new breed of climbing-wall-trained climber, and then went on to abbreviate such activists as 'IYMs'. It was this abbreviation which stuck in out minds and became a much used part of our vocabulary. I was perhaps rather unsure how to handle the criticism and never defended my corner as fiercely as I should have done, relying on Jon's socialising talents to make friends in all camps and smooth troubled waters.

Animosities reached a peak in December 1976 on Ed Drummond's notorious creation, the Linden at Curbar Edge. His first ascent had created a furore because he had drilled two holes and used two sky-hooks for aid. Though this overcame the technical crux, it still left some very hard wall climbing. The route was, however, on gritstone – 'God's own rock', as I have heard devotees refer to it – and such jiggery-pokery did not go down well. Subsequently, a couple of pegs were placed and removed, and one sky-hook-hole enlarged.

Certainly by the time Jon and I became interested in the line in late 1976, it was something of a discredited masterpiece. Livesey's IYMs had sniffed around the line and although we were aware of several abseil inspections, no one appeared to have attempted to free it or even repeat the line in Drummond's style. In line with the modern philosophy, and maybe crossing the 'IYM' threshold ourselves, we abseiled down, practised moves and vigorously wire-brushed any lichen within a metre of the holds. Then Mike Morrison came up for the weekend and our trio was together again. Snow lay on the ground but the sun warmed the crag sufficiently for us to manage the first free ascent.

It was a curious time. Whilst our convincing photographic evidence and the lack of protection went some way towards silencing critics, the clinical nature of a rehearsed climb detracted greatly from my own personal satisfaction and did much to shape my future attitude to rock-climbing. I think the real problem was that because I had abseiled down and practised the moves, I knew exactly what was coming and, more than anything else, I *knew* that I could do it before I started to climb. I had effectively destroyed the sense of adventure and uncertainty and to me the sense of achievement was correspondingly lacking. Nevertheless it cannot be denied that the appreciative comments of contemporaries and my first experience of magazine exposure were definite ego boosts. Gradually the abuse which was once hurled at me in Peak District socialising spots subsided and we became more accepted in the rather incestuous, but immensely talented world of Peak District climbing.

Things were far from perfect though. The poor minivan was tiring at last and life on the dole in Sheffield was fast eating up the pennies that I had managed to save whilst slaving away at clerical work in London. My relationship with Gerry was clearly heading towards a split, and perhaps it was my state of mind, but the Sheffield winter seemed depressingly dank and grey; it certainly did nothing to inspire me to get out climbing. It was however the great Abbeydale Road party which I can thank for forcing me out of a state of rather indecisive lethargy and prompting a change in direction.

The details should not perhaps be laboured, but let me just say that a rather fine climber of the time happened to be queuing for the toilet with no clothes on when he was caught short and decided to forget the toilet and use the open window instead. Unfortunately the landlord's perfectly polished secondhand cars were on display

down below. It would have been difficult to score a more messy
direct hit. In response to nagging by the flat occupants, the culprit
could be found at 10 a.m. the next morning ineffectually dabbing at a
shiny Hillman Avenger with a wad of damp toilet tissue. This in itself
might not have been too bad, but at some point during the party,
his trousers had been thrown out the window and were carried away
caught on a lorry loaded with stacked reinforcement grids which had
been waiting at traffic lights just outside. In fact the only clothes he
could find were an abandoned pair of jeans with an unfortunately
positioned large hole. The sight of a seriously hungover partygoer
trying to remove excreta from the furry Avenger window seal whilst
wearing nothing but this pair of trousers was the last straw for our
hitherto patient landlord. We did not stay at the flat much longer.
The new tenants turned out to be something to do with the police
who were presumably (and apparently incorrectly) regarded as nice
quiet people.

Our forced departure coincided with a planned two-month trip to
the Alps, so it was not until my return that the question of where to
live and what to do next with my life arose. Jon and Gerry returned
to Sheffield, but a couple of half-hearted visits convinced me that a
reconciliation with Gerry was out of the question and with nothing
to hold me there I gradually veered back to George's house in
Wembley.

'Why don't you look for a job, son?'

The question was inevitable and relevant. I was bored without a
job in London and was becoming increasingly listless and decadent.
It had been different in Sheffield where there was fulltime climbing
to keep me occupied until the weather deteriorated and I had
then turned first to a clerical job with the National Water Council
followed by labouring with a local builder and decorator. For some
reason it was all right to have a labouring job in Sheffield (where
at that time many other climbers made enough money to pursue
their obsessions by similar means) but in London such jobs had no
appeal.

Meanwhile George kept circling advertisements in the paper and
so I took myself in my suit with my thirteen 'O'-levels and one
'A'-level (rock-climbing had taken over at that point) along for
a clerical job interview at the Inland Revenue. Despite the good
pay offered, I must admit to having been unenthusiastic at the

prospect of working for the Tax Office and really only applied for the job to keep George happy. I purposely failed to admit to all my qualifications and projected what I thought to be an indifferent air at the interview. Nevertheless I somehow got the job and had what I felt to be the dubious pleasure of becoming Administrative Officer at Harrow Collection Office. In retrospect I realise the job was a godsend in that it restored some order into my life. In my couple of months of indecisive wavering after my return from the Alps, I had slipped into some distinctly negative habits – midday starts to the day and general lethargy (even towards climbing) did not bode well. It seemed that though I had originally left London to maximise my climbing time, the lack of pressure frequently led to leaving things for another day and generally losing momentum. My return to regular employment was undoubtedly a positive step. Weekends away became regular features, and in rock-climbing terms a healthy enthusiasm replaced an obsessive but increasingly ineffectual approach. Ambitions returned again.

Mike Morrison was still in London and we soon fell back in together as a regular climbing team. Overtime payments provided sufficient funds to replace the original minivan with the second of a final tally of thirteen such vehicles, and weekend trips to all parts of the country began in earnest. Climbing in Devon had opened our eyes to the potential away from traditional areas and, after twelve months of virtually exclusive activity in the Peak District, I felt over-ripe for checking out other interesting areas. This was not a new feeling, but one that had been growing gradually, but suppressed by the incestuous nature of the scene I had been sucked into in Sheffield. Back in London there were no such problems. London may be a long way from conventional rock-climbing centres, but it has its advantages. Whatever perverse destination one may wish to visit at the weekend, an enthusiastic partner can invariably be found, whether it be for a weekend on Scottish ice, the Dover chalk cliffs or even flying over to sea stacks on the west coast of Ireland!

Contact was renewed with old schoolfriends whose social scene was still thriving. Ian and two or three others again became regular drinking partners and disco-goers. However, the two scenes did not mix incredibly well simply because discos tended to be Friday and Saturday night affairs which clashed impossibly with weekend climbing. The sort of girls we met at North London discos also proved remarkably disinterested in my attempts to introduce them to climbing. Only one allowed herself to be taken away for a weekend. Poor Marie. On the Hanger Lane dance floor she was in her element and after a couple of successful outings to the cinema, I mooted the idea of a romantic weekend in the Cheddar Gorge. She jumped at the idea and I really thought that perhaps I was on to a winner here with a North London disco-loving prospective rock-climber.

Things went badly from the start. Knocking enthusiastically at the door of her Ealing bedsit at 7 p.m. on a Friday evening, I was greeted by a near-shaven head with vivid purple roots peering hesitantly round the door.

'Bloody hell! What have you done to your hair?'

I could not contain myself. This was a lady who had flowing blonde hair and cultivated an image of classical good looks. I just could not believe what I saw before me. There was a nasty pregnant silence during which I began to feel uncomfortable. Something was not quite right.

'Are you looking for Marie?'

Embarrassment flowed over me. This girl, who was by now looking less like Marie than ever, glared reproachfully at me. I struggled feebly to make amends but Marie had already appeared and the would-be lookalike (who I learned later was renowned for her irritability) ranted horribly. We left Ealing with obscenities still rending the evening air and general unhappiness oozing from Marie. It was not a good start.

A night out in the Cheddar Gorge started out only slightly better. Marie had somehow got the impression that we would be staying at a hotel or at least some kind of bed and breakfast accommodation. Certainly she was distinctly nonplussed when it became clear that minivan accommodation was all that was on offer. Questions such as 'Where can I have a wash?' and 'How do I get ready in the morning?' were sidestepped with difficulty. Looking across at her immaculate mascara and pristine white trousers I could sense the reasons for her concern and began to wonder at the wisdom of my romantic suggestion.

It was hot that night and we slept with the back doors flung wide open. It was about 2 a.m. when the heavy throbbing of Harley Davidson motorcycles aroused me from my slumbers. A Hell's Angel chapter was passing through the Cheddar Gorge, but although one or two of them were circling around near to the van, nothing too threatening was happening. I kept my head down and pretended to be asleep. Inevitably, though, the open back doors attracted attention; the throbbing grew closer and powerful lights lit up the interior of the van. Trembling by now, I kept my head down whilst Marie vibrated with fear at her own rate beside me. More bikes appeared and the light increased. I contemplated closing the back doors but thought of our relatively remote position and the possibly inflammatory effect of such an action. Inactivity and crossed fingers would have to do.

'Have a good night, people.'

I could not believe it. Never have I felt so grateful to be classed as uninteresting. I tried to dismiss the incident with a laugh but knew that the anxious tone in my voice gave me away. Marie was distinctly uncommunicative. It was only early Saturday morning and our supposedly adventurous and romantic weekend was not going well.

Gentle strolls and a few easy scrambles on Saturday meant that by Sunday morning I had regained some lost ground, and Marie was expressing interest in climbing something a little more challenging. Somehow we ended up in the Avon Gorge with a local climber, Gordon Jenkin. My choice of route was a bad one – an early Pat Littlejohn extreme called the Bilk – I should perhaps have anticipated that Marie would not appreciate the pleasures of this climb when she had a little difficulty with the mud slope leading to the foot. Gordon led the first pitch. It was short and not too difficult – at least when compared to what was to follow – but it did overhang gently. Marie started up boldly, but encountered some difficulty at ten metres. She had never had to put her weight on the rope before and simply would not trust Gordon to hold her. Unfortunately she was unable to make any progress or retreat. She hung batlike for an impressively long time, clearly becoming more and more distraught. Gordon tried to cajole her from above whilst I soloed up to offer advice and consolation from close at hand. I got kicked in the head whilst Gordon was on the receiving end of an impressive tirade of verbal abuse. Ultimately of course she could hang on no more and with a tearful scream swung out away from the rock towards a nearby tree branch. This she clung on to koala-bearlike, mascara running and coiffure showing distinct signs of dishevelment. Gordon tried to let out the rope and lower her but this only resulted in increased wailing and a loop of slack rope beneath her. Finally, completely spent, she peeled away from the branch and was lowered like a rag doll through the tree, landing in a dense cover of brambles and stinging nettles below.

We did not speak all the way back to London. I did see her again, back on form on the Hanger Lane disco floor. She ignored me. Her friend told me she spoke little about the weekend. It was a pity, I concluded, but beautiful disco queens seemed unlikely to be on the weekend climber's wavelength. I concentrated on climbing for a while.

With Jon still in Sheffield, Mike down in Thornton Heath and me in Wembley, it was only natural that I should make an effort to get in with a local group of climbers. I heard that a group called the North London Mountaineering Club met on a Wednesday night at the Sobell Centre climbing-wall, or to be more accurate, at the Globe pub opposite, and it was here that I gravitated. There were a few faces I recognised from weekends away, but most people seemed to be paired up in regular climbing teams or not too keen to venture on to the North Cornwall shale cliffs that increasingly dominated my aspirations. There was, however, one chap who showed interest. We were different in many ways but enjoyed the same broad approach to climbing.

Simon Fenwick was in those days the classic East End 'wide boy'. His souped-up orange Escort Sport, complete with aggressive spoilers and racing stripes, contrasted sharply with my civil-servant look and white minivan with horrendous rust stains (the result of me naïvely painting it with emulsion). His background was distinctly rough compared to mine and his stories from the Chingford disco and snooker club scenes tended to involve violence of a level that made the occasional Wembley fracas pale into insignificance.

Top of my list of climbing priorities at the time was a line up the 150-metre Henna Cliff at Morwenstow on the North Devon coast a few miles north of Bude. This cliff had first attracted my attention in E. C. Pyatt's *A Climber in the West Country* where he wrote: 'the gigantic Henna Cliff over 400 feet high has a sheer face which is too loose for the climber . . .' The grapevine had told me that Keith Darbyshire had attempted it some time in the early 1970s, and Pat Littlejohn had said that it was 'interesting'. A visit was clearly in order.

In the village pub over a tuning-up beer, the barman told us how the landlord had soloed the cliff at Henna many years before.

Unfortunately, he was unable to describe the line his boss had taken, let alone tell us exactly how to find the cliff. Neither of us had brought a map, nor had the faintest idea of how to get to the boulder beach below. Some clifftop wandering revealed a small wooden footbridge which provided an excellent abseil point, albeit to the consternation of the coastal cliff path walkers. But once established on the boulder beach, away from the public eye, an easy walk to the north revealed an excitingly large and steep cliff with only one really obvious weakness; a fault line, forming a chimney up the central part of the crag. Unfortunately the bottom seventy metres or so were gently overhanging and looked particularly unjustifiable. Knowing that Darbyshire got about fifty metres up, we searched studiously for signs of rotting slings, etc. Simon, never having seen a shale cliff before, studied the rock with interest. Eventually, unable to locate any evidence of the previous party, we had no option but to rely on our own judgement and decided to try an entry into the fault line from the left.

Being a kind-hearted soul I offered the first pitch to Simon, who to my surprise readily accepted the sharp end and started off up a projecting rib. Soon the happy tone of his voice changed. 'It's all loose,' he complained, prodding distastefully at the rock. I couldn't help thinking that from below the section that he was on appeared to be one of the most solid parts of the route. This did not seem a good point of encouragement and I remained silent. Simon inspected the rock more closely and poked it curiously with an ice-screw. 'Haven't seen this kind of stuff before,' he mused. 'I think I'll belay here.' Many swearwords later I joined Simon belayed to two ice-screws on ·a shale ramp about ten metres up. One hour had passed and it was mid-afternoon. Things were definitely not going well. I wondered whether to suggest a dignified retreat, but Simon was by now becoming uncomfortably enthusiastic, pointing out overhangs and non-existent weaknesses above. He looked at me expectantly, waiting for me to glide easily along the ramp and up the wall.

I had other ideas and reached for my ice-axe (specially resurrected from its summer hibernation). Fortunately the overlying material of the ramp proved very soft, but even so it was a precarious matter to clear footholds and edge along between the overhangs. A pinnacle I had been heading for turned out to be more of a bulge of unstable rock and a groove of worrying stability (and not inconsiderable difficulty) led to a belay ledge with marked similarities to a rotting windowbox. Simon followed rapidly, thinking (as I discovered later) that this type of looseness was quite normal on all shale cliffs.

Having completed belay formalities with only minimal structural collapse, we considered the rock above. Five or so metres above us a diagonal ramp/chimney line led up rightwards into a wide chimney and the main fault line. A short struggle later and it was more than a little disheartening to see that on closer acquaintance this turned out to be more of a diagonal U-shaped scoop of poor rock with unhelpful overhangs above and below. We had expected to be able to stomach-traverse the ramp but the overhangs above were much closer than expected and any progress would definitely have to be made in a hand-traverse position – at least after the first three metres, which looked as though they might just permit a unique lying-down back-and-foot grovel! I peered hopefully around for other alternatives, but it was clear that at the speed we were going night would fall long before we reached the top and any time wasted attempting other lines could easily cost us a night on the crag.

Placing several poor peg-runners in a particularly soft shale band I mantelshelfed into the scoop, which promptly started a gradual but determined sliding movement. Instinct took over from any climbing ability and I squirmed into a back-and-foot position. Down below faint sounds could be heard voicing increasing doubts about shale climbing. I thrutched up to the right and with great relief placed a reasonable peg-runner. From my new position the slanting chimney line above appeared fairly reasonable but an obviously difficult section barred access to its base. The difficulty consisted of a band of soft coal-like material which lay on the very sloping floor of the ramp and moved alarmingly whenever a mantelshelf movement was attempted. From below, a miserable voice advised that the weather had stopped threatening and that a steady drizzle was falling. Being amidst overhangs I was unaware of this and, ignoring the warning, continued until safely established in the base of the chimney. Still dry beneath overhangs, I squirmed up to join the main fault line on a sensational saddle of projecting rock. A lack of good belays here necessitated climbing a difficult but well-protected bulge to gain a good niche with poor ice-screw belays embedded in a curious sandy conglomerate.

I was out from under the overhangs now and where this material had got wet it was transforming itself into an unclimbable frictionless paste. Despite liberal encouragement, Simon remained soggily marooned on his stance.

It was becoming obvious that a particularly fine epic was imminent; a sea mist had now engulfed the crag, daylight was fading fast and the rain increased. Simon was about twenty-five metres below and ten metres to one side. Looking closely at the belays I was uncomfortably aware that they were not going to permit carefree, bouncing abseils. However, there seemed no option but an abseil of some sort – I vaguely wondered what Blackshaw's *Mountaineering Manual* would suggest in such circumstances. Down in the gloom Simon was sounding less than happy. He tied his end of the rope into his belay with the result that much of the strain of my weight was taken by a very poor peg a metre or so above him. Unlike Simon, I knew how insecure it was. The now soaking rock reduced friction to nil and me to a kind of slithering tyrolean. I reached the stance with great relief without it pulling. The whole situation was sufficiently adrenalin-producing for us to completely forget about the instability of the belay ledge. I collapsed quietly whilst Simon struggled to pull the ropes through. It didn't take long to realise that despite my elaborate preparations up above, they were decidedly jammed. However, if we both hung on separate ropes and one person then released his grip it was discovered that about ten centimetres of shale-sliver-infested rope would ooze through. We were not in the best of moods as we alternately hung, jumped, let go, swore and developed impressive blisters. Whilst changing over, one rope somehow managed to snake its way out of our grasp to hang uselessly about three metres out from the rock and five metres to one side. Much precious and precarious time was then wasted recapturing it. It seemed a very long time before two climbers and two ropes were eventually reunited for a final abseil in the twilight and a prusik through a waterfall back to the bridge to complete a most memorable day.

The following day at Brownspear Point a few miles up the coast a block demolished Simon's helmet and cut the rope neatly in two; back in London after his first shale expedition, it was perhaps not surprising that he sounded somewhat dubious regarding a further Henna visit. Mike Morrison, though, needed no persuasion to join me for a further attempt.

*   *   *

Preparations this time were considerably more detailed and exposed themselves to the public eye in the form of two homemade stakes and a sackful of bivouac equipment. The former we judged to be useful if a retreat should be necessary above the first overhanging band and the latter seemed advisable judging by our slow progress on the previous attempt.

Five weeks after the initial débâcle Mike and I were established at my previous highpoint above the lower overhangs, with only a distinctive rope groove in the rock to remind me of our previous epic. We were pleased to find that the next pitch, although it provided us with two difficult bulges, was easier angled and not so sustained as the previous ground – we felt in high spirits to gain thirty metres so quickly. Above us, the second band of overhangs was getting closer – a massive block with its top forming an obvious ledge split the continuation of the fault line. Two alternatives presented themselves: to our left a steep sandy fault line led directly to the top of the block, whilst to our right compact, blocky rock led to a rightwards-slanting groove from which a possible traverse line led left on to the top of the block.

'It's unjustifiable.'

Mike spoke with a huge grin on his face. Here was a man clearly operating in his element.

The lefthand line called for a short descent, so we decided to retain our height and try the righthand possibility. Poor ice-screw belays did little to encourage rapid progress but solid rock, if technically difficult and with little protection, allowed steady movement to the point where the traverse line led leftwards towards a possible stance. From close up this could be seen to be uncomfortably sloping with some precariously poised blocks at the start. A short overhanging wall separated the groove from the start of the ledge line and forced a wild swing leftwards into a strenuous position uncomfortably close to the blocks which moved but stayed *in situ*. Mike followed quickly, the encumbrance of the sack forcing him to trundle the offending blocks. Fortunately, the sun was now shining and in high spirits we contemplated the ground ahead.

From below it looked reasonable – a shallow sandy chimney led up to large overhangs which it seemed possible to outflank on the left or right. However, once engrossed it immediately became apparent that first impressions can be distinctly misleading. The walls of the chimney consisted of a crumbly yellow material and were sufficiently unstable to prevent the use of orthodox techniques.

Being too V-shaped for chimneying it provided a very absorbing cross between a mantelshelfing and bridging exercise, protected by a good ice-screw. At the overhang the possibilities noted from below looked at the best frightening and at the worst impossible. The death potential seemed excellent. For a long time I remained motionless. Up to the left overhangs appeared with a disconcerting frequency, whilst to the right an overhanging rib abutted against the main overhang, its only redeeming feature being one fragile projecting handhold. Much as it looked keen to part company with the cliff, it seemed just possible that it might last long enough to permit a wild swing out on to a small grass ledge three metres higher. Down below Mike was showing understandable concern at the lack of progress, and was keen to stress that retreat from here seemed an unappealing proposition, involving the loss of many brain cells as well as much equipment. With the future of our precious equipment at stake my renewed efforts culminated in a particularly uncontrollable swing on the crucial hold which, much to my relief, resulted in my being established safely on the elusive ledge.

We had hoped that the overhang would provide the final obstacle but half an hour later I had to admit that the slightly off-vertical ground ahead was nastily devoid of holds and frighteningly con-structed of outward-sloping shale slivers. Only eight metres up to the left a wide crack offered probable runner placements but the moves in between seemed impossible – I envisaged the prospect of a retreat and searched even more studiously for runner placements. Nothing worthwhile could be found and it became increasingly clear that either it was done without protection or it wasn't done at all. In frustration I started up yet again; sloping footholds and fragile layaways were the order of the day. Passing my previous highpoint the moves seemed irreversible and I could not help but realise that retreat was impossible without a long serious fall. With the crack almost in reach the holds thinned out even more – progress only seemed possible by balancing up on a particularly suspect sloping hold at waist level. The prospect appalled me but the lack of alternatives, combined with failing strength, prevented any further consideration . . . Heart in mouth, my weight was transferred and I straightened up; the crack was now in reach but the best hand-jamming position was still too high. Stretching higher I could feel the footholds move, my leg began to shake . . . the hold moved more . . . panic took over and I lurched into the crack, dust flew up from the back; a chick above flapped wildly, but a runner was placed and suddenly the panic was over, everything seemed under control again. The chick settled down deep in the crack, the dust settled and three metres higher I removed a seagull from a secluded niche and thankfully belayed.

Watching Mike seconding the pitch it struck me how out of place the sack containing our bivouac gear appeared on a South-West British sea cliff; however, Mike seemed quite at home with it as he joined me once more.

Above us things were finally looking more amenable – a short steep wall separated us from a slanting grassy ramp apparently leading to the top – however, we were learning not to be optimistic; most shale climbing appears about two grades easier than it actually is. Remarkably though, this pitch seemed to be an exception to the rule: the cliff appeared to be succumbing at last, and the initial wall proved as desperate as anticipated, but beyond this reasonable climbing led to within three metres of the top.

Excitement mounting I climbed the final easy wall to emerge on the clifftop path amidst the calm and tranquil scene of grazing sheep and families out for leisurely weekend strolls. The humans regarded us with indifference, the sheep with curiosity; I felt like telling them both just what they were missing and how I came to be standing on the edge of a Cornish cliff carrying an ice-axe and ice-screws, pegs, hammer, nuts, helmet, etc., and why I was tied to two long pieces of nylon rope hanging over the cliff edge. But a tug on the ropes reminded me that an impatient Mike was still twenty-five metres below and by the time he arrived the sheep had moved away and the humans were nowhere to be seen. A classic piece of practical route-naming saw the line christened Breakaway after all the little bits that had broken off.

Along with other similar lines on the shale coast it opened my eyes to the tremendous potential for adventurous and immensely rewarding climbing on British sea cliffs, and proved that my ability and self-confidence really had improved since the dithering display on Prayer Mat a couple of years before. Now I felt able to decide what would or would not prove climbable and had the confidence to launch forth. Even in the late 1970s and early 1980s, when the rush was on for new lines, few other people seemed interested in the shale cliffs, and climbing mainly with Mike Morrison, an enduringly enthusiastic and talented partner, I enjoyed many wonderfully adventurous weekends, completing 150-metre-plus routes on the huge cliffs of Bukator and Beeny, as well as numerous shorter ones.

6

In Praise of Chalk

Only fifty miles from London, the towering chalk cliffs of the South Coast provided a vertical environment that was virtually unexplored. The ever adventurous nineteenth-century British Alpinists had touched the surface but their explorations were limited to traversing the solid wave-washed rock at beach level or scrabbling on steep grass slopes where the insecurity was likened to 'delicate Alpine work'. There was one exception – the infamous Aleister Crowley, deviser of the Hellfire Club, who thrived on scandal and unconventional activity. He is remembered generally for his black magic routine with which he regularly terrorised other devotees, but to climbers for his exploratory adventures, ranging from a new route on Napes Needle in 1893 to a disastrous Himalayan expedition in 1905. He was however light years ahead of his time in his attitude to tackling vertical chalk cliffs and established the first rock-climb at Beachy Head near Eastbourne. At approaching 150 metres, the cliff here is the highest vertical stretch of rock on the South Coast and one of the highest in the country. That anyone at all was climbing at Beachy Head in the 1890s is remarkable. Rock-climbing as we know it in this country had yet to take off. Classic challenges such as Napes Needle were only climbed for the first time in 1886, an ascent which is often referred to as the 'birth' of rock-climbing as a sport. Certainly it was still very much the golden era of mountaineering, with British Alpine Club members deeply involved in first ascents in the French and Swiss Alps. The challenges posed by the relatively puny British rocks were shunned and looked on merely as a training ground.

Crowley was different. His achievements on chalk were impressively way ahead of the time and it is unfortunate that his finest route on this coast, Devil's Chimney at Beachy Head, fell down in the 1950s. The Chimney was misleadingly named and was actually a slender pinnacle projecting from the main cliff in the vicinity of

Ethelreda's Pinnacle, the prominent thumb of rock 200 metres east of Beachy Head itself. Crowley climbed this flake by *à cheval*, whilst his companions refused to set foot on the final tottering section and would move forward only so far as to give Crowley enough rope to sit (to stand would have been out of the question) victoriously on the top. His achievement is photographically recorded on the wall of the pub at the top of the cliffs. He also climbed the Very Severe stubby thumb of Ethelreda's Pinnacle. But his real enthusiasm and ability were demonstrated in his attempt at the sixty-metre-high crack in the main cliff behind Ethelreda's Pinnacle, Cuillin Crack as Crowley christened it. It is an obvious soaring crackline, clearly visible from both the clifftop and the beach. Crowley tried it in 1894. It is certainly intimidating and in those days the ground that he covered was without doubt amongst the most technically difficult in Britain. At that time 'Severe' was still a very highly respected grade and Crowley's efforts in reaching a point only five metres or so from the top involved Hard Very Severe 5a climbing on dubious rock and with dubious protection. Unfortunately for him he was unable to surmount the crux 5b bulge and then discovered that he was also unable to descend, a problem which was only resolved by the appearance of the Beachy Head coastguard. Crowley's predicament provided endless amusement for them and guaranteed that his embarrassment was well publicised in the climbing world.

Crowley's achievements were never really fully appreciated in his lifetime and chalk-climbing was amazingly slow to take off. Between 1894 and 1979 the only recorded attempt at repeating Ethelreda's Pinnacle was by the well-known team of Tom Patey and the climber/photographer John Cleare. Their inability to cross the steep loose ground leading to the foot of the pinnacle simply served, in most people's eyes, to confirm the unjustifiable nature of South Coast climbing.

It was not until 1979–80 that a small group of climbers began to appreciate the joys of this coast and take over where Crowley left off some eighty-five years before.

Arnis Strapcans got there first. I knew his name from a magazine article he had written entitled 'What's in a Name' by Arnis Arnold Strapcans, which had stuck in my mind as something of a coup commission by the magazine editor and not a bad article either. When I first met him he had just completed what was probably the second ascent of Ethelreda's Pinnacle and was bubbling with enthusiasm for the area. 'Four-hundred-foot vertical cliffs, south-facing, great lines, no crowds.'

It certainly sounded appealing and I kicked myself for not getting off my bum and checking it out earlier. I couldn't wait to tell Mike Morrison and watch the inspirational smile cross his face.

'Mike, I think I've found something wonderful to climb. An urge has to be satisfied.'

'Simply has to be.'

Next weekend we were there, along with Brian 'Blob' Wyvill, who Mike had recently teamed up with. It all looked horribly intimidating. Beachy Head itself boasted a vertical wall which to our inexperienced eyes looked completely impossible. Around Ethelreda's Pinnacle the cliff was shorter – around seventy metres – and offered more conventional-looking possibilities. Cuillin Crack was perhaps the most prominent amongst these and was the line that immediately attracted our attention. A few hours later, having not had too much trouble with the pinnacle itself, I was rather taken aback with the crack. Crowley was clearly something of a star rock-climber. The difficulty and seriousness came immediately. HVS-climbing with loose rock and unreliable protection. The crux and the scene of Crowley's embarrassment was obvious. A nasty bulge necessitating awkward jams and strenuous pulls on flints. Bordering on 5b technically, I was grateful for the security offered by a large nut that I was able to wedge across the crack. Crowley, of course, would not have had such protection and I could not help wondering if I would have succeeded had I been climbing with his equipment, or what the outcome would have been if he had been using mine.

Further east, the white cliffs of Dover are probably the best known, most photographed and sung about cliffs in the British Isles. Forming a prominent line of natural defences, they are clearly visible from the cross-Channel ferry and must attract the idle eyes of all climbers crossing the Channel to the more traditional delights of the Alps. Certainly they attracted me – up to 150 metres high and with no routes on them, they appeared to offer virtually unlimited potential, while only fifty miles north people were queuing up for sandstone outcrops like Harrison's Rocks. Research revealed that once again a couple of steep grass slopes around Folkestone had succumbed under the guise of Victorian Alpine training, while Mummery (who was born in Dover) had paid attention to the solid stretches of tidal rock. Use of ice-axes was mentioned in the intermittent literature available but with such tools being used almost exclusively for step-cutting before 1970, I had no real reason to suspect that they might prove useful on vertical rock.

My first serious visit was in late 1979 with Andy Meyers. Andy was an acknowledged sandstone expert at that time, but it was his adventurous approach to the sport rather than his technical ability on sandstone that was to draw us together as both climbing partners and friends. He took very little persuading to visit Dover 'just for a look' and so December 1979 saw two figures feeling rather small and foolish unloading ice-axes and crampons from the car at St Margaret's Bay. The Sunday morning quota of old-age pensioners followed our movements blankly from their cosy cars as we shouldered our rucksacks and headed quickly off along the beach in our plastic double boots. The cliff height was initially about fifty metres and gradually rose to 150 metres. Walking westwards towards Dover we had only gone a short distance when an obviously man-made cave at twenty metres attracted my attention. Being around a rib and out of sight from the St Margaret's Bay beach it seemed the ideal spot to assess the possibilities.

The chalk at Dover is much softer than at Beachy Head and does not weather into obvious free-climbing weaknesses. It does however boast numerous inspiring ramp and groove lines. Just to the west of the cave was a slanting ramp line which looked easier angled than anything else in the immediate vicinity. It was an ideal place to start. Feeling slightly self-conscious, I swung my axe hard at the chalk. The pick embedded itself and we both stood back to take stock of the situation.

Andy was the first to speak: 'Looks good.'

Tentatively we tested the strength of the placement. Initially it looked as if the pick might pull through waterlogged chalk. Eventually though the two of us were hanging from it together grinning inanely. It worked! The most adventurous visitors to St Margaret's Bay had by now rounded the rib and were gazing quizzically at the curious spectacle of two elated young men hanging from one ice-axe. No one said anything. Only in England can one be assured of such discreet behaviour.

For reasons I fail to recall, probably linked with worries about the state of the chalk higher up, we ended up not climbing but prematurely visiting the Coastguard pub on the seafront on this occasion.

A week later we were back. Andy and I had discussed our discovery at some length. Though the sea-level chalk appeared to be perfect for ice-style climbing, we were uncertain as to what conditions might be like higher up. The choice of a route was no problem with us both agreeing on the slanting line spotted on our first visit. The problem was who was going to lead it – which was where Chris Watts came in. Chris had recently moved to London from Norfolk and taken up climbing after having reached a very high standard in road-bike racing (there being very little in the way of mountaineering challenges in Norfolk). Andy had not climbed with him before but Chris and I had spent a few weekends together and I knew him to be a reliable and talented climber.

Being rather publicity shy and wary of the coastguards' attitude to climbers, we felt it best to tackle the climb at high tide when the base is cut off from the hordes at St Margaret's Bay. This necessitated a grovel through seriously prickly undergrowth and a fifty-metre abseil down on to the small expanse of pebble beach not covered by the tide. Initially we concentrated on demonstrating to Chris how secure the placements were and then pointed him at the first pitch. All seemed to go well. His axes thudded home (it would be a lie to say that they twanged in like solid ice placements but they did embed themselves in a comforting sort of way) and his crampons appeared to bite securely. Equally importantly, his drive-in ice-screw runners slipped comfortably in up to the hilt. Things looked good. The rope snaked out quickly and Chris seemed to be enjoying himself.

Andy was the first to notice a potential problem. Out at sea a coastguard vessel had appeared and its occupants were clearly paying an inordinate amount of attention to our activities. A rubber dinghy was lowered over the side and two coastguards prepared to come ashore. Meanwhile Chris had completed the first ever rock pitch at Dover and probably the first ever ice-style pitch on rock in Britain. Such achievements were fully appreciated by Andy and me but lost on HM Coastguard. Chris was ready for one of us to climb just as the dinghy arrived at our tiny beach.

'Who's first?'

I stepped forward quickly. 'Me.'

Andy was left to deal with the diplomatic crux of the day. He coped admirably. After the initial rather hostile reaction, the two coastguards proved to be men after our own hearts. One of them even appeared to border on the persuadable and, had he not been on duty, our team could easily have expanded to four. Andy chatted amiably for a few minutes, after which the coastguards returned to their dinghy and prepared to rejoin the pilot vessel.

Unfortunately they had a walkie-talkie and it soon became clear that those in the pilot vessel were not too keen on their colleagues departing with nothing more than an affable enquiry as to our well-being. The two frontline men returned.

'Our boss says that you have to come down.'

Andy relayed the message upwards.

'Why?'

Another pause whilst an appropriate response was sought from superior officers.

'You signalled for assistance.'

This was a confusing one. It seemed that some Channel fisherman had mistaken our ice-axe placement demonstrations for Chris as a signal for help.

'No we didn't.'

The conversation was in danger of stooping to a ridiculously immature level.

'Are you refusing to come down?'

This was unexpected, and called for a carefully chosen reply if good relations were to be maintained. Andy was up to the task.

'If it helps – yes, we are refusing to come down.'

That stumped them. We could hear Andy's 'refusing to come down' words being relayed to the boss before, with a cheery 'Good luck, lads', the frontline boys headed off and left us in peace.

The rock was considerably better than I had expected. I had feared that it would become dry, dusty and impossible to get a placement in as soon as we got above the waterlogged sea-level chalk. There was certainly some deterioration, in that the chalk became harder, but with a few swings of the axe it was possible to get a good placement every time and the adrenalin flow was nowhere near as fast as I had feared. As for the belays, three six-inch drive-in ice-screws took just the right amount of energy to place in order to inspire confidence. Chris looked very pleased with himself perched on a tuft of grass twenty-five metres up and grinning from ear to ear. By the time I reached him I was doing the same. It was 'looking good' as we kept saying to each other.

As always seems to happen when I climb as a rope of three, the stances are judged to be too small for three and the third person spends endless hours standing around seizing up. This time was no exception, so I started tentatively up the next pitch with Andy still on the beach. The tide was beginning to go out and the more adventurous Sunday strollers had left their cars and were peering curiously at us, though, like the week before, they gave Andy a wide berth and muttered quietly amongst themselves.

On the sharp end, the first thing I noticed was that crampons and my state-of-the-art flares were a bad combination. Having pinned a flapping expanse of material to the rock with one crampon, I could see Chris struggling to get a photograph before I could extricate myself from my predicament. This though was a minor problem: the chalk was definitely getting both harder and more broken up. The temptation was to make fast progress on the very tips of crampons and axes but, having got myself precariously poised in my efforts to escape Chris's photographic intentions, the adrenalin flow necessary to get re-established in a secure-feeling position was such that I veered firmly towards the slow but steady approach. The final five metres consisted of a wall of steeper and obviously looser rock which could possibly be outflanked to the right, with a crucial five-metre traverse across looser material looking to be the hardest section. Moving on to this I became uncomfortably aware that I had left the smooth faultless shield of rock that we had been climbing on thus far. Here my crampon points tended to slip down and little cube-like pieces of chalk came away and stuck to the picks of my axes. My legs started to shake as I began to place protection screws.

'We told you that you should have gone down.'

A head had appeared over the edge directly above me. It wore a peaked cap. I did not feel in quite the right frame of mind to hold a reasoned conversation with a senior member of HM Coastguard.

'Wait there, laddie – the lifeline is coming.'

This was a distinctly unwelcome development, but first things first. I said nothing but continued to hammer away at the ice-screw until it was safely in up to the hilt. Feeling slightly more relaxed, I surveyed the situation.

A chunky length of rope had appeared hanging down easy ground about five metres to my right. If I could reach where the rope was I could easily climb up to the top without its security.

'Hey – can you pull up that rope, please?'

Chris had seen what was happening and was fearful of our ascent being flawed by this unwelcome intrusion. I was not quite so sure. The ground I was on was different to anything that I had ever come across before and I was far from certain as to what to do next. Being under close and disapproving scrutiny did little to ease my discomfort. I stayed silent whilst, much to my surprise, the lifeline was pulled back up.

Other heads were now visible, two of them belonging to officers of the law. Our efforts were attracting rather more attention than I would have liked. Ruefully I remembered our decision to start off at high tide to minimise our exposure to the masses.

Feeling distinctly under the magnifying glass and accompanied by such useful comments as 'Be careful, lad,' I teetered precariously until able to thwack a solid placement into grass tufts marking the start of easy ground.

Standing on top at last, my elation was either dampened or heightened (I was not quite sure which) by the ridiculous amount of attention our efforts had attracted. The coastguards' presence was of course anticipated but the three of them were just part of the reception committee which had managed to assemble itself in the hour and a half since we had first been spotted. The ambulance-men surprised me. Someone had directed that a stretcher be taken through brambles and nettles to the top of the cliff (has the concept of gravity not been fully understood by the ambulance service?) and the two unfortunate bearers stood scratched and miserable in the biting wind. Perhaps even more surprising was the BBC cameraman who, having gone through a similar amount of unpleasantness carrying an impressively unwieldy camera through the natural obstacle course, was wandering helplessly about trying to get a good position close to the edge. His efforts were of course being thwarted by the coastguards who reminded him of the dangers of crumbly clifftops every time he was close to getting a reasonable position. He hovered hopefully, moving in for a quick bit of footage whenever their attention was diverted.

More worrying from my point of view were the two police officers who were clearly not enjoying this particular call-out and knew exactly who to vent their anger upon. One of them approached me immediately: 'Behaviour likely to cause a breach of the peace.'

I stared at him aghast. A wonderful first ascent completed and all this man could witter on about was criminal charges. My eyes were drawn down to a right-angled tear in the knee of his trousers. A bloody knee was just about visible to account for his foul mood. Words rather failed me. After taking down our names and addresses the two of them stomped off muttering that the 'incident would be reported'.

That still left six people staring in a disapproving semi-circle. Chris could be heard asking what was going on and it was clearly time to find a belay. Usually I would have belayed on the nearest bush but being very aware of the emphasis that the coastguard seemed to be placing on safety I felt it necessary to look for something more substantial. A tree well back from the edge gave something obvious to go for but just a metre short of it shouts from below revealed that I had run out of rope. This was getting embarrassing. It was clear to those around me that I couldn't reach the tree and they waited silently to see what my next move would be. The BBC camera whirred capturing a close-up shot. I couldn't help but be aware that the coastguard's lifeline was tied to the same tree and was easily within reach. But to use it would have invited comments of the 'what would you have done if we hadn't been here' variety. The problem was solved by joining two long slings together and swinging them round the trunk. Most of the assembled crew seemed nonplussed by this but it prompted renewed activity from the cameraman.

With a belay safely arranged the situation eased somewhat. One of the coastguards even admitted that he had done some winter climbing on Lochnagar and started showing interest in our equipment. The BBC man was allowed to wander freely – even taking up a particularly dangerous-looking perch on an exfoliating flake of chalk overhanging the route. Sleet was blowing in the wind by now and the ambulancemen were looking keen to get away.

Clearance was obviously required from the pilot vessel which had again taken up station a couple of hundred metres offshore. This seemed not to be as readily forthcoming as expected. Chris had reached the top and Andy was on the stance before we were able to overhear wisps of their conversation: 'The third man is looking precarious.'

The pilot-vessel men were obviously in no hurry to return to port. Peering over the edge Chris reported that Andy was still on the stance. It therefore seemed rather curious that he could be 'looking precarious'. Poor Andy, he was nicknamed 'Precarious' for some time to come.

Andy's mother recorded the news broadcast that night. It was something of a classic: 'There was drama at the White Cliffs of Dover today. Three climbers, all from London . . . refused every appeal to come down. When they reached the top, safely as it turned out, they met the wrath of the police who criticised them for their dangerous behaviour.'

Dangerous? The ice-screws had sunk in a lot better than we had expected. The climbing too was, in retrospect, enjoyable and immensely rewarding. Endless possibilities remained. A short break would be necessary to allow relations with the coastguard to cool down but in the longer term I had no doubt that the South Coast would be exerting an irresistible pull. Scottish ice could even become regarded as ideal training for the Dover cliffs.

7

Ice is Nice

It was decidedly slippery at 4 a.m. on the roof of the Kings House Hotel in Glencoe. Frost covered the old slates and stars shone through an intermittently clear sky. The Alpine Climbing Group annual piss-up had ended a couple of hours earlier and now it was time to go climbing.

Unfortunately, I was having trouble finding my partner. Chris Watts had chosen to stay the night in the hotel. Being of a less free-spending nature than Chris (and not being accompanied by a delectable damsel), I had ended up squeezed into the laundry room with an equally impecunious Al Baker. This had seemed a great dossing spot after a serious night of drunken revelry, but the morning's discovery that the inside door handle did not work got the day off to a distinctly bad start. My lock-picking talents not being up to Al's, I had no option but to wake him from his slumbers and seek assistance. He had hoped for a lie-in and was not pleased. However, being somewhat of a fan of the unusual, he brightened up at the ridiculous prospect of being locked in the laundry room of a three-star hotel. Release was of course unlikely in the near future and shouting for help at 4 a.m. on a Sunday morning seemed destined, at the very least, to reduce our popularity rating. But despite his talent, Al was having trouble. Credit cards, his house keys and a penknife all failed to do the trick. I was becoming agitated; there was work to be done. This was the third time I had come up from London to try a particular unclimbed winter line in Glencoe – and here I was wasting such a golden opportunity for action fumbling about locked inside a laundry room. Despair was setting in when a table knife came to light. What this was doing wrapped up in the dirty linen I shall never know, but Al grabbed it and attacked the lock with renewed enthusiasm. It burst open. I think he was more surprised than me.

Out in the corridor I headed off towards the bedrooms in quest of Chris, but after five metres or so I was faced with another locked door. This one was not an accidental slip of the latch: a deadlock in the middle and bolts at top and bottom effectively barred access to the main part of the hotel. The situation was becoming ridiculous. An hour had passed and all I had managed to do was get out of the laundry room. There was however a door that led outside from the short length of corridor we now had access to. Al opted to snatch a bit more sleep whilst I wandered around outside staring hopefully up at the upstairs windows. There was no movement and from a fleeting visit the night before the only window I could recall in Chris's room led out on to a sloping roof. I went round the back. Yes – I could just about make out some windows overlooking a V gully between two eaved roofs . . . and I was pretty sure which one was Chris's. The drainpipe was slippery but do-able. At close quarters though it was more difficult to be certain which window was the right one. The two that were accessible both involved a short climb up the slates and my gut feeling was that the lefthand one was the one to go for. To make matters slightly less certain, however, a bedside light was on in the righthand room. Was Chris just getting up? I decided to have a quick peek through the righthand window first.

The night before had been one of those very heavy dews followed by heavy frost which covers everything in a thin veneer of ice and a thick layer of frost. It probably looked very beautiful but did not aid progress up the slates. Poised precariously with an awkward pinch grip on the windowframe, it was possible to peer through the net curtains and see an old lady's head peeping from beneath the bedclothes. This did not look right. It was almost inconceivable that any old lady would want to spend the night in the Kings House at the time of the ACG annual piss-up but this seemed to be the real thing and not a curiously disguised reveller. Time to move on.

'Eh – you. Whut yeh up te?'

A piercing Glaswegian accent rent the air from below as the suspicious nature of my activities came home to roost.

'Looking for a friend of mine.' It did not sound very convincing. My North London accent sounded awkwardly out of place. Not wishing to draw too much attention to my crawling around on the roof, I slid quickly down the slates and headed across to the drainpipe and terra firma where I would feel happier giving a full explanation at a sensible volume rather than screaming from the rooftop. Looking back as I scrabbled across the roof I saw a light on and a face at the previously dark window. It was not Chris.

Happily, my accuser was an early riser not particularly interested in my predicament and, more helpfully, able to let me into the hotel foyer from where it was but a short run up the stairs to Chris's room.

Chris's ladyfriend did not look too pleased at my babblings about frost, frozen tufts and wonderful conditions. Chris too seemed curiously unenthusiastic but we had already driven over 3000 miles between London and Glencoe trying a line close to the gaping gash of Ossian's Cave. Also one of my favourite pieces of equipment – a battered MOAC wedge on 11 mm rope – was still hanging on the first stance where a combination of darkness and bad weather had halted the most promising of our two attempts so far.

It was well over two hours later than planned by the time Chris had been prised from the bedroom and Al had been roused again to drive us to the drop-off point. Comfort and ice-climbing weekends just don't go together.

I could not help but remember the close shaves involved on our previous attempts. Close shave number two had been uncomfortably close to the mark. The weather had been cold in Glencoe but gale force winds whipped the freshly fallen snow around in impressive flurries as we had toiled up in the dark to the foot of the ramp from which the route starts. Here great waves of spindrift poured across the wall above and formed deep drifts on the mist-shrouded slopes. Every now and then we had caught a glimpse of our surroundings but the conditions were sufficiently unpleasant for us to decide against our real objective and wander aimlessly upwards to 'have a look around' higher up. Beneath the layer of new snow large areas of the ramp were sheet ice. The dangers of Scottish avalanches had been drummed home, although I was pleased to say that I had no first-hand experience of them. We did notice small areas of new powder sliding away from around our feet every now and then but felt that by keeping away from the more open slopes we would be perfectly safe.

Somewhere near the top of the ramp the lines of mixed rock and ice that we had been following ran out into a more continuous slope of deep new snow. Chris was in front. He stopped and began prodding the snow with his axe. I was just about to step up beside him when, despite the virtual white-out, I was aware of a wave of snow advancing on us. It was relatively innocuous-looking but caught Chris with its full force, making him lose his footing and fall backwards. We had just front-pointed up a short steep section, and seeing Chris losing his balance I moved to get a good axe placement in icy ground a few feet to my left. It was too late: Chris's weight and the wave of snow hit me together as my axe swung in mid-air. Together we fell back on to fellow Londoner Duncan Tunstall (who was in the middle of the steep section) and all three of us started to slide uncontrollably. Jon Lincoln, the fourth in our party, was standing slightly to one side but was caught in the face by a flailing fist and he too joined us. By good luck or (he would say) good judgement his feet almost immediately hit a projecting rock and he stopped dead in a position where he could witness the three of us sliding off down a shallow runnel towards a big drop. It was a ridiculously small avalanche – more a little snowslide – but, despite almost stopping at one point, none of us was able to brake. I found myself lying on my back pinned down by my sack and unable to turn over. The others were clearly having similar problems, although at the time I had no idea that they were sliding down with me. I knew the terrain well, was terribly aware of what lay below, and could sense myself going faster and faster. Suddenly I was free from the feeling of being pinned on my back and was distinctly spinning round in mid-air. I hung grimly on to my ice-axe in the braking position but had no idea where the slope was or which way up I might land. I remember seeing what seemed like huge clods of snow falling with me and mentally picturing the vast North Face of Aonach Dubh with its numerous vertical thirty-metre drops. With a lung-emptying thud I landed on what seemed like a monstrous cushion and then . . . I was off again. This time though the snow was heavier and slower moving. After a few feet it stopped and I was able to scrabble to one side, sink home a secure axe placement and collapse limply next to it.

For the first time I was able to take stock of the situation. Surprisingly Chris could be seen a few feet ahead of me and close to the edge of a fifty-metre drop into a deep gully. Up until this point I had no idea that anyone else was involved. Chris seemed a trifle dazed but was moving and signalled to me that he was OK. A loud shout from behind alerted us both to Duncan's presence. He too seemed relatively unscathed and was cursing his lost glasses, which miraculously were lying in the snow beside him – except that he was too short-sighted to see them. A closer assessment of our state of health suggested that we had all been falling in a flailing ball of dropped axes and crampon-clad feet. Chris's clothing in particular was peppered with holes whilst I sported the only blood-producing injury – a small cut on my eyelid which was rapidly developing into an impressive black eye.

Jon was nowhere to be seen but at that stage we had no idea whether he was above us or somewhere over the drop down below. It wasn't long before a piercing whistle from up above answered the question for us. Scream as we might, the feeble shouts from our still-winded lungs were clearly insufficient to reassure him. We had fallen about 200 metres in total and the prospect of climbing straight back up to stop Jon's effort to summon a rescue team was not exactly appealing. More than anything else it was the potential embarrassment of unnecessary rescue which stirred me into action.

I emerged stiffly from the top of a steep grade 3–4 ice runnel.

'What are you doing?'

'Trying to get you bloody well rescued – what do you think?'

It was a uniquely happy reunion. At one point we had fallen a good twenty metres completely free and yet none of us had any real injuries to show for the experience. So by the time Chris and I arrived back at the foot of the line for a third try we felt we deserved a success this time, if the amount of effort we had already put in was anything to go by.

Our previous highpoint on one of our less epic-laden weekends was at the first stance. Getting to this point had proved to be particularly exciting but the ground ahead showed no signs of easing off and I started up with a deep feeling of trepidation. The climbing was more on frozen tufts than ice but, being a very damp line in summer, its winter garb was primarily verglas, frozen tufts and wind-blasted snow. Certainly I found it an attractive line and more appealing than the increasing winter trend of climbing snow-bound but ice-free routes. Scottish tufts can provide some of the most secure ice-axe placements known to man but here they seemed not to be very well attached to the rock. Progress was further complicated by a distinct lack of protection and the need somehow to bypass a particularly bendy and generally unhelpful sapling. But this was ground we had covered before and, conscious of the need to make up for our late start, we managed to move quickly to the previous highpoint. The nut that had been our abseil point had disappeared. I could not believe it. Had our wonderful first ascent been snatched from under our noses some time in the three weeks since we were here last?

Above us an overhanging section of dry rock, sparsely equipped with tufts, looked destined to give us an exciting time. It was Chris's turn to lead, but he still appeared to be suffering from sleeping (or not sleeping) in too comfortable a bed, so I started rather hesitantly upwards again. The tufts that clung resiliently to the fault line were still insubstantial and dry. Axes pulled through them readily. Progress was both slow and insecure, and I soon ground to a halt beneath an overhanging section of pure rock. Ice could be seen drooling over the top of this, but ten minutes of free-climbing effort convinced me that a couple of points of aid were the answer. Ethical practices on winter routes are nowhere near as clear cut as on pure rock. Over the last few years efforts have been made to introduce a very precise and purist ethic to Scottish winter climbs. Personally, I am not so sure that this is a step forward. By their very nature winter climbs vary tremendously. One day a bulge will be verglassed and desperate to climb, whereas on another occasion it will be covered with thick easily manageable ice. To give anything other than a general indication of difficulty in such circumstances seems rather pointless to me. It also risks undermining the on-sight ethics of winter mountaineering to the extent that we have already seen some first ascensionists abseiling down initially in an effort to 'improve' the style of their eventual ascent.

Excuses and ethical considerations aside, I had no regrets as I used a couple of pegs to get myself above the dry section and on to a thin veneer of ice leading up into the mist that was now swirling around the cliff. Chris came up whooping with joy and brandishing the lost abseil nut. It had been there after all but so much snow had fallen that it was buried a metre down! A storm was gathering fast and the wind whipped up any loose snow, blasting it hard into our faces. Contemplating how good this was for our complexions, we continued more quickly up a series of steep and difficult walls, until the ground eased and we had done it. We were able to race down to the car and get in a quick beer before heading back to London. After all the setbacks it was time to choose a suitable name – 'Against All Odds' seemed ideal.

*   *   *

British winter climbing had been a gradual learning process for me and it took many unsuccessful trips before I concluded that short, sharp weekend dashes from London were the most likely to be productive.

Initially I had this strange idea that the last week of February was the best time to go. This was probably because it coincided with the half-term holidays which meant that Gerry was able to join us. Arriving in Glencoe, the news from the Clachaig Inn was invariably 'Too warm in Glencoe; Ben Nevis good up until a couple of days ago.' Blindly accepting pub talk as gospel we would spend the week alternating between pub and café watching the rain. A highpoint on one week was an ascent of Great Gully on Buchaille Etive Mhor where the pitches were banked out with wet snow but Jon was at least able to christen his brand new Terrordactyl axe by traversing across to a conveniently accessible patch of ice. But our tick list of winter routes in Scotland remained depressingly unchanged.

North Wales I had never really considered until one year blocked roads prevented the journey north and we ended up in Llanberis. My eyes were to be opened. Winter climbing was one of Snowdonia's better-kept secrets. Walks with George had never really prepared me for 100-metre frozen icefalls and the wealth of unclimbed possibilities. By the end of that week I had a healthy number of new routes to my name and knew that nine days' nonstop winter climbing was pretty exhausting. But I also knew I was hooked on winter severity. If North Wales, a heavily populated climbing area, had such gems on offer, what was available in the Scottish Highlands? And on Skye? The list of possibilities seemed endless.

A week in the Charles Inglis Clarke (CIC) Hut on Ben Nevis with Victor Saunders consolidated this view. Victor was to become a major influence on my climbing, though I must admit to finding him an irritating little squirt when we first met in 1976. After all those years of grounding with George I had just done my first really exciting Alpine climb – the Cecchinel Nominé route on the Eckpfeiler Buttress on the Italian side of Mont Blanc – and was aimlessly wandering along Chamonix High Street contemplating what to do next when I was floored by someone who fired a hail of questions all delivered so furiously fast that I found it difficult to give any sort of response before the next one descended upon me: 'How steep are the steepest sections? Are the aid points in place? How long did you take? Where did you bivi? Are the belays good? What stove did you use?' The inquisition seemed endless and took me quite by surprise. I was probably very rude. Victor remembers our first meeting too. He felt that I was pompously disinterested because he didn't recognise my name. I do not know why he should have done but, suffice to say, we met again in the Wednesday pub scene in London and got on much better, which was how we found ourselves in the CIC Hut on Ben Nevis early in our Scottish winter careers.

The week that followed convinced me that whenever the weather was cold enough in the future I would simply have to go winter climbing somewhere in Britain. Ben Nevis is of course very popular but not only were the climbs superb, it also seemed that there was still considerable potential for new routes. Having ticked off the classics we finished the week with a fine line of dribbling ice which I had noticed on the walk up to the hut. Not only was it unclimbed, Shield Direct was also one of the best ice climbs that I had done. Nothing could be better for whetting the appetite.

One thing I finally realised, however, was that a whole week of good winter weather could be just too much of a good thing. It had been pretty knackering in North Wales. In Scotland the walk-in from the hut or pub to the crag every day was just that bit farther. I am not a walker. It was enough to persuade me to bring a halt to week-long exploits which ate deeply into my strictly limited civil service holiday entitlement and so often left me with precious little to show for it.

The idea of Scottish winter weekends from London tends to be greeted with horror by those who have not participated. In fact, with four drivers, even the 650 miles to Torridon can be expressed as 160 miles each behind the wheel – a much more reasonable-sounding proposition. The key of course is to ensure that plenty of sleep is had whilst not driving. With an average time of about ten and a half hours to Torridon, a 7 p.m. departure from the house I had by now bought in Cricklewood (conveniently situated at the end of the motorway) would see us arriving at 5.30–6 a.m. and getting straight into the action. Not all London ice-climbers were enthusiastic but with increasingly frequent forays the journey became second nature and the road north a sea overflowing with marker points and memorable incidents.

Scratchwood Services, only five miles from Staples Corner: it was here that Victor Saunders started on an unfortunate footing by somehow taking the wrong exit and driving back south, and nobody realised until we arrived back at the Staples Corner roundabout.

Junction 40 (M6): scene of the incident where Henry Todd acquired the temporary nickname 'Bollards' after a close encounter with a large number of them (not to mention another car) in a cone-ridden section of roadworks.

Ma Shepherd's, A74: the one and only allowable stopping place *en route* to Scotland. Anne, behind the counter, can be relied upon to keep an eye on the forecast and update us about other teams heading north. After serving up pie, beans and gravy (the cheapest fare and the best), Saturday's breakfast (cheese roll) and Sunday's breakfast (ham roll) are placed into tied Mother's Pride bags. The order of consumption is very important. Cheese rolls for Saturday, ham for Sunday. Cheese dries out faster than ham.

Loch Lomond: heroic manoeuvre by Chris Watts. Three-hundred-and-sixty-degree rotation including a reverse movement across a narrow bridge. No damage except to the nerves.

Ballachulish: the scene of Bert Simmonds' demonstration (whilst snoozing contentedly behind the wheel) that hired Sierras are ideal vehicles for surging across roundabouts and ending up in fields. He subsequently had to fight hard to avoid prosecution for driving a vehicle with no road tax!

North of Fort William: John English's durability test for Volkswagons. A ten-metre bank, partial immersion in the loch and (perhaps most challenging) a tow back on to the road by a drunken JCB driver. The Sirocco proved remarkably resilient.

The list is endless and the drives themselves became an essential part of those weekends.

Dedication, though, pays rewards. Take the 1st–2nd March 1986. An excellent forecast and a report from our man on the spot prompted my first weekend trip to the Isle of Skye.

Four thirty a.m., Saturday, 1st March, 1986. The car had stopped. The memory-jogging landmarks were behind us. In front the road dipped down into a calm sea. Kyle of Lochalsh. The Skye ferry. Bedtime. Victor and I collapsed haphazardly outside the car whilst Chris Watts and Sonja Vietoris stayed *in situ*. This was in the days before the bridge. The ferry didn't run all night and the first one was at 5.30 a.m. We had sixty minutes to snooze away.

I awoke with the realisation that a huge articulated lorry was edging its way past my head in its bid to be first on to the ferry. Its exhaust pipe spewed diesel fumes straight into my nose ensuring that pollution intake levels far exceeded my weekly London norm. So much for the fresh air of the Highlands.

By 7 a.m. we were there. Glenbrittle. This was, I have to admit, a slightly unethical trip in terms of truly 'on-sight' activity. George, having taken up winter Munro-bagging in his retirement, had been persuaded that Skye was ripe for his attention. On the Friday night he had phoned London at 6.45 p.m. to give the all-clear. A clear, crisp night with sea-level snow and a glittering frost. A short delay had occurred whilst I attended Ian's wedding reception (pity I couldn't stay longer), but twelve hours later we had arrived. Every climbing team should have an on-the-spot conditions assessor.

Waterpipe Gully was top of the list for the weekend. George had checked it out the previous day and the signs were good. Unfortunately, though, he must have been getting a bit short-sighted as he somehow failed to notice the crisply clear tracks left by Doug Scott and Colin Downer, who must have been physically engrossed in the first ascent whilst he was standing at the bottom. Such talented competition in such farflung spots.

To our surprise Victor and I were more competent than usual, and completed a second ascent with time to spare. South Gully away to our right had stopped me the previous Christmas but today the pitch that I had failed on only two months earlier was almost banked out, and having lightened our rucksacks at the bottom we managed a quick solo.

Possibilities opened up above. At the head of the amphitheatre containing Doug Scott's earlier line, the Smear, a continuous narrow ice streak culminated in an icicle-ridden overhang.

'Let's go for it, Mick.'

Victor can never be accused of dithering when he is face to face with severity, and I have to admit that the urge which overcame us both was indeed irresistible. In such situations it is of course necessary to ignore inconveniences like the late hour and having left most of the gear over 300 metres below and concentrate on the task in hand. Soloing a few short grade 4 sections saved some time and meant that the lack of gear was not really noticeable until we had gained the line proper and effectively committed ourselves.

Victor led off on our single 9 mm rope. His time was not wasted placing gear as we did not have very much. Progress was therefore still fast and after a gradually steepening ice ramp a short but expletive-packed struggle with a brittle icicle led past a small overhang to a stance from where the rest of the line was clearly visible. It consisted of a steep and narrow but continuous ice streak leading directly to the capping icicle-draped overhang. Such sights make leaving the Tax Office desk and rushing to Scotland particularly worthwhile.

'Unjustifiable – just the way you like it.'

Our standard phrase of the time came simultaneously to us both. A couple more steep and spectacular pitches on perfect ice led to the obvious crux of the route where water seeping through the overhang had frozen to form two huge icicles, one dropping from a point midway across the roof and the other adorning the lip. From a constricted belay in a shallow ice cave it looked just possible to climb up beneath the roof and cross it by transferring from one icicle to the other before moving round on to the front face and pulling on to the easier ground above. As luck would have it the ice was better here than in the icicles Victor had been struggling with lower down. A couple of home-made Russian ice-screws had survived the gear rationalisation earlier in the day and we screwed these safely in – safely was a relative term, this being before such screws were tested in the West. A series of lurches and much scrabbling of crampon-clad feet took me out on to the outer face of the outermost icicle. In such situations my poor arms have been known to let me down and a couple of times I have ended up dangling inelegantly from my rucksack straps – which I have judiciously attached to my ice-axe wrist-loops for that very purpose. Today though was to be a good day without such excitement. It was easier than it looked. A quick pull on bomb-proof axe placements and the sun was glinting on my face as the upper slopes came within reach. Only fifty metres higher Icicle Factory was over and we stood on the deserted Cuillin Ridge and surveyed the scene. Despite it being a perfect day we had seen no one since leaving the car.

The ridge too was deserted as we took time to admire the view before blundering down in the gathering gloom towards the spot where we had so foolishly abandoned much of our gear including our head torches below South Gully.

The Sligachan Hotel of the mid-'eighties was very different from the anonymity of the current establishment. Log fire, cosy armchairs and *in situ* Golden Retriever ensured the best atmosphere in which to wax lyrical over the demands of the day. Also its derelict (now demolished) garages provided superb accommodation for the discerning weekend dosser. At the time only the ladies' toilet in Glen Torridon (with its hot shower and working lights) could really be said to offer a superior bivouac.

Sunday, 4.30 a.m. Cold. Dark. The crux of a winter weekend is getting started on a Sunday. On Skye in 1986 the last ferry back on Sunday evening was at 5 p.m., so an early start was essential. The long cold spell was at last coming to a close. The wind was rising and streamers of cloud could be seen racing across the darkening sky.

A quick reconnaissance down Glen Brittle first thing the previous day had shown there to be an impressive ice streak adorning the back wall of Coire a 'Ghreadaidh. Despite the worsening weather it was clearly very necessary that this should receive some attention. A quick glance revealed no sign of the line in the guide book and, after parking at the Youth Hostel, an hour's groping around in the general direction enabled a path of sorts to be located at first light. With the wind now gusting heartily and the first snowflakes falling, air conditions promised to be better for the complexion than the day before. Chris, Victor and I groped blindly in the worsening blizzard, remembering to be revelling in the contrast between weekday deskbound dreariness and character-building weekend excitement.

A stimulating smear of ice disappearing in the clouds provided the necessary impetus and after a spot of soloing it was time to get the ropes out and get going properly. The wind whipped the spindrift into a frenzy as our stinging faces peered up to where Chris was somewhere above us in the clouds. Two long pitches and we were back to soloing again, dodging in and out of steep sections until the ground eased. White Wedding was complete and a hesitant descent was possible somewhere in the mist to one side.

Back at the car a couple of inches of snow had fallen, although a thaw had already started as the best cold spell of the winter drew to a close. A challengingly slippery exit up the hill from Glenbrittle led out on to the main road and back to Kyleakin in time for the last ferry.

Fourteen hours later I was back in the Tax Office listening to how colleagues had spent their weekends going shopping or catching up on a few odd jobs, or simply having a nice rest.

'Good weekend? Been away?' I was asked.

But when I launched into an enthusiastic summary of the delights of derelict garage dosses and the excitement of vertical ice, blank faces stared back. I might have been on another planet – or more likely from one.

The 1980s were a time of concentrated exploration and excitement in the wild North-West of Scotland. Most Scottish winter devotees tended not to venture north of the traditional cliffs of Ben Nevis, Creag Meaghaidh and the Cairngorms. So the North-West – basically from Fort William northwards – was a land of relatively untouched crags and superb unclimbed lines. Only two names spring to mind as devotees of the region before 1980. Firstly there was Tom Patey, the renowned Ullapool doctor and larger than life character who ranged far and wide from the late 1940s until his tragic death on the Maiden sea stack off the north coast in 1970. Secondly, there was Andy Nisbet, the classically modest ginger-bearded Aberdonian whose name probably appears more than any other in the first-ascensionists list of every guide book in Scotland. Aside from these two the vast tracts of the North-West had seen few regular climbing visitors – and it perhaps says something that both of these two climbed many of their first ascents alone.

Having latched on to the effectiveness of Scottish weekend 'hits' in 1979, it was not until 1983 or so that our little group from London started to brave the network of single-track roads defending the North-West. The pickings were sufficiently rich for climbing partners to be no problem. Chris Watts, Phil Butler, Jon Lincoln, Phil Thornhill and Mike Morrison to name but a few were all keen. Incidents on these weekends resulted in long-lasting nicknames for several of those involved. Phil Butler became 'Lobster' (later shortened to 'Lobby') after an unfortunate incident in the Lochinver Quayside fisherman's hut where a truly monstrous pile of lobster pots collapsed on to him while he was sleeping off the after-effects of a particularly fine night. Lobby was only able to turn on his head torch and mumble incoherent protestations about attacking lobsters until he could eventually be uncovered. Jon Lincoln became 'Carless' (with time and poor pronunciation often becoming Carlos) as a result of his persistent refusal to invest in his own transport. It was Victor Saunders' nicknames that I liked best. As I got to know Victor, everything I had heard about him seemed true: 'immensely likeable, a brilliant climber, but difficult to pin down'. 'Slippery', or 'Slipper' for short, somehow summed him up exceptionally well. It is just so difficult to get a commitment from him. Just as you think everything is under control and release the thumb pressure for a second he is off again, another train of thought having crossed his mind which, inevitably, demands full exploration to make absolutely sure that he is not missing anything, and is getting the best out of every situation. It would perhaps be best to describe him as a truly unique character. An architect by profession, he was at that time employed by Lambeth Council. I once went to pick him up from outside his office and had to park on a double yellow line. There was no sign of Victor, so I headed inside and then waited for twenty minutes or so at reception for his extension line to free. The receptionist was very understanding.

'Ah yes . . . Mr Saunders . . . A personal visit. You've been waiting some time – I'm sure he won't mind if you just pop up and see him.'

And so I popped. The open-plan office was very large with each architect surrounded by partitions covered in rather tedious-looking architectural drawings. I hesitated at the door looking for someone to direct me to his desk. The office babble though was rent by an unmistakable voice: 'I think the route goes up to the right . . . or maybe the left; it's wonderful . . . beautiful climbing . . . you will enjoy it so much . . . at least you should . . . I did.'

I homed in on a set of partitions covered with photographs of mountains. One or two architectural drawings had been allocated a small corner but Vic's boss must have been under no illusions as to where his priorities lay. Judging by the looks I was getting, breaking through to the inner sanctum was a rare occurrence.

'Victor, are you coming?'

'I'm on the phone.'

This seemed pretty obvious. I tried again.

'I'm on a double yellow.'

'I'm talking about mountains.'

Again, of this I was aware. Having now spent getting on for thirty minutes hanging around, I was increasingly aware of both the double yellow and the fact that it was now past the time we were supposed to be picking up other people in nearby Streatham. I tried something more forceful and at increased volume.

'Saunders, you slimy toe rag, I'm leaving without you.'

I could sense other architects stirring uncomfortably. Disruption, especially when caused by outsiders, appeared unusual in the world of local council architects. Victor's response was positive though.

He simply stopped in mid-sentence, said, 'Got to go. Goodbye,' and put the phone down. I had his attention at last and, grabbing the opportunity, propelled him outside and into the (still ticket free) car.

For those sufficiently committed to spend two nights a week pounding the roads to do battle with streaks of unclimbed Scottish ice, the rich pickings were spread far and wide and, at least for the first half of the 1980s, competition in the North-West was very limited. In eleven winter weekends there in 1986, I never once met another climber that I did not know! Even areas that I had always heard about and once assumed to be relatively popular seemed full of possibilities. In Glen Torridon the huge prominent icefall of Poacher's Fall on Liathach was only climbed for the first time in 1976 (by Andy Nisbet and Richard McHardy). The falls tumbling down the tiered limestone to either side regularly freeze during a cold spell and yet were still unclimbed in 1984. Umbrella Fall, at a relatively amenable grade 4 level, climbed with Lobby in 1984, showed that it was not only the desperate lines that were in need of attention – and this was on one of the most popular winter cliffs in the North-West. Other obvious lines were to follow, both on Liathach (Test Department with Chris Watts), Ben Eighe (West Central Gully with Mike Morrison), the Upper Girdle (with Chris Watts and Slippery Vic) and at Applecross (Gully of the Gods with Simon Fenwick and Great Overhanging Gully with Lobby).

All of these I found immensely pleasurable, and forays to areas even less frequented in winter, such as the north side of Beinn Dearg near Ullapool and Achnashellach, just south of Torridon, revealed equally exciting possibilities. Achnashellach was one of those areas where I was again able to tap an on-the-spot source for valuable information. Martin Moran, an ex-accountant turned Outdoor Pursuits man had established himself in Strathcarron by the mid-1980s and began to join the names of Patey and Nisbet by putting up an impressive list of first ascents in the area. On one particularly memorable occasion the team was dithering in London after an uncertain 6.30 p.m. weather forecast, before a telephone call to Martin confirmed that conditions 'looked OK' in Strathcarron. By 5.30 a.m. we had left the car at Achnashellach station and stumbled off towards the impressive High Cliff of Fuar Tholl. I was just completing the first pitch of a previously unclimbed ice streak when, horrors of horrors, other climbers appeared making a beeline for our line. It was of course Martin Moran himself who, out of all the possibilities in the area, had chosen to go for the same line as us. He did not look over-pleased to realise that it was his comments the previous evening that had spurred us into action. He completed the second ascent straight behind Christ Watts and me. Pipped at the Post was a route name we could not resist giving to the climb.

One thing I learned with repeated visits was that winter conditions in the North-West were nowhere near as unreliable as I had been led to believe. The aftermath of twenty-four-plus hours' driving every weekend somehow never seems as bad as people expect; perhaps it is the adrenalin flow; perhaps mastering the art of sleeping in the car. Either way a return to London at 7 a.m. ready for an 8 a.m. start at the office tends to pose remarkably few tiredness problems. By the mid-1980s I was still with the tax office (preferring excitement at play and relative security at work) and as I rose up the management ladder I must admit to having had reservations that drowsiness on a Monday morning could dull my enthusiasm for the endless chain of meetings. Remarkably, though, the opposite seemed to be the case. The only conclusion that can be drawn must be that weekend trips to Scotland are good for you.

Inevitably these long weekend trips were not always successful and on some occasions many miles were driven for little reward. At one stage a feet-climbed-per-miles-driven record was kept. It hovered at less than one foot per mile for several months – much to the amusement of those who were more selective about their weekends away.

There was an occasion, however, when a close eye on the weather forecast paid an unlikely dividend much nearer home. St Pancras station's drainpipe was a plum over-ripe for picking. At the time I was working in part of the Revenue's Head Office in the Strand and occasionally drove into the office past the magnificently ornate Victorian architecture of St Pancras station. In February 1987 one of the huge drainpipes on the Midland Road side of the station had sprouted a leak and in a lengthy cold spell it was gradually becoming encased in ice. Excitement was high behind the Tax Office desk at that time. Every lunchtime I would note with satisfaction the below-zero reading at the Met. Office in Holborn. Follow-up trips to the Thames to check the freeze-over potential were disappointing (it must have been bloody cold in Victorian days when it seems to

have frequently frozen over), but by Friday evening I was aware
that a couple more days should see St Pancras in condition.

Meanwhile Torridon was calling and we just had to go. On
Saturday it sleeted all day, on Sunday a 5.30 a.m. peep out from
the comforts of the Glen Torridon public toilet doss confirmed the
worst – continuous rain. There was little point in hanging about. Ten
hours later it was clear that London conditions were better than those
in Torridon. Sturdy icicles hung from the bridges over the M1 and it
looked to be a 'now or never' for St Pancras.

Chris Watts was manager of the climbing department at Alpine
Sports at the time and tended to be invited by the press to give his
opinion on climbing-related issues every now and again. Recently
he had been on a TVAM chat show telling pensioners what to do
to keep warm in a cold spell (North Face fleece jackets seem best)
and contacts at TVAM had professed themselves to be keen to film
any unusual climbing that he might be involved in.

Involving TVAM was almost to lead to failure by default. It
was all a question of timing and permission. Firstly Sunday night
was deemed not to be a good night for filming at an hour's
notice; secondly it seemed permission from the St Pancras station
management was classed as essential. But the duty manager was
more experienced at dealing with irate passengers than hopeful ice-
climbers. He deferred: 'PR Division – open 9 a.m. on Monday.'

It was getting late by now and with the forecast of more cold
weather there did not seem too much harm in leaving it for one
more day. The PR Division's telephone number was given to
TVAM and on Monday I sat back at work and let Chris handle
any bureaucracy. By 4 p.m. he was on the phone full of abuse for
every official known to man. It appeared that the man at TVAM
who had contacted British Rail's PR Division had rushed off on an
urgent job. It was not clear whether he had organised a film crew
and no one seemed to know where he had gone. It sounded like
a fellow bureaucrat's excuse for a long lunch to me, but there was
not much either of us could do about it. Chris had phoned British
Rail himself but the man he needed to speak to was in a 'meeting
of indeterminate length'. Down the pub, we supposed. But such an
important activity as ice-climbing could not be delayed any longer.

Mike Morrison had by now married and moved to Manchester.
But a 4 p.m. phone call ensured that he was back in London securely
attached to a convenient parking meter and in full belay mode by

7.30 p.m. The ice had formed in a particularly friendly position. Of three parallel drainpipes two were almost completely encased up to a height of about twenty metres. The third one was unaffected, thus enabling protection slings to be threaded round it just above the support brackets. Wonderful – a vertical ice streak of frighteningly pure (and very brittle) water ice with excellent protection – assuming of course that the Victorian drainpipe supports were up to the task. Hesitantly, I stepped from the sheet of ice covering the pavement on to the vertical world of urban icefalls, feeling slightly silly wearing plastic boots, crampons, helmet and flailing two ice-axes in a London street. My rucksack in particular attracted comment. In fact it served no really useful purpose other than the straps being a convenient place to secure my ice-axe leads – but onlookers clearly thought that I might pull out something interesting *en route*. The muttered speculation of an increasing audience was not, however, to detract from the fine climbing.

It is unusual in Britain to come across vertical sections of pure water ice. There were no twangy placements in soft white ice here, just the harshly brittle transparence of water freezing in a position isolated from the softening influence of falling snow. The encased drainpipes were clearly visible and careless blows from blunt axes could be seen to fracture right through the ice surround. Distressing. Caution was required. The crowd were looking too interested for my liking. I recalled the coastguard's comment about Andy Meyers at Dover: 'He's looking precarious.' Precarious behaviour attracts onlookers – I hoped it was more the rarity value than the likelihood of a bracket-testing plummet that drew the crowds.

I cannot claim that the climb was full of variety but it was certainly absorbing – so much so that I was initially at a loss to understand why it was getting distinctly darker as I gained height. My head torch was lurking somewhere in the depths of my otherwise empty rucksack as this was not a contingency I had reckoned on. The problem of course was the street lamps – London street lamps are much better at illuminating the street than the tops of buildings. I suppose it is not unreasonable that they are designed that way, but it made for more fumbling than usual on the upper reaches. After eight runners and an exact 19.2 metres (each section of drainpipe being 2.4 metres long) I came to the leak and the end of the ice. Looking up there was five metres or so before the gutter and some rather ornate gargoyles which looked as if they might not appreciate being hooked by axes or stood on by crampons. Discretion seemed in order and I duly lowered off from a sling stretched behind all three pipes.

Presumably disappointed at the lack of injury or death the crowd dissipated as Chris set off next. He had done five metres or so when the blue flashing light appeared. It all looked terribly official.

'You can't do that, you know.'

It seemed that British Rail officials had told the police to expect us and made it clear that they were not flattered by our desire to grapple with their wonderfully ice-clad drainpipes.

'Too late – it's been done.'

The police looked confused and peered curiously up at Chris, and the rope stretching up through the sling at 19.2 metres and back down to the ground. Somebody obviously *had* been up there. What should they do? They had clearly failed in their order to prevent the line being climbed.

'You'll have to come down.'

'I'll just get the gear down.'

This was a good response from Chris. If there was no gear left the evidence would have gone and the police would not have to admit failure.

'All right – but hurry up.'

I was beginning to like these two; they lacked the brusque authoritarian approach we had been on the receiving end of at Dover. Mike and I chatted to them as Chris climbed up into the gloom.

'How is he doing it, then?'

One of them was obviously a potential recruit to the cause. Mike's descriptions were packed full of enthusiasm and inspiration. Soon I was to witness the unique sight of a uniformed officer twanging an ice-axe into a London ice column. Invitations for him to climb the route did not receive an immediate refusal, but he seemed to judge that a uniformed ascent might not be in order.

Chris lowered back down to street level just as a very apologetic policeman was taking out his notebook and asking Mike and me to sign to say that we understood that if we climbed the ice streak we would be liable to prosecution for 'behaviour likely to cause a breach of the peace'. I was rapidly concluding that HM Constabulary's normal line must be – if in doubt claim that the peace *might* have been breached if they had not stepped in. This struck me as a challenging one to prove in court but perhaps rather irrelevant at the time, as neither Chris nor I had any intention of repeating the climb we had just done. Mike was in a different situation. He tried to squirm out of signing but having failed on this tack pleaded that the effort that he had put in driving down from Manchester surely qualified him for more than half an hour belayed to a parking meter. The police were wonderful.

'I can't believe how you do it,' said the keen one.

Their car was unmarked and one of the street lamps was broken thereby creating a dark area.

'Look – we are going to sit in the car over there and watch you, but as far as you are concerned we have gone. Be quick.'

Mike is not the sort of man to waste time under normal circumstances. Faced with such an offer, it was difficult to imagine anyone moving faster. Within thirty seconds the police had retired to the shadows and Mike was tied on ready for action.

But he was too slow – a forcefully driven Maestro with a flashing light on the roof heralded the arrival of the British Rail police. The reasonable face of the Met. melted away into the night to be replaced by abuse more reminiscent of the worst excesses of TV cops and robbers scenes.

Mike squirmed rather uncomfortably. Having just signed to say that he knew that prosecution would follow if he was caught climbing, he was at a distinct disadvantage in the altercation with the British Rail boys. His initial ploy of pretending not to hear was not very plausible and simply resulted in worse abuse being shouted at a louder volume. Mike lowered meekly back down to the ground and all three of us tried the 'we are reasonable chaps' approach that had worked so well with the Met. But the British Rail response had been hardened through years of dealing with trainloads of football hooligans and it was immediately clear that we were on to a loser.

An ice floe about six inches thick covered the pavement and was littered with pieces of ice that had broken away from the column. Not all of these were our doing but their very existence was enough to provoke commands for us to clear up 'our mess' and 'move on before you cause any more damage'. We moved on.

Naturally our first stop was Vic and Maggie Saunders in Islington. Victor is the sort of man who cannot bear to miss out on anything and is therefore ideal wind-up material. It took only a gleam in the eye to get Vic cursing and swearing that he had not seen the icicle and got there first. A second ascent rapidly moved to the top of the Saunders priority list for the next day.

The bureaucrats though had the last laugh. The cover page of the *Daily Telegraph* reported on the icicle the next day. The caption to a floodlit photo of an axe-waving fireman summed it up: 'Firemen making safe a sixty-five-foot icicle on St Pancras station last night.'

At 8 a.m. when I drove past on the way to work nothing was left but a series of fire-axe chips out of the listed-building brickwork and a six-inch ice dribble from the leak.

There is no doubt about it. Those ice lines have to be grabbed when you get the chance.

8

Taulliraju South Pillar

Alan Rouse was quite certain.

'Peru,' he said. 'It's the place for you.'

A bit later in the evening a few more beers had been drunk and he was rather more direct.

'Pull your finger out and be a bit more adventurous before you degenerate into a boring old fart.'

Alcohol-induced exchanges of abuse often contain more than a little grain of truth. It wasn't so much that I was becoming bored with mountaineering – simply that I wasn't quite sure what to do next.

Early exploits with George had of course given me an ideal grounding and over the years I had gradually been ticking off the Alpine classics in my Tax Office holidays. By 1981 when I bumped into Alan Rouse at a Sheffield party I had managed the North Faces of the Eiger and Matterhorn, the Walker Spur, Frêney Pillar and quite a few rather more obscure gems that were on my tick list. I was keen to climb further afield but the cost, hassle, high chance of not getting any climbing done and other demands on my annual leave entitlement combined to form a difficult set of obstacles. Perhaps the overriding factor though was the lack of an exciting objective. As I knew from Scottish exploits the best way to find suitably inspirational unclimbed challenges is to visit an area regularly, gradually absorb the lie of the land, assess the plums on offer and waste no time when the conditions are right.

This approach seemed inapplicable to the world's greater ranges and Rouse's jovially spoken words of abusive encouragement were exactly what I needed. A trip to Peru could, he felt, comfortably be done within four weeks from Britain. The mountains were not so high as to call for lengthy acclimatisation forays but they were significantly bigger than the Alps, steep and technically challenging, and still boasted plenty of impressive unclimbed lines.

And Rouse should know – a few years previously he had spent most of the year in South America clocking up numerous magnificent first ascents and acquiring a virtually unrivalled knowledge of Patagonia and Peru in particular.

A few weeks later I phoned him up. This seemed quite a big step – the hopeful bumbler effectively pleading for help from one of Britain's leading mountaineers. Without the party atmosphere and alcohol-induced familiarity I felt distinctly nervous.

'How about the Southern Face of Taulliraju?'

'What?'

It struck me that he could well not remember me or our conversation of a few weeks earlier. I persevered.

'My father's Pickel & Ski calendar has a photo of the Southern Face of Taulliraju in it. Has it been done?'

It all sounded terribly haphazard. I could imagine the Rouse brain computing this information and wondering how serious a response he should give. In fact considering our rather basic selection method and our unknown ability in his eyes he was incredibly helpful. He told us that the mountain had first been climbed in 1956 by a French team including Lionel Terray. As far as he knew the prominent buttress leading directly to the summit had been attempted solo by the bold French mountaineer Nicholas Jaeger, who had been forced off to the right, commenting that the central section would require bolts. All in all it didn't sound very hopeful but Rouse was not at all dismissive.

'Don't believe other people's reports,' he said. 'Just go for it.'

I studied the calendar again. Taulliraju did have a lot to be said for it. At 5800 metres the height seemed about right for a first foray at altitudes higher than Mont Blanc. Technically it looked steep and difficult and it had to be admitted that there was a nasty blank-looking section of rock at one point. A possible streak of ice (it was difficult to see clearly from the picture) gave some grounds for hope in passing this section and all in all I had to agree with Rouse's basic recommendation.

The more I looked into Peru the more appealing it became. I knew that bureaucracy levels in the Himalaya could reach laughable proportions but here it seemed that contact with officialdom was unnecessary and, as the mountains of the Cordillera Blanca are relatively close to the road, access was not a tremendous problem.

The next decision was who could I persuade to join me on this step into the unknown. None of my regular climbing partners had previous experience of this sort of thing either, so we were inevitably going to be a team of bumbly newcomers to the greater ranges game. Mike Morrison and Chris Watts were keen to join me as a rope of three trying Taulliraju, whilst John English, a London doctor whom I knew well from the North London scene, chose John Zangwill as his climbing partner, and Mike O'Brien (more commonly known by the affectionate nickname of 'No Brains') was keen to come along as a photographer and perhaps do some easier peaks with Anita, my girlfriend of the moment. It didn't strike me until we were all in Peru that we had three Mikes and two Johns in the team – a certain recipe for confusion!

From somewhere I had formed the impression that sponsorship shouldn't be too hard to get, so took on the job of writing to fifty or so commercial companies – totally in vain. We received one private donation of £50 which, after deducting postage for the rest of the exercise meant a subsidy of about £4 a head. I have never made sponsorship applications to commercial companies since. We did, however, manage to secure financial help and valuable guidance from the Mount Everest Foundation and British Mountaineering Council.

The next setback for me was a personal one. Anita and I had been engaged for a year or so but things had been going badly and a couple of months before the departure date we decided to split. Anita had been in on the trip from the start and was obviously looking forward to going. She more than anyone had read up about the area and was more conversant than any of us with the Peruvian way of life. The inevitable question arose: 'Do you think I should still come?'

The situation was far from ideal but I suppose I still had some hopes that we might get back together. Also Anita knew the other members well and had already decided on some mountaineering and exploratory objectives with Mike O'Brien. So it was decided. She would come.

The next problem was the Falklands War. The trip was to take place in May 1982 – right at the height of the conflict – and Peru was distinctly pro-Argentinian, so much so that our British Caledonian flight via Puerto Rico, Caracas and Bogotá went no further than Bogotá and was treated to a circle of armed guards whilst refuelling at Caracas. At Bogotá British Caledonian had arranged for us to continue with Aeroperu to Lima. I had never actually heard of

Aeroperu and as this was the first time I had ever flown, the trip was already opening up new horizons for me. Perhaps my inexperience in flying was an advantage when a message came over the tannoy (in Spanish only, of course) to the effect that we had engine trouble and would have to land immediately. Presumably this wasn't quite as normal as I initially thought because Aeroperu did go out of their way to be hospitable and calm the more hysterical passengers during the rapid descent and the ensuing six-hour wait at a sparsely manned airstrip somewhere in northern Peru. Liberal quantities of free alcohol were available and as we sat idly on the tarmac surrounded by empty liquor bottles (whilst offering unhelpful advice to a mechanic persevering by the light of a head torch) the general conclusion was that there are worse ways than Aeroperu delays to start a holiday. A rather catchy little advertising slogan for them, I thought.

Lima at 4 a.m. was buzzing. In response to our 'cheapest hotel, please' request, our two taxi drivers took us to a particularly nasty part of town. Armed police seemed to be everywhere and, despite trying several doorways masquerading as hotels, no one was prepared to put us up for the rest of the night. If our interpretation of their Spanish was right everyone kept saying, 'Come back in the morning,' which seemed a very curious thing to say to Westerners wanting to spend hard currency. It was not until the next day that we discovered there had been a major break-out from Lima prison which was right in the middle of our hotel-searching area. We never did find anywhere to stay and eventually got the taxis to drop us off outside the offices of a bus company which ran a regular service to Huaráz – a sizeable town in the Cordillera Blanca mountains about eight and a half hours' drive from Lima.

It was not at all clear that the spot where we had been dropped was a bus station. Certainly there were no buses anywhere – just two huge doors which were firmly padlocked. Sitting uncomfortably at the side of the road we all collapsed on to our large pile of luggage and passed the remainder of the night considering our plight.

'Nice weather,' said No Brains in an effort to inject some lightheartedness into the situation. It wasn't, of course. The thick pea-soup fog, or *garua*, had engulfed the city and seemed to deaden the noise of the night – either this or there really was less activity during daylight hours. The fog didn't keep the children away. They were all eyes and fingers marvelling at our equipment, playing with the zips and asking endless questions. With our gear in so many separate bags it was impossible to keep an eye on what was going on, so Chris unpacked the climbing ropes and tied all the bags together. This felt and looked rather silly but made us feel slightly more secure, especially when backed up by Mike and No Brains screaming at anyone who dare infringe our one metre exclusion zone.

After what seemed a very long time other people, including a German couple, started to crowd around the locked doors. The Germans were highly organised. 'Yes,' they said, 'this is the place to catch the cheapest bus to Huaráz.' Things were looking up.

The bus was revealed at 6 a.m. when the huge doors were swung open. It looked very experienced. The tyres were completely bald. One had worn right through the rubber and damaged the steel reinforcement which hung in steel ribbons. One of the headlamps was broken and the whole front end had obviously been involved in a pretty hefty crash at some stage in its career. The radiator grille and front bumper were missing and it looked altogether a mean if excessively tried and tested beast. The German couple took us under their wing. It seemed that it was essential to make sure that one's baggage went in the lock-up compartment along the side and at the rear. Storage on the roof rack was to be avoided at all costs. On our person wallets in open pockets were unthinkable and it was said to be best to somehow tie hard currency and passports to our bodies. Having dutifully acted on their advice we sat back in the boneshaking seats and prepared for our first Third World bus ride.

It was to exceed all expectations.

Whilst all the loading-up had been going on, the hordes of children had been kept at bay outside the gates. As we pulled out they surged forward to check the lockers, oblivious to the acrid black fumes spewing over them from the exhaust. Somehow one locker came open and some baggage was pulled out on to the street. One of the German couple's rucksacks was last seen clutched in the arms of a seven or eight-year-old running like the clappers down a narrow side street. I was rapidly concluding that luggage preservation is something to place very high on one's list of priorities in Peru.

So my first real view of anywhere outside Europe was through the window of a particularly dilapidated bus and accompanied by the regular rat-a-tat of strands of tyre reinforcement scouring the wheel arch to an impressively shiny state, in stark contrast to the dust and grime ingrained in the rest of the vehicle. The first thing that struck all of us was the number of people. Although it was still relatively early – certainly before 7 a.m. – the roads and pavements were packed and the air reverberated with the sound of car horns and human shouts.

Gradually our bus found its way to the shanty town outskirts. No amount of reading can prepare you for the reality. I remember we crossed a bridge and were afforded a view along the backs of the shanty buildings on top of a high river bank. Each hut had a streak of brown leading down into the putrid stream at the bottom of the ravine. At one end was a much larger bright red streak with animal limbs dotted around – the abattoir. As the bus pulled away from the bridge I caught a glimpse of a group of women washing clothes in the stream.

The bus now headed north along the desert strip between the Andean mountain chain to the east and the deep blue of the Pacific on the west. The road contoured round hugely arid and sandy slopes rising up at a steady forty-five degrees from sea level. In sharp contrast to the Amazon basin a couple of hundred miles to the east, the climate here in the Atacama desert is amongst the driest in the world. The heat was unbearable. Never one to appreciate the joys of hot climates, I found myself fading rapidly. Up until the day before, my restricted climatic experience had never revealed such temperatures to me.

My first exposure had been on the walk across the tarmac from the plane to the transit lounge at Puerto Rico airport. At the top of the gangway I had assumed that the heat was radiating from the plane's engines (remember I had never flown before) and the realisation that I was in fact experiencing normal Puerto Rican air temperature was a shock sufficient to leave an everlasting impression on my memory banks.

If anything the bus was even hotter than Puerto Rico. A glance around showed that most of the team were now out for the count. I couldn't help but feel an emotional pang to notice that John Zangwill had fallen asleep across Anita's lap. She was awake and was clearly enjoying the situation. Our eyes connected briefly and awkwardly. Staring out of the window I willed myself to concentrate on the scenery. Perhaps it hadn't been quite such a good idea for Anita to come after all.

From the coastal settlement of Paitrilca the road wound its way up to the crest of the Cordillera Negra where the air was much cooler and the first distant views of the mountains could be had – outrageously steep fangs of white thrusting into the crystal clear horizon.

Remarkably the bus was still functioning satisfactorily and, more or less on time, we bumped and rattled our way into the town of Huaráz – the Chamonix of Peru. This was altogether different from Lima. Bright sunshine replaced the dense grey *garua* and a glorious panorama of spectacular mountains dominated the skyline. Taulliraju was hidden but our secondary objective Huascarán – the highest (but technically one of the easiest) equatorial mountain in the world – stood out prominently, looking all of its 6768 metres.

Rouse had told us where to go in Huaráz: 'Hotel Barcelona, top floor – ask for Pepe.'

Pepe was in fact the son of the hotel owner but he had spotted a niche and was keen to rent floor space on the empty expanse of the top floor and look after gear when climbers/trekkers were away in the mountains. He also knew everyone who could conceivably be of assistance with the result that within an hour of arriving he had arranged for a Chevrolet pick-up and an interpreter who was to come with us to the end of the motorable road and help us hire donkeys to take our gear in to the foot of the mountain.

By the time we arrived in Huaráz we had been on the go for something like thirty-six hours and were ready for something to eat. I had heard a lot about illness in Third World countries (not to mention the Peruvian predilection for eating guinea pigs) and so approached the moment with a fair degree of trepidation. But where to go? As spoilt Western brats nothing visibly on offer seemed likely to sit comfortably in our delicate stomachs. The main thing in favour of Pepe's recommendation was the darkness and virtual impossibility of seeing what was being eaten.

'Aghh!' No Brains was the first to find something unusual in his food.

Closer inspection with a head torch (conveniently brought along by Mike Morrison) revealed there to be a lump of bone closely resembling a mouse skull in his stew. A decision was made to delay serious eating until we were beyond the roadhead and could cook everything for ourselves.

A visit to the Huaráz disco rounded the evening off but the sight of seven of us dancing around wearing putrid yellow 'British Taulliraju

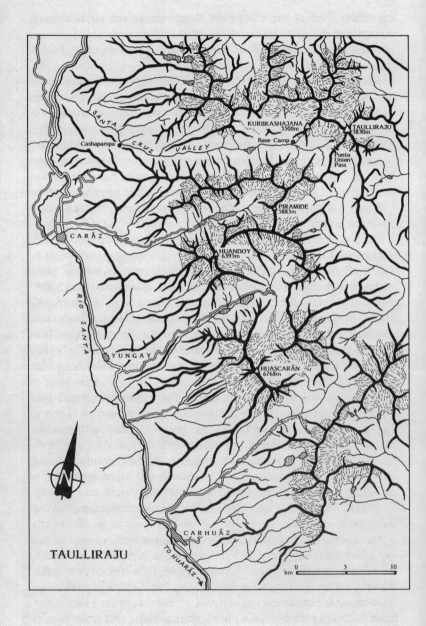

KURIIKASHAJANA
5500m
Base Camp
TAULLIRAJU
5830m
Punta
Union
Pass

SANTA CRUZ VALLEY

Cashapampa

CARÁZ

RIO SANTA

PIRAMIDE
5885m

HUANDOY
6395m

YUNGAY

HUASCARÁN
6768m

N

CARHUÁZ

TO HUARÁZ

TAULLIRAJU

km   0   5   10

Expedition' T-shirts on the day that the *Belgrano* was sunk did little to inspire constructive dance-floor relationships.

The (very experienced-looking) Chevrolet pick-up organised by Pepe turned up dead on time and took us eighty miles north up the Rio Santa valley to the town of Caráz. *En route* we passed the new town of Yungay, something of a small concrete jungle built with international support to house the survivors of the disastrous 1970 earthquake. All of us had read about the earthquake but seeing the disaster site first hand was sobering. The earthquake had triggered a huge sérac avalanche from the summit ice cliffs of Huascarán, over ten miles away. This had roared down into a large glacial lake, the moraine dam of which burst under the strain of the surging water. The resultant mass of mud, rocks and water had then cascaded down the valley straight towards Yungay. Its speed was such that it literally became airborne on the leeside of a rounded ridge a mile or so before the town.

This take-off zone was clearly visible as the only spot in the path of devastation where trees had survived. In Yungay itself only the church overseeing the graveyard survived. There were about 18,000 deaths in Yungay alone. I had never before seen such immense devastation and the scene made a profound impact on all of us. It is perhaps no surprise that mountain people tend to be more religious than plain-dwellers. If nothing else it was another reminder to be forever wary in the mountains.

Caráz, the only major town between Huaráz and the roadhead, had escaped much of the earthquake devastation. Narrow bustling side streets were thronged with old ladies battling with market crowds whilst wearing five or more colourful skirts at the same time. Much theoretical discussion was to centre around Peruvian skirts and in what circumstances how many of them might be removed.

Caráz was the last place to stock up with provisions and marked the end of the tarmac road. From here on it was challenging driving on a rough dirt track to the village of Cashapampa at the mouth of the deeply cut Santa Cruz valley which winds its way up to the Punta Union pass – 4700 metres high and one of the main passes across the Cordillera Blanca range. Away from the beaten track Peruvian rural life seemed to be progressing much as it had done for centuries. Horses pulling wooden ploughs were common in the fields and red or white flags hanging outside some mud brick houses indicated that bread or milk were for sale.

At Cashapampa José our interpreter really earned his pay as he beat down the local expectation of rich pickings from wealthy Westerners and negotiated £1 per donkey per day, and £3 for the *arrerio*, or donkey driver, and in the best negotiating tradition finger-wagging and yelling gave way to back-slapping, broad smiles and handshakes.

And so we were underway at last. With seven fully loaded donkeys and three hours of daylight to spare, our convoy straggled out of Cashapampa bound for a base camp 'somewhere under Taulliraju'. Cruz, our *arrerio*, had insisted that his father Anedo join us as 'base camp guard'. There had been lots of discussion over this, but with the Shining Path guerrillas making their presence known in the area and the ever present risk of theft, we decided that his fee of £1 per day was potentially not too bad a deal. I tried not to imagine this wiry seventy-year-old grappling with armed guerrillas, telling myself his presence was more important than his physical prowess.

An official-looking sign indicated that we were entering the 'Parc Nacional Huascarán' but no change was apparent as the well-worn path wound up between impressive cacti in a steep-sided gorge. Snow-clad mountains peeped out of an intermittent cloud cover. After only a couple of hours darkness was approaching and a halt was called.

'Which tent do you think I should sleep in?' I was aware that Anita had been becoming increasingly friendly with John Zangwill, and had perhaps purposely pushed the subject of sleeping arrangements in our two-man tents to the back of my mind. Her question, unexpected as it was, brought the subject sharply back into focus.

'Well, er, that's up to you really.'

What else could I have said? I tried to ignore the heartache of a splintered relationship as I moved in to share with Chris and concentrate on the task in hand.

Fishing is *strictly* prohibited in the National Park – it must be, it said so on that sign we passed. This did not, however, prompt the local people that we encountered to make any effort whatsoever to conceal their ten-foot bamboo fishing rods. Cruz was no exception and proved himself a worthy fisherman catching numerous large minnow-like fish from the sparkling streams. No Brains and Mike Morrison were keen to test their boy-scouting talents and compete – after all, maximum rations were now in order after our period of hesitant nibbling in the towns. The results were not impressive. In just under an hour Cruz and his father managed eight fish compared to the Mikes' one. No Brains looked particularly crestfallen – especially when the Peruvian sense of humour was turned from his lack of fish on to his prize purchase so far – an extremely odorous Peruvian donkey bag.

No Brains is perhaps best described as a professional photographer with an overriding interest in the subjects that he photographs – particularly if they have what he calls 'extravagant ethnic interest'. The donkey bag he purchased for an exorbitant price at Cashapampa clearly fell into this category to the extent that he was exceptionally unwilling to allow the donkeys or other humans to carry it. All would possibly have been well if he had not tried to supplement his diet by filling it with bananas.

After a few hours of it bashing against his legs curious stains were fast spreading through the tough but finely decorated fabric. Anedo was the first to notice. He couldn't speak English but his sign language made it clear enough that he considered No Brains to be some kind of clumsy trainee donkey. His own beasts would never let this happen. Perhaps the mashed banana could be used as some kind of fish bait? Cruz's father was by now beside himself with mirth. There is nothing that Peruvian mountain folk like more than the opportunity to laugh at gringo mistakes.

It was a rather bedraggled and strung-out team that next day weaved its way into a delightful Base Camp at about 4000 metres, with Anedo, the oldest member of the group, now carrying not only the much discussed donkey bag but also one of our holdalls that he had found lying on the track. I couldn't help but feel that there was rather more good luck than good judgement involved in us and all our gear arriving safely.

We had glimpsed Taulliraju on the walk-in. It all looked horribly steep. Our eyes were drawn to prominent ornate cornices decorating the original French 1956 route. This had been our proposed line of descent but it looked far from the easy way down that I was used to in the European Alps. In all likelihood it had not been repeated, let alone used as a pleasant descent. I shifted my eyes to the South Face – an extremely steep wall with several parallel drooling ice streaks which failed to reach the ground and emanated from a dangerous-looking bowl of what I guessed to be powder snow high on the face. Bounding the face on the right was our pillar. It looked steeper and more intimidating than in the calendar photo;

there was also a lot less snow around – a point which provoked much discussion about the pros and cons of snow-plastered walls. Still, not to at least give it a go was unthinkable. Having said this, I couldn't help but notice that it looked particularly challenging. In the naïvety of inexperience I think it is easy to feel that success on Alpine classics with tremendous reputations qualifies one for more than it actually does. At this stage we simply stared awe-struck at the magnificent scene before us and nursed splitting headaches from a Base Camp at a mere 4000 metres. The top was nearly 2000 metres higher. I took another headache tablet.

A get-fit programme was clearly necessary. Initially this consisted of consuming excessive quantities of painkillers and, perhaps more constructively, improving our diet. An inspection of our reserves revealed that a haphazard attempt at shopping in Huaráz had resulted in little more than a vast quantity of potatoes and rice to supplement the dried-food packs brought out from England. As the latter were intended for the mountains, there was unlikely to be much in the way of palate-tickling pleasures at Base Camp. Another mistake was the cook – or rather the lack of one. In pursuit of economy it was felt that such a luxury was unnecessary. Seldom have a team's abilities been so mistakenly overrated. Chris and I, who were volunteered to cook on the first night, felt left with little option but to substitute quantity for quality, so served up massive portions of potatoes, closely followed by large bowls of tinned pineapples. But a survey on the morning of day two at Base Camp revealed that at this rate we would run out of potatoes after ten days – and we were planning to spend three weeks here. Fortunately Cruz, being a typically mellow Peruvian hill farmer, had decided to hang around for a few days and was only too willing to take food orders, which included such necessities as a donkey-load of beer. Beer was not cheap in Peru and in retrospect we were very lucky to see him again, having forked out £40 up front for this essential purchase. Personally my head hurt sufficiently for me to not be very interested.

Having thus prepared ourselves in a characteristically disorganised manner we were able to leave Base Camp the day after arriving to start up our training objective of Kuriikashajana (5500m). Though we guessed the climbing to be fairly easy we all decided to take two days over the ascent in the belief that two easy days would be better for our acclimatisation than one very hard day at a height that would be an altitude record for every member of the team. As it took me all day to struggle up an unrelenting slope of tufty grass and reach the edge of the glacier at approximately 5000 metres, it was perhaps just as well that we adopted this plan.

In fact I was so knackered that the rest of the team dismissed me as a no-hoper and I woke the next morning fully refreshed to find everyone gearing up around me. Anita had, I couldn't help noticing, disappeared into the morning white-out with John Zangwill. I had tied on what began as a rope of four with John English, Mike Morrison and Chris Watts, but ended with Mike and I on our own on the South Ridge. Unbelievably soft powder snow alternated with amazing ice formations. At one point we avoided a difficult section by crawling through an ice tunnel piercing through a huge cornice. Ultimately we reached a summit of sorts but the visibility was such that I will never really know exactly where we were.

'The South Summit.' Mike at least was confident of our where-abouts. It seemed good mountaineering judgement to agree. That night we were back at Base Camp.

If nothing else we had experienced the joys of Peruvian ridges. I made a mental note to keep off them whenever possible.

Cruz's shopping trips were less effective than we had hoped. The beer was the only order that went completely as planned. One thing we couldn't help but notice was how quickly he had managed to get down to Cashapampa and back up to our Base Camp. On the way up it had taken two days (well, we paid for two anyway) whereas now it took him slightly over one day to get down *and* back again. The poor beer-carrying donkey did look a bit tired though. Its load lasted one evening. Having consumed all the beer celebrating our debatable success on Kuriikashajana it was obviously time to justify getting on to mountain rations. We set off for Taulliraju in indifferent weather up to the Punta Union pass and then contoured around to the foot of our mountain.

I shall not dwell on our first effort. Suffice to say that after only five pitches, Mike Morrison, Chris Watts and I made a hasty retreat, due to both poor weather and our total inability to climb as a rope of three. John English and John Zangwill were equally unsuccessful in attempting another line on the face.

The enthusiasm which is perhaps only to be found on expeditions that are pushed for time somehow brought Chris and me back to the foot of the face, only the day after our ignominious defeat. We both felt sorry for Mike Morrison, who had dropped out simply to give us a better chance of success. However, a rope of two proved to be much more to our taste, and we passed our previous highpoint at midday.

Our proposed line took the imposing buttress falling directly from the summit, and it was distressingly obvious that on our earlier attempt a full day's climbing had placed us only about an eighth of the way up the face. Banking on the greater speed of a team of two, we took only six dehydrated food packets and some biscuits for our second attempt. However, short technical sections between soft snowy ramps, followed by disgusting bottomless powder snow, still ensured slow progress. We burrowed a tunnel right through the prominent snow ridge of the lower buttress (in search of better snow), and nightfall found us hacking out the first of our ice-ledge bivouacs.

The situation now looked far from promising. We were perhaps a quarter of the way up the spur, the last two pitches having taken half the day, and were faced with a disturbingly beautiful snow ridge, featuring stunning butterfly-wing cornices that looked, if anything, even more precarious and time-consuming than the climbing we had just done.

We awoke despondent and cold. Chris dropped the jumars and I the abseil tape, but such minor mishaps cannot be allowed to weaken one's resolve. After two desperate excavation pitches, an icy knife-edge crest allowed easy progress for fifty metres, and a short traverse gave access to a couloir of superb ice, leading to the top of the snow ridge. For the first time we really felt we were getting somewhere.

The ground now steepened considerably. Smooth, seventy-five-degree granite slabs, glittering with snow and ice streaks, provided an inspiring spectacle, devoid of the soft snow which had plagued us on the lower buttress. But incompetence reared its head again, in that neither of us had done any serious sack-hauling before. The obvious solution was not to indulge, but, after thirty-five metres of intensely precarious mixed ground, the climbing reached a standard that would have been worrying on a summer's day in the Peak District with shorts, chalk bag et al. Here, et al included double boots, large sacks, and ice streaks. Having removed my sack, I managed a long section of laybacking up overhanging blocks, followed by delicate bridging up an immaculate groove, until I was safely installed on a small ice slope. The two hours it took Chris to prusik to the stance with two sacks amply demonstrated our ineptitude in the sack-hauling department. We subsequently abandoned such manoeuvres, and climbed with our sacks firmly in place.

Day three started with a blank twelve-metre wall, which gave rise to the first fall of the route, during an unsuccessful tension traverse. A second attempt led us to the foot of a series of shallow, curving, seventy-five degree ice runnels, interspersed with truly vertical sections of thin ice. No more soft grovelling here: superb hard climbing on mixed ground, my favourite climbing combination. Up above, disjointed runnels could be seen to terminate in a blank sheet of overhanging granite. A very difficult pegging line on the right appeared to lead to the top of a pillar, but the ten metres of rock above looked totally blank. Chris persuaded me to leave this line and continue to the highest point of a snowy ramp in the hope of a miracle. Nicholas Jaeger's prediction that bolts would be necessary seemed uncomfortably true, as two disillusioned climbers shuffled about uneasily on the highest point of the ice.

'Where now?' We both voiced our thoughts at the same time. An extremely thin crack, leading leftwards, appeared to offer the only possible line of progress, but with neither of us being noted for our pegging prowess the next hour would have provided a fine photo-sequence for the Ladybird book, *How Not to Aid Climb*. It was surprising that only one real fall resulted, although it must be admitted that my sack would not be with me today had I not tied some flailing ends round my waist to stop them getting tangled.

Luck was clearly on our side. A fine flake crack hidden round the corner would have led easily to the obvious snow band at two thirds height, were it not for the fact that we had lost most of our pegs by this time. To put it mildly, this created some 'interest', but by adopting tactics such as standing on ice-axes hooked over flakes or jammed in cracks, we managed to make progress, and by nightfall we had reached the elusive snow band, where we hacked a poor ledge out of the ice slope. It was becoming increasingly noticeable that exhaustion was resulting in a smaller and more uncomfortable bivouac ledge each night; at this rate we calculated that by the sixth night we would be sleeping on our feet!

Bedding down just before dark, we had time to study the possibilities above. A reasonable traverse appeared to lead leftwards to a bowl-like recession in the upper part of the face, but this seemed out of line and looked extremely dangerous in its topmost reaches. The only other possibility was to weave a way up the overhanging thirty-five-metre rock wall above, making maximum use of two huge icicles, which looked marginally easier to climb than the rock behind them.

After a night with this on our minds, morning brought another clear sky. A magnificent lead by Chris put us directly beneath the righthand icicle, the bottom of which hung about three metres away from the wall. A horrific off-width chimney yielded to judicious use of Friends in a crack in the right wall, and gave access to the icicle itself. This proved to be incredibly hard ice, upon which our blunt crampon points slithered ineffectually. However, after an hour's hard work and much concern (leaving Chris with a badly bruised hip, after the tip of the icicle fell on him!), we were ensconced in a unique stance, on a rock flake behind the icicle. Above us, the fringe of the final slope was five metres out and three metres above, but the icicle had proved so strenuous that we opted for another display of our ice aid-climbing abilities. After some difficulty and the loss of yet more equipment, we were safely installed above the second steep band.

Here we experienced the sun for the first time and a demoralising hundred metres of sixty-degree slope up which a fast-wilting Fowler was hauled, feeling as out of control as the sacks on the first steep section.

That night's bivouac ledge, apart from being smaller than ever, sloped to one side at about thirty degrees, which was strange considering the effort we had put into ensuring that it was level. I was fine, having Chris as a stop and pillow at the lower end. Chris, however, was not impressed with our bedroom or my sleeping habits. Midway through the night I half woke and leant across to kiss Anita who was obviously still highly placed in my subconscious.

'Aghh!' She had grown some serious whiskers. I woke with a start. Chris just cursed me for half pushing him off the ledge and returned to his slumbers. I sat there wide awake till morning.

Fortunately, the morning sun was on the far side of the mountain, so I was able to escape its influence for a while. But the previous day's exposure had had its effect. Not having been entirely *compos mentis* during the evening (and perhaps the night too!), I was labouring under a misconception with regard to the next section of the route. Above us was a vertical rock buttress, laced with just off-vertical ice runnels on the left, and bounded by a deep ice groove on the right. The groove looked infinitely the easier alternative. It was my first pitch of the day, and I thought Chris wanted us to go left, as I was certain that he had seen something wrong with the righthand alternative the night before. Chris, for his part, was keeping quiet, feeling that I must have some very good reason for going left, even though it clearly looked easier to the right.

The lefthand alternative provided the hardest climbing so far, with no runners and honeycombed ice, covered in a metre of powder and actually overhanging. This offered no protection and required an aid technique involving foot slings attached to ice-axes. Chris stared intently at the knife-blade belay pegs, whilst the high death potential was evident to us both.

When we met again at the belay-less stance above this pitch, our error had become uncomfortably obvious. Overhanging ice mushrooms above vertical ice to each side did little to inspire confidence. Chris began to point out that as a married man he should take care, a line of conversation that seemed likely to precede a retreat. Not having enough energy left to descend and try other alternatives, I scuttled quickly right before the conversation had time to develop. Luck was with us again, for after only ten metres a hidden cave provided a good stance with easy but steep ice leading right for eight metres to a junction with the South-South-East Ridge just below the top.

It was sobering to think that we might very well have descended, not knowing that we were so close to success. Three unconsolidated pitches on the ridge and it was all over. We had achieved our calendar picture and it was time to relax and admire the expansive view, stretching from the steaming rainforest of the Amazon to the east, right across to the arid deserts beyond the Santa Cruz valley to the west.

Time on a cherished summit is always precious and it was ironic that after four and a half days of perfect weather, the continuous cloud cover of the Amazon Basin should choose to swell up and engulf the summit as we sat there at 12 noon on May 28th, 1982. Sitting in the swirling cloud, we had time to consider the immediate problem of descent. Loss of equipment on the ascent meant that we now had insufficient gear to abseil down the whole route, and our tentatively hoped-for line of descent down the North-West Ridge looked unthinkable, due to wafer-thin curling cornices and delicate snow mushrooms.

There was no option but to reverse the route. By dint of down-climbing the top few pitches, and retrieving virtually every piece of gear we had left in place on the ascent, we finally reached our bivouac ledge above the upper end of the fragile snow ridge. The next morning we chose a shorter line of descent, leading down the west side of the spur to the glacier between the two projecting rock buttresses on the face. For a change we seemed to have made a competent decision. In addition to being quicker, our chosen line enabled us to avoid the unstable snow ridge and to preserve our severely depleted stock of equipment.

Collapsed at the edge of the glacier, we peeled off our Gore-Tex suits for the first time in six days! Perhaps we were unused to walking on level ground or perhaps we were just too tired to be able to control our bodies properly. Either way both of us seemed embarrassingly prone to tripping over and falling spreadeagled on the tiny sheep track we were now following. Base Camp was only a few hours down from the glacier edge and, even if there were only potatoes left, it would be great to have a dietary change and meet the rest of the team again.

'I'm sure we should be able to see the tents from this point.'

Chris was right; I thought we should too. We both peered down the valley. Base Camp was surrounded by trees so it was a bit difficult to be certain.

'Perhaps just over there, hidden by the trees.'

We carried on staggering hopefully, but with high spirits waning fast. Could everyone have gone? When we left there had been mumblings about the lack of food prompting an early evacuation but I never really believed that it would come to this.

There could be no denying it, though. The ground that now lay before us was where our Base Camp had been. The only sign that it had been occupied was a packet of dried Mountain House food with a tin of pineapples perched on top. These sat on a large stone right in the middle of the clearing. Chris picked up a note fluttering under the pineapple tin: 'Hope you had a good time – see you in Huaráz – here is the leftover food.' There was no message from Anita.

We didn't catch up with them until a few days later on the lower slopes of Huascarán, but by now we were all too gut-rotted to make a serious attempt on the normal route. On the plane home I took time to consider. On the relationship front it was clearly over with Anita. On the mountaineering front the trip had opened up an interesting array of new horizons. If it was possible to acclimatise from zero to 5800-metre peaks in three weeks from Britain, it should in theory be possible to acclimatise for a Himalayan objective within six weeks. If I took all my annual leave in one go, I could see my horizons broadening.

9

Bojohagur

We were collapsed on the floor at Victor Saunders' house in East London. 'Our leader', as everyone present insisted on referring to him (along with other less flattering nicknames), was explaining his latest thoughts on coping with the problems of high altitude. Lumps of ice in sleeping-bags was his pet subject at the time. No one else present had any experience of these but Victor was insistent that they could be a serious problem and might be overcome by the use of face masks and plastic tubing. The rest of us slouched around mesmerised while Vic gave a practical demonstration of this idea.

'Face mask on like this, body inside sleeping-bag, drawcord tight – tube enables occupant to breathe cold air from tent space. You see it helps overcome condensation forming in the down. The moisture in your breath is discharged straight into the atmosphere.'

His critical audience surveyed the scene whilst unhelpful comments poured forth.

'Why don't you seal one nostril, ram the pipe up the other one and breathe through your nose? Then you could save the weight of the face mask.' 'A tube up your bum would have the same effect with wet farts.' 'If the tube stretched outside the tent it would eliminate hoar frost on the internal walls.'

Victor adopted a long-suffering expression and placed his equipment to one side. 'OK, let's move on.'

The occasion was an early meeting of the rather grandly named British Bojohagur Expedition, 1984. Bojohagur Duanasir was an unclimbed 7300-metre peak close to the Karakoram Highway and directly above the Hunza village of Karimabad in Northern Pakistan. Victor had spotted a blurred photograph of it in a picture book given to him by a Japanese climber in gratitude for a crevasse rescue. The photo wasn't really good enough to show any definition but it did seem that it was one of the highest unclimbed summits in

the Himalaya and it's base being only two miles from the road
meant that civil servant and architect types such as Victor and I,
with finite holiday arrangements were in with a chance. Also of the
party were Doctor John English, Mike Morrison and Chris Watts
from the Taulliraju trip, Lobby, who we all knew well from Scottish
ice-climbing weekends and George, who fancied exploring a bit of
Pakistan.

The first thing that struck me was the acreage of bureaucratic
hurdles that had to be crossed to mount a Himalayan expedition.
For Peru we simply booked our plane tickets and got on with it.
For Bojohagur official permission had to be granted, a peak fee
paid, a liaison officer arranged . . . I began to wonder whether
the crux would be solving the paperwork problems or getting up
the mountain.

It was decided at an early stage that we would climb in three
teams of two and shun the use of fixed ropes or supplementary
oxygen. For all of us the attractions of this then relatively new
alpine-style approach to climbing big mountains was obvious. We
could see no pleasure or satisfaction in the laborious process of
fixing semi-permanent camps, employing high-altitude porters and
generally allowing our holiday to degenerate into an expensive logis-
tical nightmare. Expense, it had to be admitted was a consideration –
none of us was particularly well off. But finance was not the only
consideration. I found myself a hundred per cent behind Victor's
strong ethical views on the subject and could not help but feel that
the environmental impact and steamroller approach of traditional
Himalayan expeditions was rapidly becoming a thing of the past.

Much time was spent discussing what we should expect. Considering how close to the road the mountain is, there was remarkably
little information available. We knew the height to be 7329 metres
and the name to mean something like 'where the devil's horse fears
to go'. We also knew that permission for foreign attempts had
long been refused. This was nothing to do with frontline border
sensitivity; it was simply that the Pakistani authorities like Pakistani
climbers to be involved in the first ascents of their major peaks. A
list exists of peaks felt to be sufficiently important to reserve for
Pakistanis or, at the very least, joint expeditions. Bojohagur fell
into a grey area. The peak is part of the Ultar massif, culminating
in the unclimbed summit of Ultar (7388m). By 1982 Ultar featured
on the list of reserved peaks but Bojohagur did not. Perusal of the

Education with George: above left, Whitsun on the Idwal Slabs, aged 10, 1967; above right, struggling out of Skew Ghyl, Lake District, aged 13 (MF).

The cliffs of the South-West: below left, we got quite a lot of practice at dodging fulmar puke; below right, Mike Morrison pulling on to the first stance on Henna, 1979 (MF).

Great White Fright, Dover. Phil Thornhill on the first ascent (MF).

Above, three winter weekend escapees from London. The author Stephen Venables and Victor Saunders outside the CIC Hut, Ben Nevis (CW); below left, Crag Jones on first ascent of Cryogenics, mid-Wales (MF); below right, Chris Watts on Cold Hole, Achnashellach (MF).

Day three on Taulliraju. Chris Watts engrossed in the aid traverse at the ice line cul de sac (MF).

Above, Spantik from Nagar; below left, Gulam Mehedi, father of the chapel;
the porters gave us a goat-leg which somehow the author ended carrying (MF).

Above, *Deflowerer* is assembled for an assault on the Isle of Wight Needles by Nickie, Andy Meyers, Carless Lincoln and Rupert Hoare; below left, Lorraine Smythe on the first ascent of Skeleton Ridge, Isle of Wight; below right, Guy Muhleman on the first ascent of A'chailleach, Cape Wrath (MF).

Above, Cerro Kishtwar from Base Camp; below left, the road from Atholi; below right, looking down on to Steve Sustad on the last pitch to the col on day two (MF).

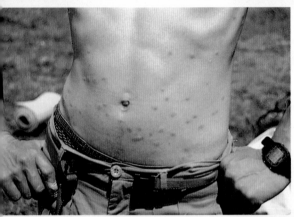

Some travelling
companions: top left,
author and friend;
above, Steve Sustad;
Victor had his own
fellow-travellers;
below left, Chris
Watts; below right
Mike Morrison
(MF).

only maps that we had confused matters even more. Some referred to Bojohagur as Ultar II, others as Ultar I, one even had an extra peak halfway along the kilometre-long ridge connecting Ultar to Bojohagur. Regardless of the confusing terminology it appeared that the mountain that we wanted to climb was only about sixty metres lower than the highest point of the massif. Victor was clearly proud to have discovered a peak which oozed such confusion. Personally I couldn't help wondering whether permission would be refused if the authorities became aware of all this. Remarkably, though, they seemed to know less about the mountain than we did and I must take my hat off to Victor who persevered endlessly to secure the necessary piece of paper which he now waved triumphantly at the meeting.

'Permission has been granted for you to climb Bojohagur Duanasir . . .'

Victor pushed his prototype face mask and tube to one side, next to his drastically modified hanging stove (which had enjoyed a slightly more favourable reception).

His presentation of the permission letter was met with appreciative murmuring. The meeting moved on to look at the other enclosures which were designed to let us know the liaison officer's exact measurements and equipment requirements. It is an enduring frustration with Himalayan trips that liaison officers are, according to the impressively lengthy rules and regulations literature, to be equipped so as to reach the highpoint of the expedition. In fact, particularly up to the mid-1980s when virtually all liaison officers were military men, a liaison officer could well have no mountaineering ability and no desire to go above Base Camp. But he had to be equipped to the same standard as the rest of the party. Arguing or skimping excessively was said to be a waste of time as if a liaison officer was not satisfied with his equipment he could refuse to allow the expedition to leave Islamabad.

Victor produced a large sheet of paper with two indistinct blue shapes on it. Just above the shapes was some writing: 'Captain Liaqat Hayat with socks.' Another sheet gave outlines of Captain Hayat's feet without socks. Slowly it dawned on us that based on this information we were supposed to purchase plastic double boots costing around £200.

And so the begging and the borrowing started. John English came up with a disgusting brown helmet, Mike Morrison offered his partially worn jeans, whilst I promised some rather experienced boots. 'Being equipped to the same standard as the rest of the team' were the key words that we would have to rely on. Poor Captain Hayat, we worried that he might be a military man used to the highest standards.

For reasons that surprised me at the time, our proposed ascent clearly captured the imagination of the grant-giving authorities and, having won the Nick Estcourt Award (one grant each year to the British expedition judged to be the most worthy), we went on to secure further financial support from the Mount Everest Foundation and British Mountaineering Council. The sums involved were not huge but they went a long way towards alleviating some of our financial dilemmas and at least meant that Captain Liaqat Hayat had one or two minor items of new equipment.

Victor and Lobby left for Islamabad a week before the rest of us. They did a fantastic job in braving the heat of the Pakistan capital in midsummer with the result that by the time the rest of us arrived a Transit minibus had been packed full of food, stoves, base tents, etc. and we were ready to leave the next day. Everyone but Liaqat was grateful for their efforts. Victor and our liaison officer had not exactly hit it off together. Liaqat was a true army officer. He liked discipline, structured plans of action and teams where all of the members jumped to the command of their leader.

Victor has a playful tendency to do himself down and understate his abilities. I find it an attractive trait as, I think, do most people. Liaqat did not.

Victor told me about their initial meeting – between the spick-and-span Pakistani army officer and the dark-skinned British architect sporting a T-shirt and a pair of very baggy Pakistani pyjama trousers. (Liaqat must have known they were pyjamas but I'm not sure that Victor did at this stage.)

'You are the leader of the expedition? Welcome to Pakistan. Where are my equipments?'

I can imagine that Victor's response left the poor man looking distinctly unhappy. 'Leader? Yes, or rather no. I think we are all joint leaders. No one is competent enough to be leader on their own. Your equipment? Ah yes, it is spread between eight rucksacks and should all be here by next week.'

The latter statement was Slippery Vic at his best. By being vague and keeping his cards close to his chest he was able to placate Liaqat with some new trainers (Brixton Market £2.99) and a smart 'silk' scarf (Brixton Market 99p). With our liaison officer's hopes raised, bureaucracy progressed smoothly and it was only when we had boarded the remarkably healthy-looking Transit minibus and were bouncing through the suburbs of Islamabad that he was able to study his equipment in more detail.

'Where is my hand-knitted wool cap?' For some reason Liaqat directed this question at me.

'Sorry?'

I looked at the list. Yes, he was right, we were supposed to supply him with a 'hand-knitted woollen cap (balaclava)'. Despairing, I looked around for support. No way could I remember sorting out such an item. John English, however, was rummaging through his bags with that especially mischievous look that comes across his face when something interesting is about to occur. In true rabbit-out-of-a-hat style he was soon waving a rather shapeless piece of woollen wear. It was an unappealing matt-grey colour and appeared to have been made from coarse llama hair. As John opened it out a ridiculous bobble was visible on top, along with what appeared to be some kind of woollen sun visor on the front. Now I saw what it was, I remembered laughing at early photos of John actually wearing it in the mountains. Liaqat looked dubious.

'It is hand-knitted?' he asked doubtfully.

Several reassuring voices confirmed this in tones which were not wholly convincing but lost on Liaqat who was struggling to get it on the right way round.

The Asian sun beat furiously down on to our metal box of a Ford Transit as Liaqat sat looking wildly eccentric with this woollen object wrapped around his head.

'You have jeans too?'

Mike Morrison's gear is more tried and tested than most. The jeans he offered were at least clean although it would be difficult to say much more in the way of positive comments about them.

'These are very expensive in England,' said Mike hopefully.

Poor Liaqat, I did feel sorry for him. His friend had been allocated to an extremely wealthy Japanese expedition and been kitted out accordingly. Liaqat looked like a man who had pulled the short straw.

The Karakoram Highway proved to be fourteen hours of incredible scenery. Sometimes described as the Eighth Wonder of the World, the road forms the main overland link between Islamabad, the north-western territories and ultimately China via the Kunjerab Pass. From Islamabad it rises gradually to Abbottabad, a temperate hill station town with extensive army barracks built during British rule. Dropping down from the Abbottabad hills, the next major feature is the Indus – a huge grey snake of a watercourse pouring down from the glaciated Himalaya eventually to cross the arid wastes of the Sind desert and disgorge into the Indian Ocean. I had never witnessed such a river before and the impact was both immediate and lasting. The valley is classically V-shaped with wild rocky slopes plunging down for hundreds of metres to the silt-laden water surging along the bottom. The force of the water is immense, like two River Thames joined together and forming a continuous boiling rapid. It was much hotter than Abbottabad here and the cold blast from the water as we crossed the bridge was most welcome though conversation was difficult above the roar.

For 200 miles the tarmac strip then clung to the walls of the Indus gorge. The road was built in the 1960s and '70s with the help of the Chinese; today it is maintained by the Pakistani army with specific battalions being responsible for their own section of road. The ground here is unstable, serious landslides are frequent and maintenance costs are high – both in financial and human terms. But the road is well used. Hundreds of intricately decorated lorries face the challenge every day – many of them are lovingly maintained old Bedfords which have been around since before the British departed in 1948. Their delicately fashioned decorative metalwork, colourful paintwork and incessant Pakistani music blasting forth from the cabs prompted Victor to refer to them as 'mobile juke boxes'.

The road signs gave only a hint of the very real dangers of the road. 'Rock Fall', a roadside sign would declare, followed by a section of uneven non-tarmac road. Above and below, sweeping scree slopes stretched right down to the river. Even in non-landslide mode the steep slope sent a steady trickle of small rocks down on to the road surface. Five hundred metres below a tangle of steel caught my eye down by the river. Our driver saw me looking. 'Forty-six dead,' he announced solemnly.

The falling-rocks signs, so similar in design to those we see in Britain, took on a new meaning. 'Have a safe journey' said a sign at the end of each landslide section. I kept my fingers crossed.

After ten hours of bouncing along in the stifling heat the landscape opened out somewhat. The Indus valley was now almost devoid of vegetation and sand dunes had become a regular feature. Glimpses of snowy peaks appeared on either side emphasising the outrageous contrast between lowland and high-altitude temperatures.

The town of Gilgit appeared on the horizon – with the surrounding land barren and rocky and temperatures soaring above 40°C it was hardly an oasis but its road link with Islamabad ensured that, if nothing else, it had almost unlimited quantities of thirst-quenching Fanta and Pepsi on offer.

By the time we arrived it was becoming increasingly clear that Victor was frequently being mistaken as a native of the area. His Pakistani pyjama trousers, which he wore incessantly no doubt defined him as an eccentric but he had to suffer non-stop approaches in unintelligible tongues which created considerable mirth from members of the team and distress for our leader. I have since realised that it is an admirably chameleon-like quality of Slippery Vic that he just seems to merge into any group of people in which he finds himself. I have never fully fathomed his ancestry but have discovered enough to know that he was born in Lossiemouth, brought up in Malaya, brushed shoulders with Prince Charles at Gordonstoun, and has substantial amounts of Russian and (perhaps) German blood. Whatever his background, his ability to fit in is truly remarkable – whether he be with Pakistani traders, Caucasian Russians or English gentry he can be guaranteed to be mistaken as one of the crowd.

Gilgit was hot – overpoweringly so. Only Victor and Lobby and of course Liaqat were able to cope with it; the rest of us, incapable of doing anything more constructive, simply lay in the shade 'guarding our equipment' in the Transit. Around us there gradually materialised sacks of rice, flour and dahl. It was all I could do to lift them into the vehicle and drink Fanta.

By late afternoon I could only bow to Victor and Lobby's ability to operate and keep the show on the road in such conditions. The poor Transit roared into life again and we were soon out on the last stretch of the Karakoram Highway leading up towards the reputedly lush Hunza valley and the long-dreamt-of Bojohagur Duanasir. Up above us Rakaposhi gleamed in the sun. Its slopes were listed in my world records book as the highest face in the world. In difficulty

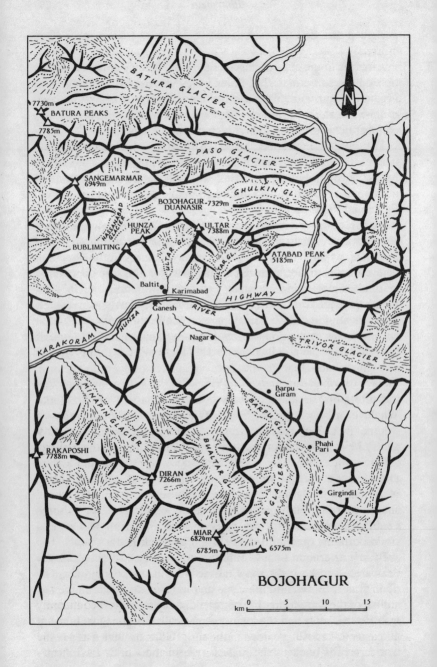

BATURA GLACIER

N

7730m
BATURA PEAKS
7785m

PASO GLACIER

GHULKIN GL.

SANGEMARMAR
6949m

BOJOHAGUR
DUANASIR 7329m

HUNZA PEAK

ULTAR
7388m

HASANABAD GLACIER

ULTAR GL.

ULTAR GL.

ATABAD PEAK
5185m

BUBLIMITING

Baltit

Karimabad

HIGHWAY

Ganesh

HUNZA   RIVER

KARAKORAM

Nagar

TRIVOR GLACIER

Barpu
Giram

MINAPIN GLACIER

BARPU GL.

Phahi
Pari

RAKAPOSHI
7788m

DIRAN
7266m

BUALTAR GL.

MIAR GLACIER

Girgindil

MIAR
6824m

6785m

6575m

BOJOHAGUR

0   5   10   15
km

terms it didn't look too outrageous but with a vertical interval of around 5800 metres, mostly on sun-drenched snow slopes, I could only marvel at the energy of Tom Patey and Mike Banks who made the first ascent back in the 1950s. I took some kind of heart from photos I had seen of Patey's frostbitten fingers. It had to be cold somewhere up there, however difficult that was to believe.

More and more mountains were coming into view now and the rocky sides of the valley were dotted with irrigated splashes of green. Water is a valuable commodity in the Karakoram and the effort put into maximising its potential defies belief. Aqueducts known as *go-tsils* weave their way for miles across steep arid mountainsides. Made watertight by mud packing between the stones they contour remarkably steep cliffs with minimal water loss. Occasionally they even traverse overhanging sections, the water being conveyed in hollowed-out logs. The drive up from Gilgit to Karimabad was an eye-opener in terms of what was possible. Mile upon mile of spectacular irrigation stonework (with just occasional green foliated streaks marking leaks) led to tenderly cultivated patches of green in the most inaccessible spots. I remember being impressed by the size and scale of the Alps on my first visit back in 1969 at the age of thirteen, but here in Pakistan in 1984 were more first impressions I would never forget.

The Hunza valley was indeed an oasis of green – completely supported by irrigation systems but green and fertile none the less. The heat up here at around 2000 metres was less oppressive – more like a very hot day in a western Alpine valley – and with the deadening heat-induced lethargy lifting somewhat, members of our team other than Victor and Lobby at last became active. John English clicked furiously with his array of cameras. Mike Morrison waxed lyrical about the 'unlimited severity' and busied himself quizzing locals on which mountain was Bojohagur. This was a subject to be treated delicately as we certainly didn't want to raise any uncertainty over the validity of our permission documents. The eye-catching granite spire of Bublimiting and the unclimbed Hunza Peak were obvious enough but the main Ultar massif seemed not to tie in very well with our sketchy maps. Knowing that Liaqat was unlikely to be impressed by uncertainty, we acted as one, confidently pointing at what we had agreed was to be called Bojohagur. In fact it looked to me like a secondary summit to Ultar but this was not the time to say so. To change the subject, we set about finding accommodation for the night and porters for the morning. To be more honest the Transit driver found the accommodation and Liaqat the porters.

Porter hiring can become a very complicated business. Victor had experience of such things on Conway's Ogre, his one previous trip to the Karakoram, but the rest of us were complete novices. Liaqat took charge. He had read his *Instructions for Liaison Officers* book and was aware of the correct procedures. Porter insurance forms were asked for along with contracts ready for signature and porter equipment such as plimsolls and sunglasses. 'Porter equipment' I knew that we didn't have, and the idea of employment contracts and insurance forms was new to me. I had naïvely assumed that a suitably sized wad of dosh (hopefully a very small one) would solve all problems. I fidgeted uncomfortably whilst Victor rustled about in his rucksack. Surely we weren't organised enough to cope with this sort of bureaucracy.

Liaqat clearly was. He was in his element now and in full army organisation mode. This was his forte. It seemed that the necessary forms had been obtained in Islamabad and brandishing these with obvious enthusiasm he berated those potential porters who had the cheek to raise the subject of plimsolls or sunglasses for such a short walk-in. And so with remarkably little fuss a team of six or seven porters had their names taken and signed insurance documents. Both of these requirements were easier said than done. Half of the porters seemed to be called by the same name and most of them signed by means of a splodgy thumb imprint. The end result was that lots of the completed forms looked exactly the same to me – but they were classed as acceptable by Liaqat which seemed to be all that mattered.

The walk-in, or rather the lack of it, was one of the key factors that had drawn us to Bojohagur. There was however a problem. The configuration of the steep ground above the Ultar Nullah meadows on the south side of the mountain were such that it seemed impossible to site the Base Camp much above 3300 metres. With the summit over 4000 metres higher it would clearly require a monstrous push to succeed on an alpine-style attempt. It also meant that the Base Camp level was hardly high enough to get a good headache going and initiate the acclimatisation process. Much discussion, bordering on argument, developed over the site of Base Camp. Our porters simply dumped the gear and proclaimed that a Japanese team who had attempted the mountain two years previously had camped here and so it must be the best site. But two to three hours of running around at higher levels failed to find a better position and with rather heavy hearts the necessary dosh was coughed up and we were left to settle into our temporary home.

There were some other problems with Base Camp. For a start, it was situated just below a shepherd's hut. The extensive flock of sheep and goats were out grazing on the higher pastures during the day but at night they descended to around the shepherd's hut and generally caused a hygiene and food-conservation problem. Poor Victor being allergic to most animals was also in danger of becoming a snuffling wreck whenever they appeared. The camp area also boasted a lovely bubbling spring, but it was not until everyone had developed frustratingly persistent diarrhoea that George discovered the spring water ran straight through the shepherd's hut before disappearing underground for a hundred metres and emerging by our tents.

Another Base Camp hazard was Dai, our cook (pronounced 'Die' and aptly named), a schoolteacher who specialised in producing food that nobody but Lobby could eat. He had been recruited early because Victor remembered having real problems finding a cook on his Conway's Ogre trip, and with this in mind Dai was snapped up as soon as he approached us in Karimabad and offered his services. Needless to say numerous other better-qualified men subsequently had to be turned down. We were too honourable, we stuck with Dai. His cooking was *awful*. Admittedly the rather bland ingredients and germ-ridden water he had to work with would have challenged a man of finer calibre but, whatever the excuses, the end results were not exactly devoured with relish. Even in retrospect I can think of only one good point about Base Camp: it provided an excellent impetus for us to maximise time spent on the mountain.

A couple of days looking more closely at the possibilities on the mountain saw a grandly named Advance Base Camp tent established on grassy slopes three hours above. The team split into two.

Chris Watts and I were keen for some challenging technical action and decided to have a look at a steep mixed buttress line, whilst the others opted for the route which a Japanese team had attempted two years earlier – a painfully long fifty degree snow/ice slope followed by a long ridge leading over several forepeaks to the top.

It was whilst wandering around outside our snowhole on the glacier beneath the face that I enjoyed my first experience of a Himalayan avalanche. Firstly, a rumbling noise from the mist-shrouded slopes up to the right of our pillar alerted me to the danger. A huge cloud of avalanche material was advancing, billowing out from an obvious runnel sweeping viciously past the foot of our proposed line. Initially it seemed far enough away to be 'oohed and ahhed' at without causing too much concern. Then to my horror it began to mushroom out magnificently, marching across the glacier like an oncoming nuclear cloud. I screamed for Chris to watch out (he was asleep in the snowhole at the time) and ran panic-stricken up the slope. The blast caught me just as I jumped down a crevasse between two boulders. Storm-force winds blasted snow into every crevice whilst I trembled in fear of a barrage of ice blocks. Nothing happened.

After a minute or so everything quietened down and I stuck my head out to peer hesitantly around the new landscape. An inch or so of snow covered everything. A couple of items of gear left outside the snowhole had disappeared but the sun had returned with customary Himalayan intensity and the danger had passed. Avalanches here were clearly unlike anything I had witnessed before.

Chris and I spent the whole of the next day staring at our proposed line. The climbing certainly looked good – lots of steep, technical mixed ground in a safe position. The approach was the problem. We would have to cross the main avalanche runnel funnelling down from huge hanging séracs up under the Bojohagur–Ultar connecting ridge – and it was pretty clear that being caught anywhere near the runnel at the wrong time would be an awful lot worse than enduring a blizzard for a few minutes. We dithered.

Mountaineering is a risky sport – some risks are worth taking. This one was borderline. Our favourite tongue in cheek adjective 'unjustifiable', was cropping up just a bit too often. Further avalanches right through the night convinced us . . . a wimp-out was in order. We would join the others on the line attempted by the Japanese in 1982.

Morning found us both in a rather sober frame of mind.

'It's not quite the same, is it?'

Chris knew exactly what I meant. The route up the South Face and West Ridge was not quite our cup of tea. The slopes to the col were long and set at a regular fifty degrees or so. They looked horribly tiring and led to a long ridge rising a further 1300 metres to the summit. There didn't seem to be anything technically interesting about the line. Naïvely I consoled myself with the thought that at least there shouldn't be too much trouble reaching the summit this way.

It wasn't very far across the glacier to join the others' line and with mixed feelings we struggled up steep moraines to join Mike and John beneath the long slopes leading up to the col at their rather grandly misnamed Camp 1. Chris was feeling bad again, so I set off alone to try and join Victor and Lobby who could be seen 600 metres above. By 9 a.m. I was wedged in a rock corner about 90 metres below what I assumed to be Camp 2 hiding from the sweltering sun by arranging makeshift shelters with my waterproofs. The next seven hours were an eye-opener in the realms of Himalayan heat survival and it was a somewhat withered version of my former self that emerged to spend the last three hours of daylight in a continuous state of purgatory, averaging thirty metres per hour in steep soft snow. Arriving at the supposed Camp 2 it was more than a little distressing to see Victor and Lobby bivouacked 150 metres higher.

'Why are you up there?' I bellowed up the slope, unable to take in that all my efforts to catch them had been in vain.

The answer was perhaps predictable. 'What are *you* doing down there?'

But by then I wasn't listening and was instead panicking over what to do next. With the onset of heavy snow I had little option but to test my sleeping-bag on its own with no tent or bivouac sack. Overpowering thirst promptly interrupted efforts to forget my whereabouts. The frustration of having a stove but no pan resulted in a mainly unsuccessful attempt to melt snow in my helmet due to the tendency of its protective paint to catch fire well before any melting was even vaguely evident.

Next day deteriorating weather drove everyone back down to brave the gastronomic hazards of Base Camp. George was by now refusing to eat Dai's offerings, Liaqat was ill and the atmosphere was becoming increasingly tense. All was not well on the mountain either. On our return it transpired that our Advance Base tent had been blown away in an avalanche. This in itself was not a disaster, but more serious was the fact that the numerous mountain goats had eaten much of our carefully protected mountain food. More amusingly (for some), they had also urinated on Victor's mountain clothing which gave him a distinctive aroma and horrendous allergy problems for the rest of the trip.

On the mountain, progress was masochistic but effective. After an all-night climbing session Victor, Lobby, Chris and I ended up on a projecting prow of rock just below the col between Bojohagur and Hunza Peak at 6000 metres. Much debilitating activity had been necessary in the heat of the first rays of the sun with the result that our bivouac was really only adequate for two, a fact demonstrated when Chris plummeted gracefully over the edge during the night. Unfortunately the quantity of sleeping tablets consumed by those still *in situ* ensured that no assistance was likely to be immediately forthcoming.

Squirming from under the bondage afforded by the suddenly tightened belay rope I was able to peer over the edge and marvel at a hand protruding from a tightly drawn sleeping-bag in an effort to release the draw cord. Chris's situation appeared particularly exciting. Muffled shouts indicated that he had lengthened his tie-in rope with a piece of dubious tape which he had been using for carrying his camera. This was now bearing his full weight. He was three metres below the ledge and six metres above the snow slope in such a way that little direct assistance was possible. As an initial helpful gesture I acted without putting my contact lenses in and slid the jumars down the wrong rope – they jammed enticingly a metre and a half out of his reach and well below the edge of the ledge. Abuse came from other stirring bodies who were displeased at having to unpack further jumars.

'What's the problem? There's more room now,' came from the back of the ledge. At last Chris was able to emerge from his cocoon only to succeed in dropping his extremely posh jacket, complete with camera, gloves, etc. in its pockets. As he completed the jumar – two zip ring-pulls attached to short lengths of tape hung forlornly from the belay rope – their true significance gradually dawned: they were from his super-gaiters which had been, and of course still were, attached securely to his boots. One boot-gaiter was tangled in the ropes with the boot attached, the other boot and gaiter were nowhere to be seen.

Morning confirmed the situation – Chris was going to have to hop back down with me accompanying him.

Three days later we were sitting down to tuck into a classic Dai dish of rice and dahl. Such are the pleasures of Himalayan climbing.

'You are enjoying the mountain?' enquired Liaqat.

Neither of us answered.

'In the Karakoram,' he continued, 'you have very big highs and very big lows.'

Most climbers return to Base Camp to recoup their strength. Ours made us feel so ill that we were back on the mountain after two days to escape feeling worse. Here I was starting up the longest route of my life and I had rarely felt so bad in the mountains. At one point a truly monstrous avalanche roared down the couloirs to the right of our originally proposed line, catching us squarely in its cloud of swirling powder snow.

Chris, Mike and I climbed through the night and reached the projecting prow bivouac where we found Victor and Lobby still in their sleeping-bags. It seemed that poor weather and general exhaustion rather than technical difficulties had prevented their reaching the summit. In fact no real technical difficulties had been encountered or seen in the way ahead and had we not felt so exhausted ourselves we doubtless would have been enthused by their news. A line of fixed ropes above us placed a fresh slant on the situation. We were aware of the existence of a Japanese team on the far side of the mountain but to find that they were attempting the same ridge as ourselves was, perhaps unreasonably, an irritant. Somehow it didn't seem alpine-style to be climbing next to someone else's fixed rope.

Chris, Mike and I pressed on to a shoulder and made an unsatisfactory bivouac. The altitude was beginning to take its toll, and sleeping tablets ensured relative relaxation.

'Morning.'

'Very good morning.'

We were woken by toothy grins and offerings of dried horsemeat by two sprightly Japanese climbers on their way to stock their upper camps. Theirs was a far more traditional expedition than ours and involved several tented camps and 1500 metres of fixed rope. They stared with interest at our bivouac sacks, doubtless comparing them unfavourably with their comfortable tents and wondering what the hell we were up to. If nothing else their ferrying activities up and down the ropes seemed to have fully conditioned them to climbing at altitude. I think all three of us felt somehow inadequate in comparison.

Before the col I had felt rather out on a limb, but now we were connected to the Japanese Base Camp by a line of fixed rope. Perhaps unreasonably, I resented this, feeling that it somehow detracted from our efforts and belittled the mountain.

Chris was the first to start up the fifty-degree slope ahead. Throwing alpine-style ethics to the wind and using a jumar handrail on the Japanese fixed rope, he slowly drew away from Mike whilst I floundered at the back, fighting a losing battle to warm my feet. Our choice of inner boot appeared to be the source of many cold feet problems and resulted in slight frostbite for five of the team. For my part I also blamed my decision to use Karrimat as an inner sole in my purposely oversized boots. The theory was that my feet would have plenty of room and enjoy the extra protection provided by a nice thick inner. In fact these soon squashed down to a useless wafer-thin layer and left my feet sloshing around like in oversized wellies.

We were painfully slow: by midday only ninety metres of progress had been made on easy ground.

The route continued up an easy-angled snow ridge which abutted against a band of séracs 180 metres above. At sea level ten minutes would have sufficed, at 6500 metres it seemed that the rest of the day would be a fair estimation. We set off together managing ten or so paces in between rests. Even with the assistance of the ever present Japanese fixed rope and by alternating the job of breaking through rapidly growing drifts, progress was made at a steadily decreasing rate. Chris was slowly drawing ahead whilst Mike and I struggled to make any progress at all. Every movement induced immediate exhaustion. By mid-afternoon the sérac barrier was only thirty metres above and a fixed rope could be seen flitting in and out of the swirling cloud to its right – nevertheless our rate of progress would only allow ninety metres' more progress that day and concern was mounting, as a suitable bivouac site was not visible.

Judging the energy expenditure worthwhile, I shouted to Chris to stop at the first reasonable site. This time luck seemed on our side, as he discovered a small ice cave on the traverse under the séracs. We set about enlarging it with surprising amounts of energy and by late afternoon it was large enough for the three of us to squeeze in and shut ourselves off from the elements. The extreme cold caught me unawares – our cave was part of an open crevasse system in which cold air seemed to circulate. Food preparation went ahead slowly and painfully as our inspired idea of a hanging stove proved somewhat impracticable within the cave. The floor was sufficiently uneven for the stove to have to be held all the time – a situation which resulted in exhaustion from sitting upright, pain from touching the wrong parts of the stove and frustration as more food ended up spilt than inside us. Mike was clearly suffering from altitude and unable to eat anything at all; we gingerly passed the urine bottle and congratulated ourselves on not having to go outside for any other functions.

In the night it snowed. The Japanese fixed rope above was deeply buried. Chris made a few unconvincing upward efforts, but we all knew we had no choice but to go down. No great difficulty could be seen ahead – the fixed rope disappeared into snow drifts but we knew from Victor and Lobby that the séracs could be passed with only one pitch of grade IV climbing. Above that, long easy-angled slopes led to a narrowing of the ridge, more grade IV climbing, and Victor's and Lobby's highpoint below the 300-metres summit pyramid. Our egos were dented but we knew there was no choice.

Slithering down the buried Japanese rope I couldn't help but notice a magnificent buttress line in the distance. The mountain that it was on I knew to be called Spantik, but I pushed the thought of it to the back of my mind. Here was a team who couldn't even walk up easy ground at 6500 metres, let alone climb a Walker Spur-type feature at something around 7000 metres. We felt as if we had had a defeat without a battle. Although we had cursed the presence of another team on the mountain, there can be no doubt that their ropes proved invaluable in speeding our descent.

Tails between our legs we waved our horrible Base Camp goodbye and turned our back on Bojohagur.

In Gilgit we met the liaison officer of the Japanese team who gave us the news that the Hiroshima Walkers Team had been successful.

Six weeks of flies, fleas, diarrhoea, sweltering heat and not only had we failed to rope a pitch on the mountain, but our modestly named competitors seemed to have engineered a fine success which left me feeling even more demoralised than before.

Back in Islamabad I contemplated all the new rock climbs I had in mind in Scotland, wondered how many of them I could have done in six weeks and understood immediately the significance of the immaculately painted slogan on the back of my pristine split-screen Morris Minor taxi: 'Pakistan – love it or leave it,' it said.

At that point there was no doubt in my mind – I would leave it.

10

The Golden Pillar of Spantik

I went to the Alps in 1985. It was wonderful. In three weeks of excellent climbing with Crag Jones I managed the Croz Spur, Dru Couloir, North-East Spur of Les Droites and a few other less significant routes. Altogether we did perhaps 4000 metres of pitched climbing. On Bojohagur I had been away for twice as long and managed no pitched climbing at all. My opinions about Himalayan climbing remained unchanged.

In 1986 I chose a slightly more adventurous area – the Caucasus – and again had a successful time, this time climbing with Victor, on mountains less than 6000 metres and a climate that I felt more comfortable in.

Victor did not share my distaste for altitude, high temperatures and bureaucracy. In 1985 he engrossed himself in the almost insuperable complexities of a joint Indo–British expedition to the disputed Indo–Pakistan border area. Even with Indian organisers and contacts in the army the team experienced its fair share of problems, although Victor and Steve Venables put in a very fine effort on the unclimbed Rimo I – which was brought to a premature halt when the hapless Venables dropped his rucksack containing such vital items as the stove, his sleeping-bag, and the food.

So Victor returned empty-handed. After three trips to the Himalaya he had very nearly stood on the summit of Conway's Ogre in 1980, and failed by a fair shot on Bojohagur in 1984 and Rimo in 1985. Having spent probably twenty weeks enduring the bureaucratic, climatic and germ-ridden challenges of the Himalaya I would have thought that the man's enthusiasm might have begun to wane. But I was wrong. We were sitting together in the Priut Hut on Mount Elbrus in the Caucasus. At regular intervals I was sick – a fact which I put down to an unfortunate slip into the toilet outflow the evening before. Victor though was not in a caring mood. He had other things on his mind.

'I've been thinking,' he said. A worrying state of affairs. I kept quiet.

'That pillar we could see on the horizon from Bojohagur. I think we might have to . . . er, have a closer look . . . know what I mean.' I knew exactly what he meant. My response was instantaneous.

'No chance.' I rushed off to be sick again. Then I did a mental re-run of the Bojohagur trip. Six weeks of fleas, flies and failure. Maximum masochism on oven-like slopes, no roped climbing at all and a serious bashing for the ego buds as a Japanese walking club planted their flag on 'our' unclimbed summit. The Golden Pillar of Spantik had indeed attracted my eye to the south but would obviously involve very hard technical climbing at an altitude higher than we had ever managed to walk to on Bojohagur. Excusing myself from the challenge by convincing myself of my desire to visit new ranges rather than return to the Karakoram, I allowed the vision of the Pillar to recede to the back of my mind once more. Victor did mention 'that pillar' a couple more times in the Caucasus but his enthusiasm was mixed in with similar aspirations towards all of the most exciting mountains known to man (and a few known only to Victor) so that I was never really forced to reiterate my views or readdress my exact feelings.

Victor, though, had not let the subject slip. It was bubbling away just below the surface waiting for the right moment to surge forth again. By late 1986 he had begun to mention 'that pillar' more prominently in pub conversation and the memories of the Bojohagur trip had faded somewhat. I studied my slides again – it was certainly an impressive objective and not one that I could let Victor rush off and do without me. Succumbing to temptation I let myself in for another six weeks in Pakistan. Friends collapsed in hysterical laughter – I had not really stopped abusing everything to do with the area since my previous visit.

After numerous changes it was eventually decided that, in addition to Victor, Lobby Butler, Bruce Craig, John English and Liz Allen were to be my fellow-sufferers.

Bureaucratic complications were evident from the start. Several other British expeditions were caught up in the confusion which was only resolved by some very devious activity involving outrageous persistence on Victor's part and a key Pakistani official being invited

to the wedding of Roger Payne and Julie Ann Clyma who were off
to the Gasherbrums and experiencing similar problems.

Though Chris Watts wasn't coming with us this time he used
his Alpine Sports-related TV contacts on our behalf to muster
some exposure. The hope was this might give us a better chance
of sponsorship this time.

And so it was arranged that the whole team would perform for the
cameras on the brickwork of the Hornsey Walls, a disused railway
cutting in North London. It was a damp June evening and an
enthusiastic onslaught from swarms of midges began immediately.
Almost as numerous were groups of snotty-nosed children, joggers
and local eccentrics who gathered to admire our performance.

An impressive array of photographers, assistants and hangers-on
had been despatched by Thames TV but it was immediately apparent
that they had no preconceived ideas on how the scene should
progress. For our part, we clambered up and down the shiny
brickwork and did our best to explain the difference between the
Hornsey railway cutting and the Golden Pillar of Spantik. Someone
from Thames TV then suggested a crevasse rescue demonstration.
It struck me that this was a little difficult to simulate in a busy
North London suburb but the media were keen, and not being
self-confident in this field we felt something had to be done. Five
minutes later I was strapped to the outside of a conveniently situated
footbridge preparing to hold Victor's simulated fall into a crevasse
(or jump from a bridge depending on your degree of realism).

The first time Victor jumped two metres or so but was judged not
to look concerned enough, so a re-run was called. By this time I had
decided that his jumping directly on to my belay on the outside of
the bridge was firstly rather painful, as my belay was not completely
tight, and secondly wholly reliant upon the questionable strength of
the bridge handrail. As I pondered these points Victor was preparing
for a second, longer fall to be accompanied by blood-curdling
screams. Too embarrassed to hold up proceedings by changing my
belay, I glumly surveyed the scene as Victor judged the slack rope so
that he would just miss the ground seven metres below. The idea
was that he would be climbing down, accidentally slip, be heroically
held by me and then jumar back up the rope, thereby completing
his escape from the clutches of the crevasse.

The cameras rolled again and Victor dutifully slipped unexpectedly from the bridge. Unfortunately his fall was equally unexpected

for the belayer as the strain of a five-metre fall on to the belay slammed me nose first into the railings. Meanwhile Victor's blood-curdling scream was stifled by his having rather too much slack for comfort and was replaced instead by a volley of swearwords as he just clipped the ground. Things were not going well – the camera team brightened up. Victor bounced on the rope and stopped a metre short of the ground spinning slowly. Hanging painfully from the belay I waited for him to jumar back up. However, shouts from below indicated a marked degree of misunderstanding between belayer and belayed.

'Lower me down,' hissed Vic.

'You're supposed to jumar up.'

'No – no. Slack!'

There seemed little option but to lower him to the ground, upon which he untied and walked from the base of the 'crevasse' to the camera crew. This was certainly a novel twist to crevasse rescue – I doubted whether the real thing would be so easy.

The others stood around equally confused until our expedition doctor, John English, stepped in and volunteered to pretend that Victor was injured and demonstrate how he could jumar out with him on his back. I was to belay Victor – presumably in case he fell from John's back – whilst the camera crew were to home in on John's heroic efforts. The rest of our party were beginning to feel that perhaps our efforts were becoming over-optimistic. They did not have long to wait before their suspicions proved to be firmly based. The watching crowd had increased somewhat and developed a nastily expectant hush.

John wore two slings around his neck: one under his right arm, one under his left. The idea appeared to be that Victor would sit on his back with a leg through each sling. Reaching as high as possible with his jumars John stepped up and left the ground – the cameras whirred. It was the sort of manoeuvre one would not dream of making in a crevasse. Still belayed to the bridge rail, I watched with interest as Victor's weight gradually pulled the intrepid duo over backwards until Vic's back was firmly in contact with the muddy floor of the railway cutting.

'Pull!' he screamed at me.

As he was lying on his back the rope from his waist came up along John's back and across his neck before snaking up to my position on the bridge. I pulled as hard as was possible in the circumstances.

John was already distinctly red in the face from the constriction caused by the strategically placed slings that Victor was sitting in. My pulling was the last straw. As the rope to Victor tightened and cut deeply into his ear, he released the jumars and both doctor and leader collapsed in the mud.

By the time we got on to the interviews credibility seemed to be so lacking that any thoughts of a confident selling exercise had slipped to the back of my mind. Damage limitation seemed more appropriate. But I was wrong – the camera can lie. The end result was a few sequences of intimate struggles with the brickwork, followed by selective extracts from the chat, enhanced by suitably ego-boosting comments from the interviewer.

Needless to say no sponsorship resulted directly from the TV efforts but Victor did persuade Barclays Bank to sponsor us to the tune of £450. In addition the North London Mountaineering Club contributed £50 and a further £2600 was secured via the Nick Estcourt Award and grants from the Mount Everest Foundation and British Mountaineering Council. I began to feel that the grant-giving authorities had more confidence in our abilities than we did. Two serious hurdles had been overcome though. We had permission and now we had enough money as well.

It seemed that 'Spantik 1987' was going to happen after all.

Relaxing at lunchtime I closed my office door and sat back to contemplate what I should have learned from our ineffectual performance on Bojohagur. What had a Japanese walking club got that we hadn't? 'Five thousand metres of fixed rope' was an obvious answer that sprang to mind, but this was not a style of approach that held any interest for us. What else, then? A higher Base Camp would help, as would a better acclimatisation programme and not falling off bivouac ledges and dropping boots. All of these things would have to be addressed once we got to the mountain. The one thing I was able to pinpoint which caused me great problems in Pakistan was the food – not only Dai's germ-ridden nasties but the food in general.

Prior to the Bojohagur trip I had been a serious chops, peas and potatoes man. Trips to Indian or Pakistani restaurants were definitely off the agenda and in Pakistan I had eaten local food only with extreme reluctance. In retrospect I had to admit that those most keen on Pakistani cuisine in Britain certainly seemed to fare better when faced with the real thing. Victor and Lobby for instance actually seemed to enjoy the local food whereas staunchly British eaters such as Mike Morrison and me seemed to be felled with diarrhoea problems at the first contact. Perhaps a serious training programme in the most germ-ridden Eastern eating houses in London would prepare my body? I resolved to try.

My local Indian was named the Pink Rupee. When I was last there it was very good; back in 1987 though it was not.

My first tentative visit had the expected effect on my bowels whereas those whom I was with remained perfectly healthy. At the very least a bit more effort was required on my part. In the three months before leaving I ate more mounds of detestably unpleasant food than ever before. Some of the establishments that I visited would previously have been well off the acceptability scale. Chris Newcombe must take credit for finding the worst in an impressively bad selection. Chris is a devotee of Eastern eating and led me proudly to a memorably downmarket takeaway near his home in the North London suburb of Barnet.

It seemed to be a one-man band run by a particularly harassed and sweaty Pakistani. Chris assured me that the food was 'ethnic'. I wasn't exactly sure what he meant by this but the surroundings looked promising. Formica panels around the walls peeled ominously whilst the polystyrene tiles on the ceiling displayed stains of a distinctly unattractive nature. What was once a fairly large room was crudely partitioned with an irregular hole cut to act as a serving hatch from the rear kitchen to the front part, where queues of anxious eaters were presumably expected to line up. A peep through the serving hatch confirmed my initial impression that this was likely to be the ultimate challenge in my food training programme. I had already graduated to somehow forcing down the hottest curries that were being thrown at me but for pure germ-ridden slurry this place looked to be streets ahead of the competition. There was only one other person on the public side of the hatch. She was about forty-five, heavily made up, and revealed rippling waves of fat thighs by wearing a disconcertingly short plastic skirt. She was engaged in an emotional argument with the proprietor. Chris was a regular (he actually likes this sort of thing) and knew them both well. Tonight, though, his cheery greetings were ignored.

It seemed that the fat lady on our side of the hatch was in fact married to the sweaty one-man band on the other and their argument revolved around whether or not his wife was an active

East Barnet prostitute. It seemed a curious argument to have in public but somehow summed up the place as a no-holds-barred establishment. I wondered how much care and attention went into the food preparation. The fact that the prostitute (Chris felt sure that she was) was eating a bag of chips clearly purchased elsewhere did not bode well. I had indeed reached the zenith of my food training programme.

Next morning my consumption of the hottest ethnic meat dish on the menu produced the now familiar ring-sting but by lunchtime there had been no further ill effects and there was no doubt about it, my body was ready – at least for unlimited quantities of curried slurry if not the full range of Pakistani food germs.

Once again Victor and Lobby had gone ahead, so the Transit minibus was waiting for the rest of us, along with Iqbal Ahmed, a keen mountaineer and civilian doctor who was to be a model liaison officer and contrast sharply with our previous experience. I couldn't help but notice that much of the food on board was rice and dahl but, aware in advance this time of Victor and Lobby's enthusiasm for Eastern staples, I relaxed, comfortable in the thought that I had managed to slip a few tins of Marks & Spencer steak into the bright blue barrels which had been freighted out separately and were now wedged in behind the back seats. I had even managed to conceal a few tins of carrots and peas. The fact that these were ninety per cent water and freighted at a charge of over £1 per kilo did not cause me to hesitate for a moment. I sat back contentedly imagining the joys of tinned steak with peas and carrots at Base Camp. What better food can there be to stock up before a major effort?

This time we chose to travel the Karakoram Highway at night. Not only would it be cooler but we would be unable to fret over the terrifying drops and exciting driving styles. The experience had not lost all its piquancy however. Every now and then a sickening swerve would indicate to the semi-comatose team that our driver had either fallen asleep at the wheel or met another vehicle on a bend.

The Hunza valley had changed a lot in just three years. Trekking had taken off and accommodation of all shapes and sizes was proliferating wildly. Hotels ranged from the super luxurious down to numerous one- or two-bedroom establishments. Shunning them all, we escaped quickly and our jeeps took us to the village of Hoppar on the far side of the main valley.

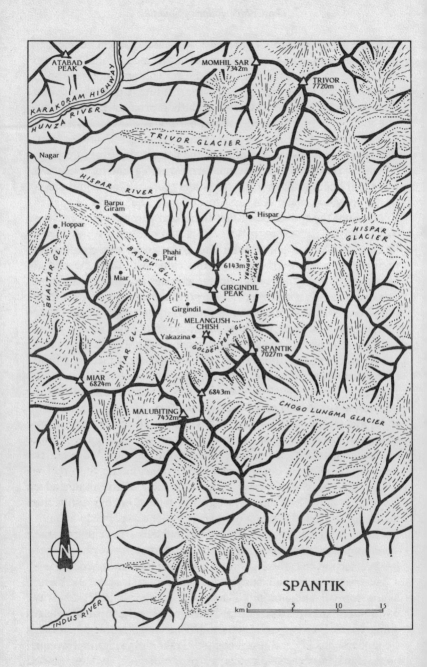

ATABAD
PEAK

KARAKORAM HIGHWAY

HUNZA RIVER

MOMHIL SAR
7342m

TRIVOR
7720m

TRIVOR GLACIER

Nagar

HISPAR RIVER

Barpu
Giram

Hispar

HISPAR
GLACIER

Hoppar

BUALTAR GL.

BARPU GL.

Phahi
Pari

6143m

YENGUTZ HAR GL.

Miar

GIRGINDIL
PEAK

Girgindil

MELANGUSH
CHISH

MIAR GL.

Yakazina

GOLDEN PEAK GL.

SPANTIK
7027m

MIAR
6824m

6843m

CHOGO LUNGMA GLACIER

MALUBITING
7452m

N

INDUS RIVER

SPANTIK

km 0   5   10   15

Here we found a class of hotel that I had not previously experienced: 'Hoppar Hilton', a sign proudly proclaimed. I looked around curiously. The jeep track up from the Hunza river had been steep, sandy and uncompromising. At one point a bridge had to be repaired before our journey could continue. In short Hoppar did not seem to be the sort of place to sport a state-of-the-art five-star hotel.

'Accommodation, sir?' A smiling face had appeared from nowhere. They tend to do that in Pakistan. I had learned to be cautious of the first man on the scene. Ending up with Dai as a cook on Bojohagur had taught me that.

'Where and how much?'

The man's grin broadened. Here at least were people who *wanted* accommodation. All he had to do was prove that his was the best on offer. 'At Hoppar Hilton,' he enthused. 'Very good quality tents.' Those in earshot made little effort to conceal their mirth. Fortunately his prices were somewhat lower than his more famous namesake's and after a quick comparison exercise failed to locate any competition we settled down into our 'luxury' accommodation and began to address the joys of hiring porters.

This time we were faced with a proper walk-in of five days or so and with a total of seven of us in the team (eight including Iqbal) our portering needs were such that we would just about move into the ever mushrooming scene of porters to carry the food for the porters who were carrying gear for other porters.

Eventually we settled on thirty porter loads and, having invited applicants to report the following morning, retired to consider progress so far. Certainly from my point of view we were not doing too badly at all. Having left Britain on the Saturday we had travelled almost nonstop and were now at the roadhead on Monday night. Only one day of my thirty days' holiday entitlement used up so far.

Next morning we suddenly found ourselves in a rather more complex situation than we had bargained for.

We had unwittingly chosen a non-Hoppar man as our cook. Rajab Zawa was a recommendation and a very good one too. He was, in fact, from the region of Nagar (as this side of the Hunza river is known), but did not come from any of the five small villages that make up Hoppar. This seemed to cause problems. Rajab's employment not only meant that we could no longer employ equal numbers from the five hamlets, as custom dictated, but also caused some consternation in that a cook's job is highly rated and had been given to an outsider.

The porters of Nagar have a frightening reputation for violence and hard bargaining. As tempers rose it seemed that we had got off to a rather bad start. I recalled a cautionary tale involving the death of two German trekkers who had disagreed over porter prices, and Doug Scott's trip to Diran which resulted in gun threats and most of the porters behind bars. With such a legacy of extreme negotiating tactics, a cautious approach seemed desirable and it was with some trepidation that we faced up to nearly a hundred would-be porters and the daunting task of choosing just thirty of them.

The whole process seemed far more regimented than I had expected. Firstly, there was a sort of union official whose job seemed to be to ensure that we employed the correct number of men from each hamlet. Secondly, the appearance of a local policeman, complete with prominently displayed gun, implied that the whole process might need some forceful controlling.

In an effort to make positive headway we quickly chose a head porter and sought his assistance in the task ahead. This much prized position not only secured him a higher pay rate than the others but also seemed to give him instant authority over the increasing number of hopeful porters milling around. Ibrahim was a wily character whom I was never quite sure how much to trust. He wore the ubiquitous modern Pakistani mountain footware of plastic shoes with no laces and almost always carried a gun. This, he assured us, was for killing ibex.

Those who had been chosen by Ibrahim and passed by the union man subjected themselves one at a time to a medical examination by John. There wasn't exactly a lot that he could check apart from their physical appearance and whether or not their hearts were beating. Initially, those before him looked fit and healthy and were passed without comment. Soon, though, some more ageing and bedraggled specimens came up for inspection. One of them was clearly well over fifty and could have been nudging seventy. With plenty of strong healthy men still to come, John gave him the thumbs-down. Uproar resulted. It seemed that a highly respected village elder had been turned down. Claims as to his physical prowess flowed thick and fast, his age was stated as thirty, his strength was compared to an ox. John tried to stand firm, the choice was ours after all. Confusion reigned supreme.

It seemed that if we didn't employ this man, Gulam Mehedi, then several of the other porters wouldn't work for us and a complete reassessment of the spread between the hamlets would again be necessary. The policeman began to finger his gun nervously whilst the union man addressed us in his most persuasive manner.

'Gulam Mehedi . . . very good man.'

'Very good man' was fast becoming a stock phrase, as was 'Check his credentials.' But the sheets of paper waved in our faces were usually illegible accolades which I imagined being scrawled by frightened trekkers at gunpoint.

Ultimately of course we had to back down. Gulam Mehedi was to come with us and the 'medical check' was reduced to John poking a stethoscope in the general direction of each chest presented to him and making a half-hearted attempt to look proficient.

'Apparently,' he said, looking at a particularly hollow chest, 'they are all very healthy.'

The porters were now insisting that a direct route across the Bualtar Glacier to the abandoned settlement of Shishkin was impossible. The claim was that this used to be the norm but the glacier had become increasingly crevassed, necessitating a full day's walk up one bank, a full day to cross and a day back down the other bank. It was all getting horribly time-consuming and potentially expensive. There only seemed one way to check out this latest problem. Bruce and I excused ourselves from the mêlée and set off to have a look at the lie of the land.

Sitting on top of a huge moraine we marvelled at the tangled ice floe below. I had to admit that there was a grain of truth in what the porters were saying. About three or four miles upstream a truly massive landslide spilled out on to the glacier. Presumably it was this that had the effect of increasing the flow rate to the extent that the glacier was clearly advancing rapidly. A huge pile of moraine was being pushed down towards the Hispar river and below us the glacier heaved and groaned with disturbing regularity.

Bruce spoke: 'I've never been on a glacier before.'

This was, to put it mildly, something of a surprise. I had climbed with him a fair bit in England and for some reason I had formed the impression that he had done a lot in the New Zealand Alps. I wondered if Lobby realised his partner's mountaineering inexperience.

Bruce, though, is nothing if not adaptable. Soon he was clambering amongst the tottering ice towers, soloing around on bits that had me

dithering, and generally putting more than his fair share of energy
into locating a direct route across for the porters. It was there, of
course, weaving ingeniously in and out of the difficult areas and
enjoying regular use by the locals. It took us less than two hours
to reach Shishkin.

Back at Hoppar the argument about the number of stages was still
continuing. It was of course not helped by the fact that none of us
knew where we were going or had a clue how close to the mountain
it might be practical to have a Base Camp.

Ultimately the walk-in was agreed at five stages with our route
across the Bualtar Glacier being part of day one. Bruce and I at
least felt that our little foray had been worthwhile.

John and Liz strode past me with their umbrellas up. I had never
dreamt that such items would ever be necessary in the arid waste-
lands of the Karakoram. But I was wrong. As they bathed in their
respective pools of shade I was reduced to wrapping my dampened
shirt insecurely around my head in an effort to prevent imminent
sunstroke. In the distance, partially hidden by the lateral moraine
of the Barpu Glacier, was Barpu Giram, the reputedly lush summer
goat-grazing meadows. They didn't look very lush, in fact from this
distance it was impossible to see any vegetation at all. What I could
see, though, was the immense pillar of Spantik piercing through
the heat haze and dominating the horizon. The late afternoon sun
picked out features which allowed me to get a better idea of what to
expect. There was an occasional discontinuous groove or crack line
but nothing which looked as if it might provide fast or technically
reasonable climbing. I sat down exhausted on a boulder that was too
hot to touch. Even John and Liz seemed to be staggering a bit now.
If nothing else it would be cold up there but try as I might I couldn't
really convince myself that I would feel more competent at getting on
for 7000 metres than I felt now. This was increasingly worrying. The
closer we got to the mountain the more I remembered our Bojohagur
failings and wondered what the hell we were doing here.

Barpu Giram did little to lift my spirits. If I was reborn as a goat
this is the last place on earth that I would wish to be. Sparsely
arranged spiky tufts of dry grass looked far from appetising and
the few unfortunate creatures that had been dragged up here lay
forlornly in the dust doubtless wishing they were somewhere else.

'I think we will have to buy a goat.' It was Iqbal's voice which relayed this stunning message. Who would ever want a goat reared primarily on dust? Even more to the point, who would ever want to *buy* one? After an hour or so of negotiating I had an answer to both questions. The porters *wanted* a goat and *we* would buy them one. Our purchase was said to be a traditional gift for porters passing through Barpu Giram. It was also said to be traditional for the porters to give their employers a leg. Somehow I ended up carrying this. It protruded awkwardly from my rucksack and doubtless contained many of the most active inhabitants of Barpu Giram: fleas.

On day three of the walk-in it rained. This was unfortunate. I had not banked on rain. John and Liz grinned sweetly from beneath their umbrellas whilst the porters looked miserable and struggled to wrap themselves in the plastic sheeting we intended to use for a Base Camp kitchen shelter. By day four the rain had turned to snow and the porters were reduced to cutting hair from a solitary yak for a bit of extra warmth. On day five we ground to a halt.

'They say that this is it.' The tone of Lobby's voice dragged me harshly out of idyllic tea-stop mode.

'Base Camp?' I stared around me quizzically. OK, it was a good campsite but the base of the spur was miles away out of sight round a bend in the glacier. Their line of argument was immediately clear: This place, they said, 'is Yakazina – where you asked us to bring your equipment.'

It was the classic claimed 'misunderstanding' argument. Iqbal had a go at persuading them to continue but to no avail. Ibrahim fingered his gun disconcertingly, saying that there were ibex in the area. It seemed that a stalemate had resulted and, as I sat down on a boulder to nurture my headache, Lobby and Victor (who were clearly able to summon more in the way of energy reserves than anyone else) headed off round the corner to check exactly where we were in relation to the spur. Our situation didn't look at all hopeful. In fact it was becoming increasingly tense. Iqbal, who of course understood much more of the local dialect than we could, was noticeably twitchy. I busied myself searching for my headache tablets and avoiding eye contact.

It was just over an hour before Victor and Lobby returned. They looked pleased. The foot of the spur was still a few hours off but what they felt to be a perfect Base Camp site was only an hour away round the corner.

'If need be we can ferry the loads ourselves,' said Victor. I contemplated the five carries (at least) that would be necessary to get the gear up this final stretch. This wasn't like the Alps at all.

I must say that I have to take my hat off to Victor for what happened next. He climbed on to a boulder and, against the advice of Iqbal and Ibrahim, appealed direct to the porters, through Ibrahim as an interpreter. He reminded them of the goat we had bought them, our acceptance of their increasingly short walking days and emphasised their importance to us and the respect he had for their perseverance in continuing with the walk-in despite the adverse weather conditions. He culminated with a plea for them to carry for one hour more to 'save our expedition', as he put it.

It was Gulam Mehedi, whom we had tried to reject down in Hoppar, who started the tide turning in our favour. A great hulk of a man, completely bald, and kitted out with traditional gear to the extent that he shunned the ubiquitous plastic shoes and preferred long strips of leather wrapped firmly around each foot, he was clearly a much respected elder and when he stood to say a few words to support us, a mood swing in our favour was immediately perceptible. Smiles began to replace looks of intransigence. At length Ibrahim turned to Victor, who was still standing uncomfortably on his boulder.

'They will carry on for you.' Smiles all round.

One hour later we were at Suja Basu – a grassy meadow with fresh running water and a clear view of the pillar. The porters were paid off, with a special thank-you for Gulam Mehedi, and at last we were on our own with only the mountain to climb. The bureaucratic and man-management challenges were behind us. It was 14th July, 1987 and we were at about 4000 metres. I wondered if we had passed the crux – but nursing what was by now clearly an altitude-induced headache and seeing the route in its entirety for the first time, I concluded that we probably had not.

Morning on 1st August, 1987 – this was the fifth consecutive day that neither Victor nor I had moved from the tiny two-man tent perched at 5800 metres on the Golden Pillar of Spantik. Outside the snow fell incessantly. My diary entries revealed my enthusiasm level: '30th July – didn't even bother to put contact lenses in today. Nothing worth seeing.' '31st July – this is purgatory, eight hours trying to sleep and sixteen hours bored – every day. Snow completely covers rucksacks now.' '1st August

– snow waist deep now – unbelievable misery – can't stand it any more.'

I had never seen so much snow fall and endured such acute boredom for such a long period. We had food for fifteen days and intended to carry seven days' worth with us from this point. That allowed us eight days to wait for the weather. This was day five of that contingency time. I couldn't help myself expressing this timewasting in work terms. My colleagues would be completing their daily cycles – get up, wash, breakfast, go to work, morning in the office, lunch, afternoon in the office, travel home, evening meal, evening entertainment, bed – and through all of this we stay put in our 2m×1m tent. Four complete days later and we were still in the tent. That's like getting up on a Monday, working for four days and on Friday morning noticing two people who haven't moved from a 2m×1m rectangle all week!

Neither of us had anything to read and conversational standards fell to an alltime low. With alpine-style Himalayan climbing having a lot to do with controlled starvation, it was perhaps natural that the subject of food should surface every now and then. In particular I recall an outrageously long conversation about the nutritional value of bogies. Both of us developed habits that were irritating to the other. Victor prattled on endlessly about whether or not the tent needed a 'bell end' whilst I spent literally hours picking dirt out from under my fingernails with a penknife and flicking it around the tent.

On the morning of day five I cracked: 'Victor, I can't stand it any more.'

'Me neither.'

That evening we were back in Base Camp. Four inches of snow covered everything. John and Liz had already gone home and Bruce was feeling his Himalayan inexperience and becoming increasingly uncertain about committing himself.

Spirits were decidedly low, the sparkling Base Camp water supply was reduced to a slush trickle and visibility was down to twenty metres. A murky grey shroud of mist enveloped both tents and morale. England seemed very appealing. I remembered why I had vowed never to return to the Karakoram.

It was 3rd August. I was booked on to a plane from Islamabad on 16th August and with the route likely to take about ten days from Base Camp things were looking decidedly tight. The temptation was to give up and go home but after all the effort that had gone into planning the trip and getting this far I felt obliged to have one final attempt. If the weather cleared sufficiently by the 7th we would go up, if not it would be back to England for me.

After our four days of purgatory in the tent I suppose we could have guessed that both the 4th and 5th August would prove to be fine and clear. The evening of the 5th found us back at a flat area on the moraine which we rather grandly called Advance Base. It was obvious this was to be our last chance of success and although high cloud skimmed the sky, any cautious optimism that had built up over the last two days was held in close check.

The alarm bleeped at 11 p.m. – it was time for the lower spur again. We knew the route well by now – fifteen minutes up the moraine, forty-five minutes across the glacier, an hour and a half of grade II–III ice-climbing, and four hours of steady plodding, probably in knee-deep snow, to reach the hanging glacier bivouac and the start of the real difficulties. We had left all of our food and most of our hardware here on previous forays, so at least this time our sacks were relatively light, and with a midnight start we were able to avoid the debilitating effect of the sun and arrive back at the all too familiar tent platform by 6.30 a.m. Although almost halfway up the buttress in terms of height gain, we now had the difficult climbing ahead in the form of a horrendous-looking 1000-metre buttress. Of course having arrived not long after daybreak meant we still had the whole hot day to sit out. This time I had brought along *Gorky Park*, but I am glad to say it had to wait until the return plane journey to be finished.

Things were looking good – the fine day gave way to a starry night and by 6 a.m. we were heading for the technical climbing at last. Previous forays had culminated in 100 metres of rope being fixed on the first two pitches of the slabby lower section of the pillar. Throughout the bleak days of waiting it had looked as though this pathetic achievement would be the highpoint of the expedition. Twelve months of planning and preparation, so much physical effort – all for two pitches of roped climbing. The only positive point seemed to be that this was two more than I had managed three years previously on Bojohagur – and in fact the only two roped pitches I had managed in the Himalaya up until this point. This time though we were in with a chance and a breath of enthusiasm crept to the fore. It was sixteen days since our previous visit to the highpoint and although our ropes were still in place they were often deeply buried in powder snow and intermittently frozen in. The 100 metres which was fixed was about Scottish grade 4 standard, and in retrospect fixing it was a complete waste of time. (The rest of the terylene that we had brought from Britain didn't even make it beyond Advance Base.) In a fit of weight-consciousness we had taken only one pair of jumars between us for the route. Thus it was a comic pair who ascended their laboriously prepared fixed ropes by soloing up next to them, each protected by a single jumar which had to be removed every now and then to pass lengths frozen to the ice. We concluded that the price in wasted energy far exceeded the half hour saved.

Our exploratory probe had left us with the impression that there was enough ice in grooves on the slabs to give continuous grade IV climbing – perhaps with the occasional harder pitch – leading up to a prominent depression in the face which we dubbed the amphitheatre. It was therefore something of a shock to leave the end of the fixed rope and immediately find ourselves on sustained and insecure grade V ground. The problem was that only certain grooves were climbable. However, with an inch of powder snow plastered everywhere it was difficult to pinpoint which grooves held the most ice. The end result was much whimpering on the part of the leader who was forced to make regular character-building tension traverses between hopeful-looking lines and much penduluming activity from the second. As we stuck strictly to alternate leads, the pleasures of the different techniques were shared equally.

Despite the unexpectedly hard climbing, progress was surprisingly good. By late afternoon we had completed eight pitches and could see into the amphitheatre for the first time. It was not an encouraging sight. Fifty-degree slopes in the back ran up to a steep corner system which provided the only feasible exit but looked considerably steeper than the ground we had been climbing. I hoped that conditions up there would be more conducive to steep climbing, although I could think of no real reason why they should be. In fact as the corners received minimal sun they presumably experienced minimal freeze/thaw and would, therefore, be even more powder plastered than the lower slabs. Common sense was clearly something to be pushed to the back of the mind; we would simply have to look and see.

Of more immediate concern was the late hour and distinct lack of bivi sites. In fact I couldn't remember passing one all day. Ice, where encountered, was never more than five centimetres thick and the underlying rock was set at a uniform sixty degrees. A small flake proved to be our salvation – not spacious enough to pitch the tent on but at least allowing us to sit in balance. The tent fabric doubled as a bivi bag and probably more due to exhaustion than comfort we both enjoyed a reasonable night.

The next day started well with relatively firm snow allowing rapid progress to the chimney/groove system exiting from the amphitheatre. It was my lead – awkward back-and-foot work and for the first time real problems with the cold. Even with considerable adrenalin flow I was having trouble warming my hands. Air temperatures on the pillar were boasting the usual Karakoram extremes. Facing north-west it was in the shade during the morning and sufficiently cold to dissuade us from any earlier start than 7 a.m. But by 11 a.m. the sun was overhead and the Fowler body could be seen to wilt. However, here in the chimney it was 9 a.m. and cold; technically the ground was 'good V', which means that I was finding it desperate. Ice smears at the back gave some assistance but what ice there was became increasingly brittle as we gained height and the temperature dropped. Progress was accomplished by shattering the ice, staring at the blank rock underneath and grovelling furiously using any minute rugosity that crampon points could hook on to.

Encouraging comments of the 'Go for it' variety floated up from down below.

'I am,' I grunted. 'I am.'

Up to this point all the rock encountered had been a form of marble but I had now reached a shale intrusion which formed a prominent seventy-five degree chimney fault leading up to the right edge of the buttress. An encouraging amount of ice was visible in places, but as Victor soon found out this was far from being an asset – it was so brittle that it shattered like a pane of glass at each blow; axe placements were shallow and hardly instilled a feeling of security. The whole feature was reminiscent of North Devon's shale coast in a hard winter, packed with slivers of shale projecting ten centimetres or so through the ice and obviously more frozen in place than attached to the rock beneath. Victor's lead was steady and impressive, teetering from sliver to sliver for fifty metres with only similar slivers offering dubious spikes for protection. Another similar but easier pitch saw me approaching the right edge of the front face of the pillar when one of my worst nightmares came true. I simply had to crap there and then. Waiting was out of the question.

'How do you go to the toilet when you are hanging on a steep face for days on end?' This favourite post-expedition question from work colleagues ran through my mind. Usually there is no problem; with a bit of care and attention one can hang on the belay and do the necessary, so to speak.

Here, though, I was in mid pitch; even worse I was spreadeagled on sixty-five-degree bottomless powder and unable to secure myself in any way. A short buttock-clenching traverse saw me on a slightly easier-angled slope but there was no time for any further niceties such as searching for belays. Feeling horribly insecure I untied our two ropes and tied them around my ankles. This at least got them out of the way, meant that I wouldn't drop them and perhaps most importantly meant that I was still tied on after a fashion. Thereafter I shall spare the details. Suffice to say that my bottom was cold for a long time afterwards and that crapping on a fifty-five-degree bottomless powder slope is not something I would recommend.

Feeling rather unsettled I returned to the climbing. Above me the short slope eased as I gained the right bounding edge of the pillar. Across to my right monstrous ice cliffs overhanging awe-inspiring avalanche-ridden gullies seemed surprisingly close, whilst further right again was our proposed line of descent: a snow and ice spur of a modest angle low down but increasing to a steep-looking ice slope in its upper section. A surrounding fringe of cornices looked potentially exciting at the top but worries in that direction were a long way off yet. Also evident from our viewpoint was the fact that the summit snowfields were anything but straightforward – it would be challenging enough just reaching the flat area above the descent ridge. All in all it was not really very encouraging from the point of view of the descent; we had been aware of potential difficulties when studying the ground through binoculars but from closer quarters it seemed more problematical than expected. It was still preferable to descending the spur, which often seemed to lack good belay points and the lower slopes of which we knew became dangerously avalanche-prone in bad weather.

Turning back to the problem in hand, we had reached an area of snowy ledges leading up to a hard-looking powder-blasted corner above which our proposed line was out of sight. We had also just moved out of the extreme cold of the shade and into the enervating heat of the sun. Progress withered to a halt. Although the sun was out it was obvious that we were in for a period of snow. Huge grey clouds were racing across towards us and no further incentive was needed to pitch the tent as soon as possible.

A third of the floor area hung over thin air but the other two thirds gave reasonably flat sleeping quarters, and as long as we avoided the lighter area of groundsheet all would be well.

Soon the familiar sound of snow drumming on tent fabric brought back nasty memories. I engrossed myself in *Gorky Park* whilst Victor busied himself with the continuous brewing technique, struggling to melt vast quantities of powder snow. Most commendable, I thought.

'Lazy bastard,' said Victor.

Fifteen hours later – at 6 a.m. the following morning – it was still snowing heavily and fifty centimetres of new powder threatened to nudge the tent from the ledge. Nevertheless the ground ahead did not seem to be avalanche-prone and after an initial dither we decided to press on. Route-finding would be a problem if the bad weather persisted but at least we had seen the first 100 metres the afternoon before and so knew where to start. A sixty-degree snow slope leading to the powder-blasted corner looked easy but proved to be ten-centimetre deep powder lying on smooth slabs. It gave climbing at least as difficult as the vertical corner which followed although that consisted of ninety-degree brittle ice and required continuous clipping into the ice-axes, not to mention the masochism involved in clearing fifteen centimetres of powder from the ice.

By midday things were looking better; we had managed 200 metres and the weather was clearing again. A fine ledge (the only one on the entire pillar) provided a welcome stopping point and, as Victor pointed out to me, an ideal opportunity to do all the things that ledges or flat ground allow one to do in comfort. Unfortunately it was too early for us to justify spending the night here.

From Base Camp the binoculars had shown that the next section consisted of very steep rock walls with a series of parallel snowbands running diagonally from left to right. All but one of the bands had appeared to lead to rock walls set at an extremely high angle which, when considered in the context of the temperature extremes and altitude, could well present insuperable problems. It was therefore vital that we chose the right line.

From our vantage point on the platform we peered hopefully upwards. The strata of the rock was such that numerous left-to-right slanting grooves ran up an overhanging rock wall for about thirty metres to where the angle eased and we knew the snowbands began. With me taking the easiest option by tackling the shortest groove, Victor was treated to the entertaining spectacle of me demonstrating my incompetence at aid climbing. The hail of lighthearted abuse was difficult to deny but the end result was effective and we gained the base of a snowy ramp. The bad weather was back with us by now but at least we seemed to have chosen the right line. Easier ground, with only short hard steps, led up into the driving snow until we found ourselves in a steep and horrifyingly constricted chimney – an exhausting pitch which fortunately was Victor's lead. It was now well past our usual bivi time but absolutely nothing suitable was in sight. The last thing I wanted to do was climb on into the biting cold of the night. But what could we do?

More very hard climbing led to a horizontal band of ice; it was getting dark by now and, despite initial opposition from Victor, I insisted that we should spend the night here. In the rush to get ourselves established I managed to pull the wires from the back of my head torch and consequently enjoyed intermittent periods of unwanted darkness for the rest of the route.

It quickly became apparent that things were not going as planned. Wherever we started cutting, the ice turned out to be only about five centimetres thick – we couldn't even place a decent ice-screw, let alone cut a satisfactory bum ledge. Victor went unusually quiet and I cursed and swore – very much aware of who had insisted on stopping here.

One ten-centimetre diameter stone projected from the slope and two hours of effort punctuated by numerous tangles (and fumbles in the dark from me) saw us 'sitting' on a ten-centimetre-wide 'ledge' both struggling to get our feet on the solitary stone. Victor decided to tie his rucksack in to the belay and spend the night standing in it whilst I opted for relying more on the support given by my harness. Both of us were suspended from the same jammed nut, whilst tied-off ice-screws held the tent/bivi bag in position. Equipment fell to the bottom of the tent fabric pulling it tight and smothering our faces. Something told me that it was not going to be a pleasant night.

'As bad as being sat in the Tax Office?' quipped Victor, keen as ever to bring my employers into the conversation.

'No. Worse.' My answer required no hesitation. 'Squeezed next to you all night – awful prospect.'

'Likewise,' came from somewhere in the dark next to me.

There is nothing like a bit of feeble abuse to keep the spirits up.

The onset of snow was almost the last straw; it was not so much that it snowed heavily but the expanse of face above caused waves of spindrift to engulf us at regular intervals. The valance around the tent entrance proved to be a perfect receptacle for this and it soon piled up on top of the entrance zip, effectively blocking our only means of escape. Every now and then one of us would uncontrollably scream obscenities – unable to suffer the claustrophobia a moment longer – rip open the zip for a breath of fresh air and suffer a face full of powder snow, some of which inevitably found its way deep into the warmth of our sleeping-bags.

Suffice to say that the night was long and miserable, although fortunately the weather turned out to be better than it had sounded; our spindrift problems were caused chiefly by shifting snow higher on the mountain, rather than actual precipitation.

The dry cold air and heavy breathing was by now irritating our throats. Both of us had niggling coughs and for me there was a definite sensation of something stuck in my throat. During the night I made several disgusting attempts to cough up this blockage, and when I managed to, just as we prepared to leave the bivi, a strip of flesh appeared, perhaps one centimetre long and half a centimetre wide. I stared aghast at what I had done. There was an awful hiatus as I wondered whether I would be able to speak properly and how much pain there would be in swallowing. Tentatively rediscovering the qualities of my throat and larynx, it was with more than a slight feeling of relief that I found everything seemed to function normally. There still seemed to be a frog in my throat but there was no way that I would be making any effort to clear it further.

This aside, the morning's preparation was a nightmare of cold fingers, wooden toes and assorted tangles – it was truly a pleasure to be on the move again. Day six from Base Camp started with a couple of standard insecure pitches taking us to the start of the final snow ramp which could now be seen to lead to a fortuitous gap between the top of the pillar and the séracs, which were draped from the summit icefields. A monstrous 100-metre high ear-shaped sérac was visible overhanging the gap through which we would have to climb. The ramp was about two metres wide and continually hard – one pitch in particular being a nightmare of scraping crampons on seventy-degree rock, no runners and the prospect of a big, big fall down the vertical wall below as a penalty for any mistake. It was a fine nerve-wracking lead by Victor which led to a point directly beneath the exit gap and – less favourably – exactly in the line of fire of the giant ice ear (not to mention lots of associated smaller ears). The last hard pitch loomed above, an eighty-degree corner choked with powder overlaying a veneer of ice. Both of us glanced anxiously at the thousands of tons of ice poised directly above. Careful movements were the order of the day – no hefty thumps on peg-runners here, more delicate taps and gentle clips into deftly inserted axe placements. It was a hard pitch, both mentally and physically, but the end was in sight – above it only fifty metres of snow slope remained. Somehow Victor found the energy to produce the necessary waist-deep trench and we were on the plateau at last. All technical difficulty lay behind us. I flopped limply on to horizontal ground; the immediate pleasure was a properly erected tent and somewhere flat to lie down. Any elation could wait till later.

In England I had confided in friends that I would be satisfied if we managed to climb the pillar but could not get to the summit. Now we were actually here, it seemed unthinkable that we should not try.

But success was far from a certainty. Morning revealed the top to be a depressingly long way off. We had originally planned to take all our equipment part way and collect it whilst heading down towards the 'descent spur'. Now, however, it seemed that progress would be challenging enough just with light sacks, so our tent and hardware were duly left behind.

Plodding limply in Victor's steps I had no doubt as to whether we had made the right decision. It was all I could do to keep going at all – our rate of progress was so painfully slow and the summit so distressingly distant it just seemed inconceivable that we would ever make it. With sufficient rests the pace could be maintained – the difficult part was keeping alive the will to continue when it seemed such an impossible task in the time available.

Cold was also becoming a real problem. The powdery snow at this altitude was making our feet uncomfortably cold. Hands were fine – if our fingers became cold we could quickly warm them down our trousers or under armpits. Feet, however, were logistically more difficult to warm in this manner. For me the best technique seemed to be to lift them out of the snow and (energy permitting) shake them vigorously in the air. This looked rather silly and didn't aid progress too well; it also prompted Victor to get the camera out a lot.

'Must send these shots to your boss,' he kept saying.

Inevitably the result was that foot-waving stops were kept to a minimum and cold feet were something we had to live with. Frostbite, though, is a deep concern of mine and I found the time when I had no feeling in my toes deeply disturbing.

The day developed into an endless masochistic trudge. Surrounded by magnificent views I could only stare blankly at the tracks and envelop myself in the exhaustion of every step. At best we sank in ankle deep – at the worst genuinely waist deep and always in the penetrating cold of feathery powder snow. Victor was a tower a strength on this sort of ground. I found the lack of any firm footing and the constant struggle to stay upright totally enervating. Give me technical climbing any day.

It seemed incredible that the summit was getting closer but at 12.50 p.m. our efforts were rewarded – we could go up no more. At 7027 metres our goal was achieved, everything suddenly seemed worthwhile – from the masochism of the last six and a half hours to the bureaucratic hurdles of the last eighteen months.

We stayed for forty-five minutes waiting for the never-to-appear hole in the clouds before scurrying back to the tent, hotly pursued by crackling electricity and swirling spindrift. Now we had only to get down. A glimmer of elation grew in the depth of my heart.

Two long days later we had cautiously crossed crevasse minefields, abseiled from powder-snow mushrooms, lowered each other through cornices and very nearly been avalanched, but success was ours. The glimmer had developed into a hearty glow. Safe at last, we had completed the untrodden descent spur and could now wallow in the warmth of Base Camp and relish our cook's hugs and flower garlands.

It was Thursday evening – I had to be back at work on Monday morning. The journey was a little tiring but suffice it to say that on Monday the civil servant shoes were duly in position under the civil servant desk. My other life had begun again.

11

Meanwhile Back in Britain

In the years leading to Spantik it had become increasingly clear to me that Britain was still blessed with a vast number of spectacular unclimbed summits – sea stacks. A quick glance at the Ordnance Survey maps showed a liberal spattering in areas not usually frequented by climbers – North-East Scotland, Shetland, Cape Wrath, the Isle of Wight . . . the list was endless as were the possibilities. I could sense an irrepressible urge beginning to flow over me.

Early days involved swims to exciting Cornish off-shore islands which boast fine rock-climbing faces. Lye Rock and Long Island north of Tintagel bring back memories from those early days. Long Island, in particular, occupies a firm niche in my mind. It was an early exploit with Victor and having arrived on top after a 130-metre climb I lost my balance whilst untangling the rope from my legs and fell against a projecting edge of shale. The razor-sharp slivers entered between my cheekbone and eye resulting in impressive quantities of blood and necessitating a challenging return swim, lots of bemused clifftop strollers and a magnificent rock removal and stitching job by a Tintagel doctor who was interrupted from mowing his lawn on a Bank Holiday Monday. Bloodbath seemed a fitting route name.

My interest in these off-shore challenges began because I could see obvious rock-climbing potential just a stone's throw from my by now habitual shale-climbing haunts on the North Cornwall coast. Further research revealed the more well-known stacks to be in remoter settings in the far north of Scotland. Tom Patey, the roving Ullapool doctor, had been a stack-climbing devotee and was responsible for virtually all the major stacks climbed in the 1960s and '70s.

It was trips to his classic routes on the Old Man of Hoy, Am Buchaille (Cape Wrath) and the Old Man of Stoer (Lochinver) that persuaded Chris Newcombe (an old friend of mine from the North London scene) and me that there was a lot to be had from this branch of climbing, and a new phase of sea-stack development could reap rich rewards. Am Buchaille and the Old Man of Stoer had necessitated short swims but the many possibilities revealed on Ordnance Survey maps and picture postcard books on the British coastline showed that a boat would be well worth having. Patey was clearly of the same view. His final sea-stack trip in May 1970 was a boatborne visit to the Maiden sea stacks off Whiten Head on Scotland's wild and beautiful north coast. Tragically he fell to his death in an abseiling accident on the descent, his old wire figure-of-eight descender somehow becoming detached from his harness. The incident robbed North-West Scotland of its most active pioneer and the climbing scene of a much loved and admired character. In terms of stack-climbing in Scotland, it resulted in a virtual cessation of activity.

When my interest was fired in 1986–7, it was difficult to think of a single worthwhile sea stack that had had a first ascent in the post-Patey period. There was no doubt that the potential was there but northern Scotland is a long way from London and how would we get hold of a suitable boat? Getting local people to drop us off would be risky and owning a boat ourselves would pose transportation problems.

Chris though was not to be defeated. Seldom have I seen him so enthused and willing to overcome so many apparently insuperable obstacles. The first was that his efforts to hire a boat were not met with any great enthusiasm. The usual exchange was along the following lines.

'I'd like to hire a boat for the weekend please.'

'Certainly, sir. What sort are you interested in?'

'Er . . . a small one, perhaps an inflatable.'

'What are you going to use it for?'

'Er . . . as transport to unclimbed sea stacks.'

'Any nautical experience, sir . . .?'

The dialogue then trickled out into refusal after refusal. Chris was persistent. He finally located a boat-owner in the well-known British port of Basildon who was sufficiently disinterested in our safety to hire us a leaky fifteen-foot inflatable on a strictly 'no questions asked' basis. This fine craft came with oars but little else. Basildon was not exactly convenient as it entailed considerable extra mileage on a Friday night to pick the thing up. Chris was not to be deterred. There was, as he kept reminding us, 'work to be done' on the sea-stack front.

He was undeniably right:

Handfast Point, the chalk headland two miles east of Swanage, sported a selection of challenging unclimbed chalk stacks. Old Harry was the best known and had been an objective of mine for several years. Twenty-five metres high and overhanging on all sides, it stands as a prominent sentinel, the most seaward of a series of more squat, less impressive towers stretching out into the Solent. The inner towers I knew to have already been climbed. In fact I well remembered the redoubtable Arnis Strapcans standing at the foot of Old Harry's House after stunning his audience by successfully demonstrating the 'how to retrieve your ice-axe when you have just abseiled from it' technique.

Old Harry himself had rebuffed would-be suitors for many years. Their efforts had ranged from attempts to throw a grappling hook from the nearby Old Harry's House to bolting and using six-inch nails. As far as I could work out the wind had curtailed the line-throwing efforts whilst sheets of rock parting company with attached climbers stopped the bolters and nailers. I must admit to once having been a prospective nailer myself. Back in 1979, several years before the advent of the boat idea I had braved the ten-metre-wide channel with Andy Henderson. Andy is about six inches taller than me and could just about walk along keeping his nose clear, whilst I was forced to flounder alongside. On that occasion the blank rock looked impossible to free climb, and shivering violently in the winter temperatures we retreated to a Swanage ironmonger for a supply of six-inch nails. Perhaps fortunately the weather was bad the next day, our aided attempt never materialised and the nails subsequently spent several years rusting in my garden shed.

Eight years after this débâcle I was back with Chris, Lynne (Chris's wife) and Lorraine Smythe, my girlfriend of the time. This time we were seaborne, with the Basildon Bombard inflatable providing the transport. Transporting the thing had been eased by Chris using his work pick-up. Having converted the pile of boards and rubber into a vaguely seaworthy craft, a rather uncertain crew pulled away from a sandy beach one mile east of Handfast Point. Our aim was to row around the Point and inspect from close quarters the two attractive chalk pinnacles on the Swanage side. Unfortunately, our arms were not up to the challenge. Despite regular changes at the oars it seemed impossible to beat the current round the headland and gain the promised calm water beyond. Lorraine was disappointed that the current wasn't in the other direction. Filled with civil servant caution I wondered if that might not have been worse. It also occurred to me that lots of the stacks we had pinpointed for our attentions were in the Pentland Firth – an area renowned for its dangerous currents. I couldn't help but feel that an engine was looking to be an increasingly worthwhile investment. On this occasion, though, a disorderly retreat was inevitable.

In May 1987 – two months before the Spantik trip – we were back as proud co-owners of the Basildon Bombard. At £400 for the boat, oars *and* a 2.8 hp Seagull engine, we were well pleased with our purchase, especially compared to the £50 per weekend hire charge. *Deflowerer*, as we christened her (thinking of all those virgin stacks out there), was not exactly a master of the high seas but she was not completely insubstantial either. Being approximately five metres long with a sturdy wooden floor and five tough inflatable compartments she could take four in comfort and survive climbers jumping in from at least three metres. We had in fact tried her out a few times before revisiting Old Harry but with Lynne and Lorraine always along I couldn't recall any problems fitting her together. This time was different. There were four of us – Mark Lynden and Andy Meyers had joined Chris and me. Andy was 'into sailing boats', which meant that the rest of us irrationally looked firmly to him when we hit problems with rubber-boat inflation.

Swanage had been chosen as a potentially more convenient launching spot than the sandy beach to the east of the headland. Its advantages were only to become evident as the boat somehow failed to fit together as easily as when Lynne and Lorraine had been around. Swanage in May is a popular place. A crowd of interested onlookers leant over the railings above us and interjected unhelpful comments every now and then. Somehow it seemed impossible to stretch the fabric sufficiently to fit the floorboards and keel in. We tried with various combinations of inflated and deflated compartments but nothing seemed to work. Meanwhile the slipway was effectively blocked with our tangle of rubber and wood until some nautical types in the launching queue behind us stepped forward to offer assistance and get us off the slipway.

Since buying *Deflowerer* a few bits and pieces of safety equipment had materialised. We had even spent some money on flares. Lifejackets, however, were inexcusably lower down the list of priorities. I think it was because we had been given some by Jon (Carless) Lincoln (who had found them lurking under a pile of rubbish in his parents' garage) and somehow convinced ourselves that these were OK. In fact they were of very questionable use. One was clearly for a four- to five-year-old and the others were to spend more time being used as seats than round our chests.

Anyway, fully equipped or not, the trusty 2.8 hp throbbed heartily (so much better than oars!) out towards the distant stacks on the Swanage side of Handfast Point. The stacks here are considerably bigger than they first appear. Of the three most spectacular ones Tusk Pinnacle, sometimes known as the Wine Bottle, is the highest and most slender – a forty-metre needle with a tottering razor-sharp summit ridge. But this time we had come for Old Harry – rather lower but clearly offering the most technical climbing challenge.

Something had changed over the intervening years. I wondered whether it was the physical appearance of the stack but I couldn't be sure. Nothing seemed to have fallen off and in fact subsequent inspection of my old photographs confirmed that it must have been my perception of the problems that had changed. On my last visit I had remembered it as resembling a huge ice-cream cone, overhanging on all sides and with no line of weakness whatsoever. Now the seaward face seemed to boast a line which might just be free climbable. There was even a small ledge at half height which should provide a comfortable spot to belay.

Inflatable boats do seem to be incredibly tough. Our hesitant manoeuvrings towards a possible drop-off point saw the rubber compartments scraping nerve-wrackingly against the sharp edges and barnacle-covered rock at the base of the stack.

'What's all this water in here?'

Mark was the first to notice a problem. There was already five centimetres in the back of the boat and the level seemed to be rising. Chris and I took the first opportunity to get on to the stack whilst Mark and Andy began bailing furiously. Comfortable in the fact that we were on terra firma and the boat was unlikely to sink Chris and I addressed the problem in hand.

Although awkward for the first three metres the ground was nowhere near as difficult as I had envisaged and we were soon safely established on the halfway stance beneath the final ten-metre overhanging wall. Exfoliating chalk and insecure flints caused problems here, as did a not inconsiderable amount of technical difficulty. Fortunately ice-screw protection was reasonable and the final fringe of overhangs was reached without too much adrenalin flow.

The crux was the last two metres where the chalk seemed to be held together by the mat of vegetation on the flat summit. The final move, a difficult pull with a loose flint in one hand and a poorly rooted grass tuft in the other remains etched on my mind.

Self-congratulations seemed in order as I lay panting in the scant vegetation on this windswept untrodden summit. Something was wrong though. What was this rusty reinforcement rod protruding from the foliage? It could only have been put there by one man. Simon Ballantine – the man famed for introducing the reinforcement rod to Dover chalk. The bastard! He had beaten us to one of my key objectives . . . and on home ground too. I understood now how Martin Moran must have felt on Fuar Tholl when we rubbed his nose in it with the inflammatory naming of Pipped at the Post.

A phone call the following day confirmed my suspicions. A few months before, Simon and John Henderson had waded out, climbed the stack and swum back to the mainland. In sharp contrast to the competitive environment in more traditional areas, they hadn't even bothered to report such an important ascent!

Having quizzed him thoroughly I had to give it to them that their efforts showed considerably more willpower and imagination than ours. Noting a conveniently low spring tide they had gone for a 5 a.m. start and waded out wearing wetsuits and rock boots and carrying ice-axes, ice-screws and a two-kilo lump hammer. Having reached the top via the landward side using a combination of ice, rock and aid techniques, they then slept there for a few hours, intending a simultaneous abseil when the tide went out. However, a change of plan suggested itself as they realised that they were in with a chance of making the pub by lunchtime. A premature abseil was the result, after which, having pulled down and coiled the ropes whilst treading water, the intrepid duo did not let the weight of two axes, five kilos of hardware and the two-kilo hammer prevent them from swimming thirty-metres to the nearest beach and prusiking up their rope to fence posts on the clifftop. A commendable performance all round though I am still at a loss as to why they named their route the Witch's Tit. Breasts on broomsticks were certainly not something I noticed in the vicinity.

We did have one shot left in our own locker. Down in the boat Mark tied on the blue stuff sack.

'Pull it up,' he shouted and as an afterthought, having surveyed the amount of water still in the boat, 'Get a move on.'

Chris and I were not used to erecting small geodesic tents. In theory it was all very simple. The two poles should fit neatly through the fabric sleeves and tension the fabric by clipping into eyelets in the four corners of the groundsheet. Something seemed amiss though. The poles seemed to be too long. Mark was an expert in such things. He was also getting impatient. His water-level instructions were more abusive than helpful. We had hoped to win a sponsorship deal by letting the tent manufacturer use spectacular and unusual shots in exchange for mountain bivouac tents. But our best efforts at photography still made the tent look disabled. The results met with complete rejection by the manufacturer and lots of piss-taking comments for some time thereafter. Such is life. Mark subsequently confirmed that we had the wrong poles and the whole incident faded into the category of 'useful knowledge gained'. It did cause a stir amongst the South Coast walking fraternity for some weeks however.

By the time we were all back in the boat the water level had stabilised but was still high. Curiously it seemed to go down slightly as we chugged back in the general direction of Swanage.

'Who put the bungs in?' Chris directed his question at me. All eyes were drawn to the cords which should have been taut if the underfloor drainage bungs had been in place. They were slack. I had learned at least two things on the Old Harry trip. Firstly check the pole lengths on geodesic tents, and secondly remember to put the bungs in before launching. The climbing wasn't bad either.

Owning the boat naturally prompted closer perusal of those stacks and cliffs I knew which did not lend themselves to a traditional landborne approach. Even in the South-East the possibilities were inspiring. Andy Meyers was perhaps the expert on the key area around the Solent. He worked for Plessey at the time and had access to a small sailing boat owned by Plessey's sailing club. He was keen to frighten others (and sometimes himself) by braving all but the worst Solent seas in this seemingly fragile craft. Ultimately he decided that fiddling with electronic gadgets was not for him and he left Plessey (and the boat) and trained to become a commercial pilot. One must hope his apparent need for a steady surge of adrenalin is not transmitted to his paying passengers.

Working on Andy's advice the huge cliffs on the Isle of Wight stretching from the Needles along to Freshwater Bay were subjected to a closer inspection, though the boat was only felt to be necessary for the Needles themselves. This fine line of stacks, named after a larger more slender pinnacle which collapsed in the 1890s, was duly visited on a magnificent May day in 1988. The history of first ascents here is hazy to say the least. John Cleare in his book *Sea Cliff Climbing in Britain* attributes the first ascent of all three to Robin Collomb. When I telephoned him, Collomb attributed the first ascents to Cleare. Both were insistent that they personally hadn't climbed them. In fact the only confirmed ascent of any Needle that I could trace was by the RAF who apparently used the area as a training ground and periodically dropped poor defenceless crew members on to the central summit where they were then abandoned for many hours in the middle of cold, windy winter nights. Presumably this built their characters immensely.

Technically the Needles are all relatively easy but the attraction of such climbs is of course not so much the difficulty of the climbing but the overall situation and adventure involved. Although it initially sounds silly, comparisons can be drawn to Himalayan climbs, where the walk-in, ethnic environment and climb all combine to give the overall experience. The advent of *Deflowerer* and sea stacks provided an ideal excuse for visiting new places whilst at the same time tackling spectacular unclimbed summits. Another real bonus seemed to be that Molestable Young Ladies tended to be far more keen on nautical excitement with some climbing thrown in, rather than concentrated activity on serious and often rather loose unclimbed cliffs. Perhaps I speak from a prejudiced viewpoint but certainly this was the case with Nicki Dugan whom I first got to know well through sea stacks. Starting with the Needles we did quite a few together before she became my wife!

The Needles are well known to be defended by serious currents and it was perhaps fortunate for my future in sea-stack climbing that the day we chose was perfect in every way. Cloudless skies allowed the hot sun to burn down on to a near-millpond sea, and in between climbing all three Needles we were able to stop for tea and scones with the lighthouse keepers who seemed pleased to have us interrupt the potential monotony of a four-weeks-on/four-off timetable. (Surely a remarkable work routine considering that Yarmouth on the Isle of Wight is no more than half an hour away by fast boat!) We even enjoyed a guided tour of the lighthouse itself, taking in the built-in beds curved to the shape of the wall, the toilet with a view and the diesel generator engines which have been in nonstop use since they were installed in 1948. The outer Needle was particularly interesting: not only has the end of it been completely cut away to make room for the lighthouse but the inside has been hollowed out to act as storage space. One lighthouseman described being inside the store when a freak wave hit during the October 1987 storm which caused so much damage throughout the south of the country.

'It shuddered quite a lot,' he said, 'and water spurted in around the door.'

Handfast Point and the Needles were early stack climbs for me. In fact they could to a certain extent be looked on as consolidating confidence in *Deflowerer* to the point where I felt brave enough to face up to the more serious nautical challenges posed by the high seas and dangerous currents off the north coast of Scotland, Orkney and Shetland. Our first visit was to the Maiden, the scene of Tom Patey's tragic accident, and use of Chris Watts' Renault Espace solved *Deflowerer*'s transport problem. Being blessed with perfect weather and calm seas, both the Maiden stacks were climbed in a memorable hitch-free weekend.

George had been persuaded to interrupt his munro-bagging to act as boatman and even the long chug across the exposed seaward end of Loch Eribol hardly stirred the adrenalin glands beyond acceptable levels. Doubtless we were lulled into a false sense of security. Epic-free trips to the far north were unlikely to continue.

Nicki was keen to visit John o' Groats, a name to conjure with but a place that we would probably never have visited were it not for the fine selection of stacks adorning the area. The innocently named Clett Rock was our first objective. Lying just off Holborn Head near Scrabster harbour it is visible from the Scrabster to Stromness ferry and had first attracted my attention some years before when on the way over to Orkney to climb the Old Man of Hoy. Also there were the stacks off Duncansby Head at the extreme north-eastern tip of the mainland. These, too, simply *had* to be visited. It was time to test *Deflowerer's* seaworthiness to the limit.

Clett Rock was one of the very few impressive Scottish stacks which had first been climbed without Tom Patey. In 1970 R. Jolly, M. Willis and D. Young made a semi-aided ascent up a series of overhanging grooves on the western end. Aid was used as necessary, but even so at Severe and A2 the line looks particularly challenging and to the best of my knowledge remains unrepeated. We had a completely free ascent in mind. Whether or not this was a realistic objective we didn't have a clue, but when in doubt one simply has to try such things.

Two cars were necessary to transport team and boat to Scrabster. Carless being still without a car (but presumably with a very large bank account as a result) persuaded an old friend of his, John Cuthbert, to make the trip and Nicki and I made up the rest of the team. The nearest launching spot was Scrabster, about two miles from the stack. We all felt vulnerably small squeezing alongside the comparatively huge Orkney Islands car ferry in the harbour. The looks we got from passengers and harbour staff alike did little to inspire confidence. I got the impression that *Deflowerer* was generally regarded as more suitable for an indoor play pool than the challenges of the Pentland Firth. To have the courage of one's conviction is vital in such circumstances. I pointed this out to John Cuthbert who was looking rather hesitant.

'My first time in an inflatable,' he replied.

From close up Clett Rock was stunning, 200 metres long, twenty metres wide and fifty metres high, with vertical or overhanging walls protecting its grassy summit at every point. Active armies of squawking fulmars patrolled overhung ledge systems, apparently gleeful at the prospect of doing battle with a climbing team. Fulmars will need little introduction to those who climb in northern Scotland. They are possibly the most objectionable bird to frequent these shores. Originally here only in small numbers, they have steadily taken over from the lovable puffins, the razorbills and guillemots to dominate large areas of the North. Their defence mechanism, which comes into play when they are just mildly concerned, is to regurgitate the contents of their stomachs with unerring accuracy. Anyone who saw Zoë Brown on the receiving end during the last Old Man of Hoy outside broadcast will know what I mean. Suffice it to say that they are out of favour with climbers and ornithologists alike.

Bird life aside, the scenery was inspiring. At half height on the western end we could just make out a rotting abseil sling left by the first ascensionists and trace the line of their ascent. On the landward side swirling currents filled the thirty-metre-wide channel between Clett Rock and the dripping verticality of the Caithness coast. An impressive sight indeed.

The north side seemed to offer the most promising possibility but a boat-scraping three-metre swell looked problematical. Fortunately, this was not breaking against the rock so it would be more a matter of jumping off at the right moment than worrying over when the boat-swamping mega-wave might break. One person would of course have to stay and look after the boat, as mooring it to the stack is a nonstarter even in the calmest seas. So Nicki and I both had several attempts before managing to establish ourselves on a large but outward sloping greasy ledge. Carless and John stayed in the boat to give each other some company and moral support whilst we grappled with the severity.

A groove line cutting through imposing ground proved to be of a reasonable standard and led to a point beneath a band of overhangs which looked likely to give the crux of the climb. The fulmars eyed us speculatively. The difficulties ahead looked challenging enough without the distraction of gushing bird vomit. Looks did not prove deceptive. Hard climbing with little protection led to a long, long reach for a prominent flat hold on to which a desperate mantelshelf was necessary to reach the end of the hardest section. More reasonable climbing then led to the top, untrodden for eighteen years. We found the remnants of the first ascensionists' cairn, but in the absence of any *in situ* stake our own abseil points had to be hauled to the top. These consisted of a metal fence post found on the drive up and half of one of the oars which had broken during some over-enthusiastic fending off. Such implements would have proved perfect for the job had the summit soil been more substantial. Although it was comparatively large in area, perfunctory prodding revealed an average depth to be twenty centimetres or so, hardly sufficient to hold a stake worthy of a fifty-metre abseil. The swell below was by now increasing and one or two curious onlookers were visible peering across from the mainland. Slate-grey clouds rolled in from the north and a situation of considerable interest was obviously developing.

At length marginal anchors were placed and in a gentlemanly

way I went first. The end of the abseil was in a shallow zawn on the seaward side of the stack which meant the swell tended to break against the back wall and bounce back as a breaking wave. This state of affairs proved particularly testing as Nicki dangled on the end of the abseil rope attempting to release herself at the right moment, whilst I struggled to manoeuvre the boat beneath her. At exactly the wrong moment a rolling bank of swell exploded against the back wall and simultaneously the engine cut, the boat was awash and Nicki was unsuccessfully trying to escape the clutches of the sea by climbing hand over hand up the abseil rope.

Substantial bailing and engine-drying operations ensued and, as Carless and John had their turn on the stack I began to feel distinctly unwell in the swaying boat. By the time we were ready to pick up Carless the swell was worse than ever and, being in need of manoeuvrability, yet fearful of the engine being swamped again, it seemed that the only option was to keep the engine running, bounce the nose of the boat off the rock, and for Carless to jump at the instant the boat hit the rock. A reverse gear would have been useful.

Putting the plan into action was more problematical. The by now huge swell meant that a moment after impact the prow of the boat scraped horrifically down the barnacle-covered rock and flopped neatly beneath a one-metre overhang before beginning to rise again. John and Nicki frantically pushed at the rock whilst I experienced the memorable sensation of being lifted out of the water still grimly hanging on to the engine controls.

Carless was forced to jump from about five metres whilst Nicki and John pushed their hardest, trying to ignore the water now pouring over the sides. With a tremendous popping and rasping noise the front was suddenly clear but Carless was on board and I and the engine were soaked.

Frantic use of the one remaining oar resulted in serious adrenalin flow but we managed to make an effective enough escape to less violent waters where the engine could be restarted and a safe return made to Scrabster. Another stack ticked and time to contemplate the rest of the weekend.

The North-East of Scotland enjoys rather more climbing potential than the average climber is aware of – so much so that the Caithness Club have produced an excellent little guide to the area. In 1988 I knew little of this and relied on the *Scottish Mountaineering*

Club Journal and less expert sources of information. Tourist office postcards are remarkably useful in identifying interesting coastal features. Thurso is no exception and my objectives folder contained several postcards showing 'Stacks at Duncansby' which I had picked up when passing through on trips to Orkney. Perusal of the Ordnance Survey map shows Duncansby Head to be the north-eastern tip of Scotland and the stacks to be on the east coast. A quick look at the postcard over a Thurso curry (I now like to keep my digestive system ready and waiting for Himalayan challenges) convinced the team that a visit was called for the next day.

Deflowerer is heavy. I think we were all left with this feeling uppermost in our minds having hauled the mass of rubber, floorboards, engine and extra bits and pieces 200 metres from the cars to an idyllic sandy beach on the northern side of Duncansby Head. This was as close as we could sensibly get and, though it meant we would have to round the headland, it certainly gave a wonderful camping spot and idyllic views out across the Pentland Firth to the Orkney Isles.

Thirty minutes later there was a lot more uncertainty in the party. Nicki once sailed round Cape Horn and was clearly the most nautically aware person aboard. Carless couldn't claim to be a born mariner but what he lacked in experience he more than made up in determination. Personally I had grown more confident about *Deflowerer* but had no real idea how close to the limit we might be operating. I was uncomfortably aware that the sea here was unlike anything I had come across before. It seemed that a strong flow up the east coast of Britain was meeting an equally strong current flowing eastwards through the Pentland Firth. The Pentland Firth water could clearly be seen to be slipping underneath the east coast water. Amidst the generally choppy seas an area of smooth visibly moving water seemed worth avoiding. Carless was at the controls and heading straight for it.

'Turn back.' Nicki was volubly certain of the best course of action.

'Get out to sea.' I felt that the sea looked friendlier in that direction.

'You're just being unnecessarily wimpish.' Carless was certain that everything was under control.

John Cuthbert kept quiet and looked unhappy. As he pointed out later, the current we were riding was probably stronger than

Deflowerer's engine so the options were rather limited anyway. Carless turned as we were being sucked towards the meeting point of the currents. It was too late to avoid problems completely and with a very noticeable increase in speed we sort of scuttled sideways across the fastest area of water to smack into a series of standing waves littered with white horses. The problem was not so much whether *Deflowerer* might sink – that seemed unlikely – more how we could minimise the risk of her capsizing. It was windy off the Head itself and every time the bow rose up beyond the crest of a wave there seemed to be a very real danger of a gust flipping us over. Aside from Carless, who was clearly enjoying himself, the others had now gone very quiet. Either they felt more comfortable than me or they were too frightened to speak. At my insistence we each took a corner position and leaned out as far as sensibly possible. It was perhaps a token effort at improving stability but by this time I was firmly of the view that any little measure to increase our chances was worthwhile. It was very wet and frightening hanging over the edge as the boat plunged into the calm of deeply angled troughs only to surge back up into the gusting wind on the wave crests. Both were equally worrying. In the troughs there was a real danger of the bow diving into the depths and the back flipping whilst on the crests the gusts could be felt lifting the front to the extent that a backwards flip was again a distinct possibility. Even Carless began to look slightly concerned.

Probably more due to the effect of the currents than any seafaring experience on our part, the stacks of Duncansby gradually came into view. As a bonus the wind, sea and currents all calmed down as we bumbled our way round the point into less exposed eastern waters. I tried not to think about the return journey.

The stacks did indeed look impressive. As the adrenalin flow receded the stumpy stack of Little Knee was the first in view, to be eclipsed by the magnificent sight of the Knee itself. This knobbly monster towers fifty metres or so in waters which appear to be perpetually ridden with strong currents and standing waves. Defended by angular overhangs on all sides and with a fearsome-looking summit block it would have to wait for another day, as would the eighty-metre-high wafer-thin Witch's Hat stack. Today we would concentrate on the easiest but highest objective: the Great Stack of Duncansby. Although we didn't know it at the time, this had enjoyed a previous ascent back in 1960. The landward side looked easiest and, as Carless set off soloing, the remaining three of us chugged around taking photographs. A keen wind was still blowing but the calm sea and weak sun contrasted sharply with the harsh environment off Duncansby Head. Judging by the speed of Carless's ascent (and descent) the difficulties were not great and as we changed over in the boat the threatening storm clouds promised to be more of an inconvenience than something which might stop us getting to the top.

There was one pitch of about Very Difficult standard but it was only thirty minutes or so before the remaining three of us were standing proudly on the summit. It was Carless's turn to chug around taking photographs. From our vantage point we could see him manoeuvring in the clear sea. Occasionally we would even see a guillemot diving in and swimming spectacularly in pursuit of a fish lunch – amazingly graceful compared to their airborne clumsiness. The clarity was so good that such sights were easily visible. So were the areas of shallow water – one of which Carless seemed to be heading straight for. As he was at the engine controls and engrossed in photography, looking over the side in an apparently safe area was clearly the last thing on his mind. A sudden bang followed by a high-pitched scream from the engine confirmed the worst. Broken engine. Carless was adrift with one oar.

As is so often the case in such situations things went from bad to worse in nothing more than a few seconds. The storm which had been threatening suddenly broke, and with the deluge a keen on-shore wind picked up. Being perched on the summit over sixty-five metres up there was little that we could do other than watch the drama unfold and take bets on the likely outcome. It certainly wasn't looking too good. Carless was hanging over the bow paddling furiously, first on one side and then the other, but still he seemed to be losing ground and getting pushed towards vertical cliffs dropping straight into the sea. Selfishly, I pondered our own predicament, stuck on top of a stack without a boat. But Carless was set to excel himself and a mega-diagonal rowing effort saw him controlling his drift to the extent that he somehow ended up in the lee of the stack rather than smashed against the cliffs. Once out of the wind he was able to row in towards us and, to everyone's considerable relief, secure himself and await our descent. I, for one, was very pleased. It would have been extremely unpleasant and embarrassing to be stuck overnight and have to be rescued.

We were not down yet, however. The torrential rain had dissolved the steep sections of mud and grass into frighteningly frictionless terrain. Whereas on the way up we had, moving together romped up this ground, we were now reduced to pitched down-climbing with runners to protect the last man. John seemed not to be used to this sort of thing. One pitch, although not difficult in ascent, was almost vertical. Nicki descended first and John second. She had placed some protection which John had to unclip from the rope below him and reclip into the one between him and me. An overhang at the top of the pitch prevented me from seeing exactly what he was doing. In fact it never crossed my mind that all might not be clear until he reached the first runner and an uncertain voice wafted up through the sheets of rain.

'What do you want me to do with this runner?'

Peering over the edge I could just about make out his questioning expression. It was wet and cold, and I was feeling irritable.

'Give it some clip, man – clip the bloody thing in.'

I have to admit that I may not have been a hundred per cent clear. John's expression was not that of a man enlightened, but then he didn't seek any further clarification and carried on down. I settled down on my muddy foothold of a stance and peered closely at my belay – a thread though a pile of loose blocks. It was nowhere near as good as I would like, but combined with the weight I would be able to take on my feet it would be sufficient to stop a slip. In the rush to get on to the stack and bearing in mind the apparently easy climbing, I had not brought my belay plate and was belaying with the rope around my waist.

Voices drifted up from below, suggesting that John was nearing Nicki's stance. When she had gone down she had shouted something about crossing a grass slope to reach a belay and I assumed that with the rope now running quickly through my hands, John was on this last stretch. When the rope ran out then, I had no hesitation in disentangling myself from the waist belay to give him those extra few centimetres he clearly needed to join Nicki. The jerk when it came was sudden and unexpected. It caught me at just the wrong time as I brought the rope up from my waist and over my head. The effect was that the strain came across the back of my neck pushing my head down towards the slope. Inevitably I began to lose my footing and scrabbled feverishly in the mud in an effort to both maintain my position above the overhang and minimise the strain on the belay. I stopped the fall with the smallest of safety margins.

'What the fuck is going on?'

At least I was still *in situ*, but feeling more than slightly flustered.

'Sorry,' came wafting up from below. To John of course it was 'just a little slip' as he transferred on to the grass. To me it was potentially much more serious: the strain had only half come on to the belay but even that was enough to cause some slight movement of the blocks which formed the thread.

I was still swearing quietly under my breath when more shouts from below suggested that John was safe and I should see about getting down myself. The mud was indeed treacherous and it was immediately clear that a second's loss of concentration could result in an uncontrollable slip. It was difficult to believe that less than an hour previously Carless had soloed up and down this line. The edge of the overhang held more shocks. Looking down I saw that the runners that Nicki had placed looked solid and reassuring. Unfortunately the rope hung about a metre free of them down to the grass where John had slipped. The karabiners hung uselessly against the rock. I was not pleased.

'Why the fuck have you left these unclipped?'

My words were carried away in the downpour as a tightening of the rope to my waist suggested yet more misunderstanding. For the second time in ten minutes I found myself scrabbling to prevent a tight rope from below plucking me from above the overhang.

On reflection of course my anger was misplaced. I remembered the look of incomprehension on John's face and realised it was down to me to make sure he had understood. Too late to do anything about that now. After a couple of abortive attempts I had to conclude that the prospect of a thirty-metre fall was too much and retreated upwards to the pile of blocks that had formed my belay. An abseil was unappealing but by leaving a sling and a karabiner entwined through as many only slightly insecure blocks as possible, I was able to rig up a top rope which gave a sufficiently strong sense of security to descend the pitch without further incident, retrieving the runners on the way.

Carless was looking uncharacteristically crestfallen. The rain was dripping from the end of his nose as he prodded hopefully at the engine. The propeller and drive shaft had escaped any serious damage but the pin necessary to transmit the drive to the propeller had sheared and disappeared. This was of course a safety feature of the engine. Any sensible crew would have carried a spare and fixed the problem within minutes. We did have a spare once, but search as I might it didn't seem to be around any more. I seemed to remember it on the bench in my shed at home. Much deliberation saw a temporary solution in the form of a thin knife-blade peg hammered in between a fortuitous flange and one of the propeller fins. It worked on a quick trial but no way would it be sufficient to get us back round Duncansby Head. It might just do to get us to the nearest landing spot on the mainland – but where would this be?

The tide seemed to be high and for as far as we could see the mainland was defended by vertical cliffs or very steep slopes dropping straight into the sea. To make matters worse the increasing breeze had formed a steady swell which now smacked disconcertingly into the cliffs at regular intervals. There was a glimmer of hope. At one point a small beach of large weed-covered boulders was visible and if the tide continued to go out it looked as if the exposed boulders might stretch to a point where 100 metres of very steep grass would lead to the clifftop. We elected to wait for the tide and row, use the engine, flap our feet behind – whatever was necessary to cross the 100 metres of sea and reach the mainland. I had more or less come to terms with losing *Deflowerer* but at least felt that we personally had a good chance of survival.

The arrival of a small fishing boat put matters in a slightly different light. A rescue would be embarrassing and surely we were just being wimpish about the wind, swell and lack of easy landing spot?

'Excuse me.' Nicki was the first to try and attract their attention. The gentle wording of her appeal combined with her naturally soft voice failed to attract a response.

'Hello.' Carless was next. His shouts were louder but still betrayed a feeling of uncertainty. One of the two fishermen looked up, gave a cursory wave in our direction and continued hauling in his lobster pots.

Hello can, I concluded, mean different things depending on how it is said. We all felt too sheepish to try again and we were left to contemplate the stupidity of our situation as the fishing boat chugged off into the distance, leaving us very much to our own devices.

The tide was going out. After an hour and a half we decided to go for it. The area of exposed boulders was bigger now. With the engine a definite uncertainty we would have to rely on one and a half oars to paddle across. The penalty for being blown off course would be a deadly experience at the base of the steep cliffs dropping straight into the water. An unhealthy silence had developed as Carless manned the engine (a curious responsibility for him considering his treatment of it a couple of hours previously!). John took the complete oar and I the broken one, and we paddled furiously, while liberal swearing from the stern indicated that Carless was spending the entire nerve-wracking 100-metre crossing failing to start the engine. Our hastily arranged plan was that as soon as we hit rock Nicki would jump off the bow and John and me off the sides whilst Carless's weight in the stern would ensure that the front was raised sufficiently to see us carried well on to the boulders.

A particularly large wave caught the boat and lifted us forcefully. We jumped as planned but a second wave crashed into the back of the boat forcing it forwards. Nicki's legs were caught between boulders as *Deflowerer* neatly rose and flattened her. She was only under the water for seconds but it was a distinctly unhappy bedraggled looking head which protruded from beneath the rubber as the water receded. Panicky scrabbling saw her escape before the next wave came in but a nastily bruised leg did not bode well for a death-defying scramble up the cliff.

The boulders were remarkably rounded and so covered with slippery weed that it was an easy enough job to slide the boat above the watermark and take stock of the situation. It was decided that Nicki and I should scale the cliff and tour North-East Scotland to locate somewhere that could supply the necessary pin for the engine before the tide turned. The local villages were no help, and even Thurso and Scrabster could not come up with the goods.

Seagull engines are as plentiful as seagull droppings on the South Coast but not popular in the north of Scotland. Perhaps they are judged insufficiently powerful to cope with the infamous Pentland Firth currents. A twenty-mile trip to Wick revealed no shops which could help us and as a last resort we found ourselves on the quayside optimistically pleading with fishermen who might by chance have a Seagull engine and spares concealed somewhere below deck. It was a long shot but in the absence of other alternatives, we had little to lose. Initial responses were far from encouraging.

'No, man, never heard of 'em.'

'Only seagull round here is the feathered kind.'

But persistence pays: on the fourth or fifth attempt one man thought that his boss 'might have a Seagull engine somewhere'. He had no spares but on our leaving a £5 deposit, he was kind or stupid enough to extract the vital pin from his boss's engine on the understanding that we were to return it the next day.

And so four hours after leaving the boat I arrived back at the bay, breathing heavily, but with the vital part. Nicki hobbled behind, struggling to convince herself that exercise is the best cure for a hurt leg. Only two hours or so of daylight remained but having seen how the Wick boatman had removed the pin from his engine, it was a simple copycat reversal of the process to repair ours. We could then contemplate that we still had to get back round Duncansby Head to the safety of our calm little launching bay. The currents seemed to have strengthened and the line of standing waves now stretched prominently out far into the open sea.

Rounding the tip of the headland was not going to be possible anywhere close to the land. We would have to head a mile or so out to sea where we hoped the currents would be less strong. With only three reasonable lifejackets and no need for all four of us to go in the boat, Nicki stayed to witness our efforts from the clifftop as the trusty Seagull roared into life.

'I'll call the rescue if I see you capsize.'

Her parting words were comforting, if not inspirational. Later she admitted that our small craft was lost to sight almost immediately and she didn't have a clue where we were until we gradually came into sight at our little bay. I don't know who was most relieved to see our little team reunited. Scottish stacks rarely disappoint.

The Needle is very much the 'other' sea stack on the island of Hoy. In fact, as its famous companion the Old Man is not completely surrounded by water at any state of the tide, there are those, myself included, who would say that the Needle is Hoy's *only* sea stack. Pedantic quibblings aside, it is certainly the most varied in terms of approach. Nicki and I had spotted its distant silhouette from the Scrabster to Stromness ferry and first inspected it at close quarters on a Christmas/New Year exploratory trip. It exceeded expectations and quickly rose to the top of my list of things to do.

In May 1990 George was continuing his Munro-bagging activities in the far north when his avid attention to local weather forecasts and on-the-spot experience led him to believe that a settled weekend was likely. He knew about my urge to head out to Hoy and on the Thursday evening the crucial telephone call was made. It was time for a long weekend in Hoy. Nicki was keen and Steve Sustad, a mellow but extremely talented American whom I had been climbing with regularly on the chalk cliffs, made up the third member of the team.

I had first met Steve through Victor Saunders and in fact it was probably a mutual understanding of Victor's approach to life that brought us together. Having both climbed extensively with him we were full of admiration of his abilities and amazement at his antics. Our combined Victor stories gave us virtually unlimited conversational fodder.

Steve's reputation as a tough and talented mountaineer was widely known and epics such as his near alpine-style success and harrowing retreat on Makalu's South-East Ridge with Doug Scott and Jean Afanassieff have gone down in mountaineering folklore. I first met him in the Palm Tree pub in the East End of London where the North London Mountaineering Club unofficially meets on a Wednesday evening. Falling into conversation with him, I found that he was far from the intense determined mountaineer that I had, for some reason, expected.

Not only did he seem to be very mellow and modest about his achievements but he also had a predilection for what might be termed 'adventure climbing', by which I mean anything from sea stacks to frozen London drainpipes to the chalk coast of Kent. In short he was an ideal companion for a three-day trip to Orkney. George came, too, plus Nanda the dog. We had reluctantly already decided to leave *Deflowerer* in London.

The Needle is one of those special stacks that looks more and more exciting the closer one gets to it. Approaching from the Glen of the Berry across open sheep-cropped grass slopes, the summit sticks up higher than the adjacent cliffs and beckons irresistibly. From the cliff edge the view is even more dramatic. The cliffs of Hoy drop sheer for seventy metres into the waters of the Pentland Firth whilst only ten metres off-shore the stack towers up to a small flat summit above brooding overhanging walls which girdle it completely at about half height. This was Steve's first sight of the Needle and his usual laidback attitude was being replaced by a look of boyish enthusiasm. An adventure was in store.

'I can't swim very well,' he complained, 'so you or Nicki will have to abseil into the sea and swim out to rig up a tyrolean traverse'.

With anyone else I would have argued. But I remembered Steve's open-fingered 'swimming' technique off Lover's Leap Rock on the West Coast of Ireland and the sight of nothing but the top of his helmet bobbing out of the turbulent water every now and then. I agreed to go first.

The abseil was long – two ropes tied together – and it seemed mildly ridiculous stripping off and abseiling wearing nothing but a harness. Disconnecting myself from the rope was interesting too. I just thanked my lucky stars that the sea was outrageously calm for the area and the odd dip below the surface was of no real concern. But what next? From the point where I had entered the water it was a good twenty metres across to the stack. Only seven metres across the opposite side of a narrow inlet was a reasonable ledge. From there it would only be another seven-metre swim to gain the stack. Twenty metres looked a long way and I too am not noted for my swimming ability. I chose the ledge. Just after I had dropped into the water I became aware of the seal. The water glistened on its whiskers. If I had been viewing from the safety of a boat I would no doubt have appreciated the proximity of this beautiful creature. At close quarters one can feel very vulnerable – especially when wearing nothing but a harness, even more so when it decided to dive. Where had it gone? What was it doing? I continued hesitantly, one hand clasped protectively around my balls and the other flailing wildly, until I was able to clamber out on to the ledge I had been heading for.

A diagonal abseil saw Nicki and Steve join me in an unsportingly dry and orderly manner. Then it was necessary for us all to swim across the short deep channel to gain ledges on the stack itself. Steve listened with interest to Nicki's stories of climbing through hordes of puking fulmars, before setting off up a vertical wall liberally endowed with horizontal slots well decorated with the telltale projecting white bottoms.

Nicki's nose shrivelled at the stance. Steve, though, was in full climbing mode, oblivious to all discomfort.

'Rewarding activity,' he spluttered as the fulmar puke started to fly. 'Glad the next lead's yours.'

The stack overhung all the way round at this point and the climbing looked far from easy. Rounded edges and poor protection combined to produce a memorable pitch, followed by easier ground to the top.

The summit was a small but spectacular platform which George did his best to capture in photographs from his clifftop viewpoint. The results would no doubt have been more captivating had Nicki not been curled up in a ball of agony with fulmar puke impregnated in her contact lens.

Descent offered no options. We would clearly have to swim back to the mainland, but we could jumar up our abseil rope or swim away southwards and scramble to the clifftop. Nicki and I chose the latter whilst Steve, being only too aware of his aquatic uncertainties, opted to jumar. Half an hour later all three of us had become separated.

Nicki, being the strongest swimmer, had swum off into the distance whilst my leapfrog-from-ledge-to-ledge technique was soon abandoned in favour of a character-building scramble up to the clifftop. I arrived back first. Steve was still jumaring with the clothes and Nicki was nowhere to be seen. But my ensuing cold wait was soon relieved by the sight of a naked lady skipping along the clifftops from the south. The sheep paid little attention. George adjusted his glasses fractionally before Nicki sank crutch deep into a spongy area of bog and was jumped on by Nanda. My father did not know her very well at that stage but in full gentlemanly mode produced a raincoat to cover the mud-splattered goose pimples of his future daughter-in-law.

My relationship with Nicki was becoming increasingly serious by this stage. Remembering Marie in the Avon Gorge, I was nervous that débâcles such as Duncansby and Clett Rock might have a detrimental effect on our relationship. This appeared not to be the case. In fact it seemed that the reverse was true. Before we were married in 1991 she admitted that bird puke, challenging seas and adrenalin-packed climbing provided a combination that was fully approved. I walked up the aisle comfortable in the knowledge that Scotland's sea-stack calls would continue to be answered.

12

Kishtwar

I was lying curled up in my nice warm bed comfortably dozing before the alarm. A little voice spoke very clearly in my ear.

'Daddy. Have you got a hairy bottom?'

Tessa, our two-year-old daughter, had climbed into bed and now looked at me quizzically. This was clearly a very important question which required a considered answer.

'Just the right amount of hair,' I heard myself saying after a moment's sleepy thought.

'Mine is not hairy at all.'

This was undeniably true. I hesitated for a moment wondering whether to prolong this conversation or suggest that we go downstairs for breakfast. Before I had answered, though, a new subject crossed her mind.

'I want to draw a mountain with Daddy on top.'

This was a line of conversation that I felt more comfortable with.

Staggering downstairs I poured the cornflakes and placed her scrap pad and crayons on the table. This was becoming the usual, and very pleasant, way to start the day.

'I am going to draw Cerro Kishtwar, Daddy.'

Her pronunciation was perfect although her drawing bore little resemblance to the unclimbed mountain in the Indian Himalaya that was beginning to dominate my thoughts again. It did have a stick man purporting to be me on top though. Very promising.

Driving to work I took time to consider Cerro Kishtwar further. I had been there before, back in 1989. On that occasion a mystery virus downed the usually hyperactive Mike Morrison just below the bergschrund. His illness was later diagnosed as something normally caught from sheep – a subject that Mike seems to have been rather reluctant to expand upon. The result was a frustrated team who could do no more than stare at the mountain in perfect conditions and wonder if they would ever return. It seemed that my first venture in India was even less successful than my first trip to Pakistan. At least we crossed the bergschrund on Bojohagur. Cerro Kishtwar was a name given to this fine peak by Simon Richardson in 1988 after a fancied resemblance to the spectacular fang of Cerro Torre in Patagonia. It has no local name and was unclimbed in 1989 but photographs of its spectacular profile were beginning to appear in the climbing magazines and I had that uncomfortable feeling that it would attract some able suitors before I felt the time was right to return. I was right. In 1991 two British climbers, Andy Perkins and Brendan Murphy, tried a line of ice streaks clinging tenuously to the very steep North-West Face. After seventeen days of extremely difficult capsule-style climbing they rounded the North Buttress on to the North-East Face, only to find more difficult climbing and grind to a halt four pitches from the top.

I chewed these points over whilst driving to Long Eaton station. 1993 had developed into what seemed the right year to return. Having agreed an alternate-years greater-ranges schedule with Nicki, this was to be a Himalayan year but, having moved into another part of the Revenue in Nottingham, there had been a tremendous personal upheaval caused by moving house and Nicki's watercolour conservation business at the same time. To complicate matters further we had bought an uninhabitable wreck of a house just south of Derby and then got involved in moving both Marjorie (Nicki's mother) from Portsmouth and George from Wembley. All in all, it proved to be a rather full year, which necessitated an easy-to-organise expedition. Having been to Cerro Kishtwar before I felt I knew the system inside out, so it seemed the ideal objective. The time to settle an old score had come.

Mike was a little uncertain about whether or not he had fully recovered from his 1989 virus but No Brains, who had been with us in Peru, was keen to climb with him, so they teamed up. For my part I tend to stick with those I know and trust in the big mountains. Knowing how irrepressibly talented Victor is above the bergschrund, I reasoned that if I could get him that far we were in with a chance. He was keen and we looked forward to teaming up together on a big mountain for the first time since Spantik.

I sent off the necessary application forms and peak fee to the Indian Mountaineering Foundation and waited . . . and waited

. . . and waited. Nothing happened beyond an acknowledgement that our application had been received. Reminding letters and faxes in our best polite Indi-English were unsuccessful in eliciting a response. In desperation we contacted other British teams hoping to climb in India that year. Duncan Tunstall and Chris Pasteur were to try Nilkantha near Josimath and Noel Craine, Paul Pritchard and Johnny Dawes' party were to have a go at the East Face of Meru in the Gangotri. They too had heard nothing.

We were due to leave on 23rd August. By the beginning of August it was clear that all was not going well. Worse still, our team was beginning to fall apart. No Brains was becoming increasingly uncertain due to problems at home and disturbing news was reaching my ears about Victor. Victor is one of those people who would like to keep everyone happy all of the time. In terms of tempting mountaineering objectives he also finds it difficult to say no.

And so when, having arranged to come to Cerro Kishtwar, he subsequently received an invite to climb on K2 immediately beforehand it was inevitable that he should say yes. I was unhappy. It seemed to me that if he gave his all on K2 (and I couldn't imagine Victor attempting such a project half-heartedly), then he would not have enough energy left for sustained technical climbing of the sort we would undoubtedly encounter on Cerro Kishtwar. Victor though was his usual effervescently evasive self.

'It will be fine,' he said. 'In fact better, because I'll be fit and acclimatised.'

I remained unconvinced and drew up contingency plans. It was agreed that if Victor was not in Delhi to meet us on 23rd August I would telephone Steve Sustad in Shropshire who would drop everything and get on the first plane to Delhi. Perhaps the most revealing part of this arrangement was that I believed him.

Victor headed off for K2 according to plan and I had no reason for heightening my concern until I got a telephone call from Andy Perkins who had just returned from Gasherbrum IV, a mountain very close to K2. He opened in a worrying manner.

'I saw Victor last week.'

'Yes?' I was hesitant. Victor could have got up K2. Andy could be phoning to tell me – or he could have bumped into him in Islamabad *en route* for Delhi. Such possibilities seemed distinctly unlikely from the tone of his voice.

'He says he might be a bit late for Cerro Kishtwar.' The news was not entirely unexpected. How late? I tried to elicit a bit more information from Andy. It seemed that when he saw Victor he was just about to have a final try at the mountain.

This would, I guessed, take up to a ten-day round trip from Base Camp. Andy and I chewed the timescale over on the phone. It didn't look good. In desperation I telephoned Victor's wife Maggie, who had an itinerary for the K2 trip. It showed the envisaged departure from Base Camp date as being virtually the same as our supposed meeting date in Delhi.

I had to stop dithering and replace Victor. A fax was sent to Skardu telling him this and Steve, in his usual laid-back way, stepped in at a week's notice. I was incredibly grateful. Although I had never been on a mountaineering trip with Steve, I had climbed Scottish winter routes and Dover sea cliffs with him and had no qualms about the change. I could now return to worrying about things at the India end. To think that this was supposed to be an 'easy-to-organise' trip!

Colonel Amit Roy, Director of the Indian Mountaineering Foundation, was obviously getting used to my early morning telephone calls.

'Michael – very nice to speak to you again. Permission? No, no, nothing from the Ministry yet. Yes, you are right – time is short. A problem? No, I don't think so. It is very difficult.' Then I received what I felt to be the ultimate accolade for my hassling skills.

'I will see the Minister myself,' he said, 'and I will wear my uniform.'

Of course I knew the real trouble was the political hot potato of Kashmir, repeatedly fought over by Muslims and Hindus. Three weeks before we were due to leave a bus was stopped between the towns of Doda and Kishtwar and thirteen people were taken off and murdered. This was on the road that we had followed in 1989.

In the week before departure I phoned the Indian Mountaineering Foundation every day and also took to hassling the key Under Secretary at the Home Affairs Ministry whose name and number had been given to me by the Foundation. Ultimately the liaison officer's measurements were read to me over a crackly phone line and Steve's details were faxed through for immediate clearance. By the time we left on 22nd August the liaison officer's details had been confirmed in writing but there had been no movement on the Home Affairs Ministry approval front. Never before had I left Britain feeling so uncertain about what I was letting myself in for.

Colonel Amit Roy looked surprised to see us.

'What are you doing here?' seemed not to be an over-positive greeting. 'Did you not get my letter?'

The 'easy to organise Kishtwar trip' file was bulging impressively. I extracted a bundle of letters.

'Which one?'

He looked quizzically through the mound of paperwork but clearly failed to find the one he was after. He called for his own file which was even bigger than ours, and waved a letter confidently in our direction.

'This one.' We all crowded round it. I certainly didn't recognise it, neither did I like the turn that our initial meeting was taking. Amit Roy was pointing at a paragraph which looked to be horribly clear: 'You may plan your expedition only after clearance from Ministry of Home Affairs.' There was no doubt that this is what it said, it was also addressed correctly. I stared at it glumly. This was not a good start.

No Brains, though, had noticed something: 'It's dated the 19th August,' he pointed out. 'Today is only the 23rd, you knew that we were leaving London on the 22nd.'

More people were called into the office. Much arm waving and shouting in Hindi resulted but of course the situation remained the same. Permission had not been granted but then neither had it been denied. We tried a new tack. It seemed that it was the word 'Kishtwar' that was one of the biggest stumbling blocks, with the town of Kishtwar being increasingly terrorist ridden. It could not be denied that the peak had been nicknamed 'Cerro Kishtwar' and that we had applied for permission to approach via the town of Kishtwar. We had also called ourselves the British East Kishtwar Expedition, which didn't exactly help. Perhaps we could approach via another route and rename the peak – or at least emphasise its proximity to the Ladakh border. This we suggested to the Indian Mountaineering Foundation. Last minute alterations do not go down well at the best of times. Suggestions were made and notes taken but, squirm as we might, we could not escape from the magic word 'Kishtwar' which seemed to be getting a more and more negative reaction.

By the next morning gloom and despondency were settling in. We retired to the Indian Mountaineering Foundation climbing-wall to await the outcome and while away a few exceedingly hot, sweaty hours. At least one expedition has ground to a halt here due to broken limbs. Dangerous places these climbing-walls – but at least broken limbs are conclusive whereas Indian bureaucracy can leave you on the edge for ever.

On our third day in Delhi I resorted to my best civil servant technique to bluff my way into the Home Affairs Ministry.

'No callers until 11 a.m. and then appointments only.'

I tried a new tack. 'I must telephone Mr Deepakwallah from reception.'

I was inside. And while the security man's attention was deflected by some other importunates, I sprinted upstairs to the first floor which, as luck would have it, appeared to be the bureaucratic nerve centre of the Home Affairs Ministry. A throng of generally irate foreigners milled around on the landing awaiting their turn to present their case for such things as visa extensions. Not having an appointment, a confident approach was necessary. An official sat forlornly at a desk guarding access to the corridors of power.

'I have to see Mr Deepakwallah – I spoke to him from Britain.'

'You must see his secretary first.'

Luck was on my side again. I was fortunate enough to bump into a lady coming out of another office. 'Permanent Secretary', it said on her door. This sounded exceptionally important. The time had come for a convincing performance. Years of Inland Revenue training were to be put to the test.

'I wonder if you could help me, madam. I seem to be having a little problem with some of your staff.'

She invited me into her office. I couldn't believe it. If my understanding of the grading structure was right I had the attention of somebody who had the authority actually to do something. I spread my map out on the table and explained the problem briefly.

'We would like to attempt this unclimbed mountain on the Ladakh border, approaching via Manali and the Rohtang Pass. We do not want to go anywhere near the town of Kishtwar or the troubles in Kashmir.'

There was a pregnant pause as she studied the map.

'Yes, your plan is very sensible. Come back this afternoon with three copies of your map and I will arrange the authority.'

We chatted over pleasantries for a couple of minutes before I was free to let my elation boil over and dance down the stairs, out past the perpetually hassled security guard and back to the photocopier at the Indian Mountaineering Foundation. It was going to be all right after all. Cerro Kishtwar, here we come!

'Sorry, you cannot use the photocopier without the personal authority of the Director.'

The man who was physically preventing me from using the photocopier was absolutely adamant.

'Where is the Director?'

'He will not be back until tomorrow.'

It doesn't take long to get back to reality in India. A photocopying/long-distance-telephoning-type shop obliged and I was back at the Home Affairs Ministry.

'No admission without appointment card.'

Why does every step here involve going back to square one?

The first floor was more challenging this time. The Permanent Secretary was not in her office. But a man who sat in the corridor said helpfully, 'I will take you to your file.'

This sounded interesting. We passed under a prominent sign saying 'Strictly Nationals Only' into a large open-plan office. Buff-coloured files were piled high on every desk. Curious faces turned to look in my direction. I sensed this treatment was unusual. I was shown a desk and a file with 'British East Kishtwar 1993' neatly typed across the cover was placed in front of me. Judging by its dog-eared appearance my frantic efforts of the past few weeks had at least prompted its handling. I waited expectantly.

'We must have approval of your revised approach route from the Indian Mountaineering Foundation. Three copies are needed.'

The official was insistent, pleas to see the Permanent Secretary again proved fruitless. Perhaps he felt sorry for me. I was allowed to phone Mike back at the Indian Mountaineering Foundation. My clerical man disappeared as I struggled with the phone. Getting through was not easy.

For ten minutes I had little to do other than re-dial the number and inspect my surroundings. Fans whirred on every desk. Paperweights struggled unsuccessfully to contain piles of paperwork. I had just got through to Mike when I became aware of another voice bellowing in my ear.

'You are using my telephone, and my desk – why are you here? You are not a National. Did you not see the sign?'

The usual occupant of the desk was not impressed. Arm-waving confusion and much use of Hindi erupted simultaneously – but the message got through. Mike would bring the necessary authority as soon as was humanly possible.

'Now it is time for lunch. You must return at 2 p.m.'

After lunch we presented three copies of our revised approach route, but it was not on the correct Mountaineering Foundation application form.

'We must follow regulations,' pronounced the clerk.

A controlled loss of temper seemed in order and had the desired effect of winning another personal audience with the Permanent Secretary.

'Leave it with me and call back tomorrow morning for your permission letter.'

To me she was a jewel of serenity and common sense amidst a sea of incomprehensible chaos.

I slept well that night and before leaving for the Ministry next morning felt confident enough to broach the matter of a liaison officer with the Indian Mountaineering Foundation.

'Very sorry but your liaison officer has been allocated to another expedition. We will sort it out. Don't worry.' I sensed the ride ahead was not going to be as smooth as I would like.

At 3 p.m. the next day Mike and I finally walked into the sumptuous office of the First Secretary. This really was rising through the ranks. As far as I could work out we had reached the top. Certainly I felt uncomfortably self-conscious in my rather indelicate East/West mix of smelly T-shirt and baggy shalwar suit bottoms. Mike too seemed uneasy in his very short shorts. Our path to this point had been via another day of misunderstandings and unavailable key officials. Now our time had come. Flanked by the Permanent Secretary and various other apparently high-ranking dignitaries, the First Secretary rose to welcome us. It felt not unlike some strange kind of investiture procedure. I braced myself for a long speech. But the key man was clearly not one for unnecessary rhetoric.

'Hello. Very nice to meet you. Here is your authority. I hope you enjoy your stay in the mountains.'

Everyone shuffled out of the office. The Permanent Secretary, who had by now almost adopted us, invited us into her office for a cup of tea. I took a moment to read through the authority letter. A phrase caught my eye.

'The Home Affairs Ministry is content with the expedition's revised plans *as long as they are approved by the Defence Ministry*.' I turned to the Permanent Secretary and enquired why nothing seemed to be straightforward. Her answer was simple and irrefutable.

'We work as we were taught by the British.'

Mike and I could not help but smile. By the evening of our fifth day out of Britain I felt completely drained but we at last had all our gear, all the necessary pieces of paper and all our climbing team. Victor had presumably received Maggie's fax – or in any event he had not appeared – and all we needed was a liaison officer who was duly chosen from volunteers who happened to be in action on the Indian Mountaineering Foundation climbing-wall.

Deepak Jilani was the Indian bouldering champion. He had done some mountaineering before but had not been unduly impressed. Having been called in by the Director, his first question was about the bouldering potential at Base Camp. Try as I might, I could only recall a scree slope above our tents. Deepak dithered and then for better or for worse he decided to come.

Manali lies in the Kulu Himalaya – about twelve hours' bus ride from Delhi. It wasn't really in the right direction for Cerro Kishtwar but at least it was in the foothills and away from the stifling heat of the city. I began to feel more alert again. There were problems of course, not least being our rapidly depleting funds, the apparent lack of public transport beyond here and general uncertainty as to where the roadhead was. In the circumstances, negotiating a cost for our two jeeps from Manali to the roadhead was, er, interesting.

The road though was magnificent. Steep twisting hairpins rose up the heights of the Rohtang Pass at over 4000 metres and then made a slightly more gentle descent down to the Chenab river valley on the far side. To the north and north-east we could see the recently opened Inner Line areas of Spiti and Ladakh. Hardly any foreigners (and very few Indian mountaineers) have visited these areas since 1948. There is such a lot of climbing still to be done in India.

Our route was to the west following the churning grey mass of the Chenab river down to the town of Atholi – only a few hours' drive

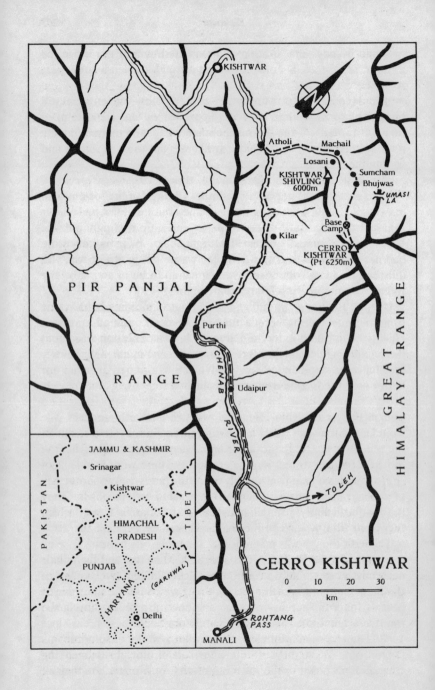

KISHTWAR

Atholi   Machail

Losani   Sumcham

KISHTWAR
SHIVLING
6000m

Bhujwas

UMASI
LA

Base
Camp

Kilar

CERRO
KISHTWAR
(Pt 6250m)

PIR PANJAL

Purthi

RANGE

Udaipur

CHENAB RIVER

TO LEH

GREAT HIMALAYA RANGE

JAMMU & KASHMIR

• Srinagar

• Kishtwar

HIMACHAL
PRADESH

PUNJAB

HARYANA   (GARHWAL)

• Delhi

PAKISTAN

TIBET

CERRO KISHTWAR

0   10   20   30
km

ROHTANG
PASS

MANALI

upstream from the political flashpoint of Kishtwar. The road in the upper Chenab valley does not connect with that leading in from Kishtwar to Atholi. We knew that there was a gap but the time and porterage costs necessary to bridge it were unknown which could still bring the expedition to a premature conclusion. Our jeeps bumped on into the night. We ticked off the small villages on our inadequate map, trying to judge how much further we had to go to Atholi and willing the road to continue.

Just past Udaipur the jeeps stopped. I guessed that we were about 150 kilometres short of Atholi. If this was the end of the road we had blown it.

The landslide looked pretty substantial in the light of the headlamps. At least our drivers thought so. Negotiations were short-lived and acrimonious. No they were not going to wait till morning. No they were not going to try and cross now. Yes they were returning to Manali immediately.

It was a miserable team that crawled out of sleeping-bags at first light. The debris sprawled across the road was indeed a serious obstacle which would need a bulldozer to clear it. It was difficult to be too irate over the jeep drivers' entrenched views the night before. Our reactions varied considerably. No Brains was for giving up our efforts to reach Cerro Kishtwar and tackling something more readily accessible instead. Mike Morrison and I seethed with frustration working out dates, finances and alternative lines of approach.

Steve's Himalayan experience was standing him in good stead: 'If there is nothing to do . . . do nothing,' came from deep within the Sustad sleeping-bag.

Various locals began to appear. Many of them smoked short curly pipes with huge chunks of cannabis wedged in the bowls. They looked particularly relaxed and regarded Steve in a way which suggested that in travelling terms at least they were on the same wavelength.

By lunchtime there was still no progress. Mike was tearing his hair out whilst I can scarcely have been any less agitated. No Brains was clearly beginning to despair. Steve, though, was lying on our pile of gear saying how nice it was to be able to enjoy his reading in the warm sunshine. We had a lot to learn from Steve.

A dusty blue truck rumbled into view and twenty or so occupants jumped out. Whether they were some sort of official roadmending crew or simply a truckload of commuters I wasn't sure. As they all

continued on in the vehicle afterwards I can only assume they fell
into the latter category. Their prowess at landslide clearing though
was such that they could easily have excelled in the former. The
landslide that I had formerly classed as clearable only by bulldozer
was, within half an hour, modified to the extent that the truck with
all of us aboard was capable of a teetering but effective crossing.

After an hour or so the truck stopped. The road did continue but
the universal opinion of those on board was that this place – Purthi
– was where we should alight and hire mules for the ninety or so
kilometres left to Atholi.

Mules are truly wonderful animals. Each one will carry ninety kilos
at a 1993 cost of 200 rupees (about £5.50) per day. They don't go on
strike, they don't need additional animals to carry their own food,
and they move more quickly and work out cheaper than porters. In
short, give me mules any day. We hired four to take us firstly down
the Chenab gorge to Atholi (an estimated three days) and then on
to our Base Camp (another four days).

For a walk that was supposed to be *down* a river valley there
seemed to be an awful lot of up and down on the way to Atholi.
Road building was very much in evidence with crèches for the
roadworkers' children perched beneath shattered overhangs and
above huge drops into the churning mass of the Chenab river. At
one point a blast from the far side of the gorge sent splinters of rock
showering on to our mules which retreated in disarray and needed
persuasive handling by Ashok our mule man to run the gauntlet
for a second time. Steve seemed to like walk-ins, so much so that
I didn't really see very much of him. Whilst I lumbered along at
the back in my own private heat and dust haze he surged ahead
– at one point to the extent that he followed a false trail and
mistakenly gained about 600 metres up a side valley. I couldn't
believe his fitness level. However would I keep up with the man
on the mountain? Sitting behind a Tax Office desk had clearly not
been good training for this sort of thing. I stumbled along in my
own hot and sweaty world of exhaustion. Somewhere ahead of me
were our mules. My only hope was that I would be able to catch
them up every night.

Ashok turned out to be a remarkably fast and determined mule
driver. Our second day started at around 6 a.m. and was still going
strong when I caught up with a struggling mule in the dusk at 6 p.m.

It seemed that I had come across a mule that was as tired as me – a definite first.

Towards the end of three very long days we were approaching Atholi when we realised that our mules had fallen behind. A lengthy wait in the sweltering sun still did not bring them in sight. I began to fear the worst. There was an awful lot of crucial (and valuable) equipment in Ashok's hands. Occasional accidents are inevitable – one of our mules had fallen down a moraine bank in 1989 – but the possible disappearance of all four mules and two mule men was potentially embarrassing to say the least.

Steve wandered back along the part-blasted road to see what had happened. He returned after an hour or so: 'Not very good at climbing, these mules.'

It seemed that a blast from the road builders had blocked the track with huge splintered boulders right in the middle of a section where the road was being fashioned across a vertical cliff. The mules were unable to negotiate this obstacle and there was nothing that we could do but continue to Atholi and wait for the blockage to be cleared. It had been so hot slogging along the dusty road that the idea of returning for tents and sleeping-bags appealed to no one. In any event we had been to Atholi before and knew an excellent place to spend the night on a cool wooden veranda in an open grassy area called Gulabhar.

The gun-toting army officer peering over the sandbags at Gulabhar bridge was not convinced by our story. As foreigners with no equipment and thin stories about mules 'somewhere behind', suspicions were immediately aroused. We were led away through a clearly tense army camp to the local police chief to have our stories checked out. We had clearly underestimated the effect that the Kashmiri troubles were having in the upper Kishtwar valley. Naïvely I had assumed that the killing of thirteen people on the Kishtwar–Doda public bus, reported in Britain a few weeks before, had been an isolated incident. Now it became clear that the terrorists were waging a war designed to focus world attention on the Kashmir problem.

A Swiss engineer working on the Kishtwar hydro-electric power scheme had been kidnapped and rumours were rife of atrocities against local dignitaries and further plans to involve foreigners.

Deepak did a sterling job convincing the police chiefs that our motley crew was in fact an 'authorised' party, so having been reunited with Ashok and the mules early next morning, we were allowed to beat a hasty exit up the side valley towards the village of Machail along the track ultimately leading to the popular trekking pass of the Umasi La which crosses the main Himalayan divide and gives an idyllic trek from Kishtwar to Ladakh. Four years before we had bumped into several trekking parties (one of which had employed a porter to carry a mountain bike over the pass!); this year we saw no foreigners at all. The troubles were hitting the tourist trade hard.

Atholi onwards was still the beautiful, relaxing walk through forested tracks and small unspoiled villages that I remembered from four years previously. We could have been a million miles away from the tension and troubles only a few hours below. Our main problem now was the weather – it rained, and looked set to continue. I had pleasant memories of strolling up these paths with Nicki in 1989. Then all had been sparkling sunlight and sharp shadows, interspersed with relaxing cups of tea in the numerous tea stops. Now I trudged along in the mist, boots squelching, whilst water seeped visibly into some of the mule loads. I consoled myself with the fact that as I could now keep up with the mules I must at least be getting fitter (or the mules more tired).

Gaining height towards Machail it is difficult not to be aware of the changes in religion. The main Chenab valley is predominantly Muslim, complete with mosques and regular amplified calls to prayer. From Atholi up to Machail the Hindu gods become more prominent with small but ornate temples along the way. Above Machail – only about a day and a half from the Chenab valley – we were in a Buddhist world. Losani, just beyond Machail and Sumcham, and at over 3000 metres the highest village on the Kishtwar side of the Umasi La, boasts fluttering white prayer flags and inhabitants distinctly Tibetan in origin. The change is truly remarkable over such a short distance.

At Sumcham it was still raining. Ashok was beginning to look distinctly unhappy. He hadn't been beyond Atholi before and having to trust our assurances was making him a nervous man. The rest of us were enjoying Sumcham. The atmosphere was so much more relaxed than in the bureaucratic world down below. At previous tea stops negotiations were necessary over every cup. Here tea and food flowed freely, despite our protestations. The way ahead, however, was distinctly rougher than that travelled so far. I could only hope that the weather would improve and Ashok would get into the mellow but tough mood of the Sumcham inhabitants. Before moving on it seemed to be obligatory to meet the village elder. I had met him four years previously when he had been claimed to be ninety. He certainly looked it but his tough leathery skin and sacking dress did not a conceal a determined twinkle in his eye. This time he looked much the same but was claimed to be eighty-five. I pointed out that he had lost five years instead of gaining four but, after a short consultation, the village spokesman remained confident.

'The mountain air,' he said with a broad smile, 'is good for his health. It makes him younger.'

With smiles all round our dripping party left Sumcham and crossed the flat plains of Bhujwas beneath the towering North Face of Kishtwar Shivling, first climbed by Steve Venables and Dick Renshaw over ten years before. The top was wreathed in cloud but it looked worryingly hard – harder than I remembered it looking. I hoped Cerro Kishtwar wouldn't look harder this year. Certainly I didn't feel up to any hard climbing just yet. The walk-in was proving to be quite challenging enough now a rapidly developing altitude headache had arrived to accompany my squelching boots and general exhaustion.

By late afternoon we were wandering around on steep slopes somewhere between the meadows of Bhujwas and the ablation valley where we wanted to have our Base Camp. We were lost. None of us could remember the route we had followed before. Steve was very understanding.

'I like incompetence,' he said. 'It adds something to a trip.'

I smiled weakly, not sure if he was joking.

Ashok was clearly not joking. He frowned, contemplating a mule's leg, cut whilst stumbling on a boulder slope. 'The mules can go no further.'

It was difficult to say if he was right. They certainly weren't looking very frisky but then they were probably as wet and miserable as we were. An interim compromise was reached. *We* would carry the loads to a flattish area 100 metres higher and negotiate properly there.

I don't think I had ever tried to carry ninety kilos before and I certainly will never try again. Only Ashok could make the slightest impression on a full load. The rest of us struggled pathetically with forty-five-kilo half loads. I felt literally squashed into the ground by the weight. Admittedly I was still not feeling my best but all the same I thanked my lucky stars that I was not born a mule.

The atmosphere was damp and dispirited as negotiations started again. Initially there was stalemate. Ashok refused to consider reloading the mules and demanded additional payment for something that appeared to equate to distress already incurred, presumably by the mules. Then we got down to the nitty gritty – money. It seemed that in return for a further 2000 rupees (approximately £60) he would 'do whatever was necessary' to get all of our gear to Base Camp. Funds were running distressingly low with nearly all the contingency funds having been used up during the lengthy stay in Delhi and expensively indirect approach route. Even so, the expedition would come to a grinding halt if agreement could not be reached. It took an hour or so but a compromise was reached for 1000 rupees (I preferred to think of it as £7.50 each). We would spend the night where we were and, with mules fully rested, Ashok guaranteed somehow to get our gear to Base Camp the following day. He was true to his word.

Weather forecasts were not available at the head of our ablation valley and it still rained. It rained for ten days. Not only did this dump lots of new snow on the mountain, it also left us a mere eighteen days to do what we had come to do. The part of me that never gets reconciled to the pace of Himalayan expedition couldn't help but consider that we could have done several good routes in the Alps by now. Instead we sat in damp tents in moods varying from the mellow Sustad ('plenty of time to read my book') line to the caged animal ('I've got to get out climbing') Morrison approach. Deepak too was suffering mental anguish.

'My boulders,' he lamented, 'are too wet for climbing.'

Acclimatisation forays resulted in a gear-stash at the foot of the face and by the time the weather improved Steve and I had worked out that our proposed line should take about eight days from Base Camp and we had thirteen days left. Bad weather or not, it was time to go.

It took six hours spread over the evening of one day and the early morning of the next to reach the foot of the face and whilst we were doing this the weather had gradually improved. By the time we crossed the bergschrund it was fine at last. We had already got farther than last time and were underway at last.

Crisp front-pointing up deep convoluted runnels allowed quick progress.

'Shit.'

Steve is not prone to unnecessary cursing, but the sound of disgruntled mumbling continued. Even the word 'down' surfaced at one point. I had guessed the problem. The sight of his ice-axe pick broken clean off at the shaft simply confirmed my fears. To get a replacement axe would take three days – one down to Base Camp and two back up. Perfect weather would be wasted. But axes can be swapped between climbers, and seconding with an adze surely couldn't be too difficult? The dither was short, the result decisive. On we went.

Snaking up left we headed for the start of the huge ramp line cleaving the North-West Face. Apart from the adze angle being perfect for slicing ice chips down his neck, Steve was flowing quickly up the short awkward steps that we came across. I kept well clear in case he suggested swapping tools. Eventually, steeper steps were called for and out came the ropes. After a total of eight weeks' climbing in India I was about to start my first roped pitches!

Soon the ramp opened out above us and we could see more definitely what was involved. I had been concerned that it could be powder snow intermittently plastered on to steep granite slabs, but from this angle it looked at least to have a thin snow covering most of the way up. The only real gap came in the first section and fortunately this fell to Steve. The broken axe was duly swapped and with two picks Steve climbed rapidly to where the ice petered out, whilst I wondered how I was supposed to climb the eighty-degree ground with only one pick.

A long tension traverse to the right saw him gain a very thin ice streak dribbling off the edge of the ramp. This looked hard to me but whoops of joy from above suggested good ice and Steve was soon re-established on the main ramp line. My efforts were less controlled. A crampon-screeching out-of-control pendulum left me dangling on smooth walls somewhere near the ice streak, and it took some furious scrabbling to make an axe placement and gain the streak.

The ice here was indeed of styrofoam quality but Steve's enthusiasm had masked the fact that it was only five centimetres or so thick. I thrashed wildly about with the pick and adze. In fact the adze worked remarkably well, the main problem being that it was best to flick the corner into the ice, which enabled me to have my turn at experiencing the joys of ice chips directly down the neck. Somewhat disgruntled by this, I arrived at the stance to be greeted by still more enthusing on Steve's part.

I was still concerned about the snow above. Although it was six or seven centimetres thick, the layer of ice beneath it was by no means constant and it was clear that at least some scrabbling on seventy-degree slabs would be necessary. Steve though seemed not to be at all concerned.

'More challenge, Michael. Just the way we like it.'

I wasn't so sure but at least a fortuitous line of flakes on the wall above looked likely to provide a reasonably comfortable night, although no chance of pitching our tiny two-man tent. Instead I wrapped myself in the tent fabric while Steve buried himself inside his bivi bag. This was to become standard practice at bivouacs.

It was time to dig into our mountain food. The question of what to eat on a multi-day mountain route seems impossible to solve definitively. Weight-saving usually wins out over taste-bud titillation. Prior to this trip I had made do with a standard diet comprising half a Toffee Crisp bar for breakfast, the remaining half, together with a boiled sweet, for lunch and evening meals alternating between salami and cheese and dehydrated food. I can't say that I was ever strongly of the view that this diet was nutritionally supreme or particularly right for me. I stuck with it simply because I can't claim to be particularly adventurous in such matters and it had certainly got me by in the past.

Steve was a packet babyfood fan. 'Ideal for mountaineers,' he had told me back in England. 'Easy to digest and full of nutritional value.'

'What's in it, then?' I had enquired.

'Not sure really. Mashed-up rusks I expect.'

I wasn't really convinced but a change is as good as a rest. Normally Steve stocks up on such things in England. This time we chose to take advantage of the 'we sell everything' supermarkets in Delhi. The resultant dish was not exactly inspiring.

'What have you done to it?' enquired Steve.

'Mixed it up using my best Cordon Bleu skills. What do you think I've done to it?'

'Difficult to say.'

We sat quietly trying to digest the lumpy mixture and contemplating the days ahead when this stuff was to form the majority of our food intake. Steve's efforts at breakfast proved marginally better but there was still plenty of room for improvement. Those with more refined culinary tastes would doubtless have instigated an immediate retreat.

Above us the ramp stretched away towards a sharp col on the North Buttress. There was clearly no reasonable bivouac site below the col and so our aim had to be to reach it, come what may. The distance involved looked to be about 250 metres: 180 metres of sixty-five- to seventy-five-degrees slabby ground topped by a seventy-metre vertical and overhanging section.

From my photographs taken on the 1989 trip I knew that the thickness of the ice on this upper section was particularly suspect. Photos from that year show sections of what look like thick black verglas with numerous small embedded stones. This year the spell of bad weather meant that everything was plastered in powder snow, although a curious speckled appearance visible from the glacier had me worried. On closer acquaintance this turned out to be the rippled nature of the underlying rock which was exposed through the new snow in a fascinatingly regular pattern. It did not look at all easy and seemed an area pregnant with serious and time-consuming difficulty. Progress was unnerving but steady. A fault line in the back of the corner provided intermittent protection possibilities and gave us sufficient confidence to venture out on to the protectionless sections of thin brittle ice on the slabs. By alternating the leads – and the axe – we reached the steep section below the col at 3 p.m. Three and a half hours of daylight left to climb seventy metres.

I started to get that uncomfortable we-are-about-to-get-benighted feeling. A couple of possibilities presented themselves but, after a time-wasting grovel in an overhanging chimney of surprisingly rotten rock, a steep rocky groove line, followed by a traverse back into the main corner, seemed the only option. Being a north-west face there had been virtually no freeze-thaw since the bad weather and powder snow was blasted into every crack, pouring past me in a continuous sprindrift flow as Steve fought to clear vital holds. Even with them readily visible it was a hard pitch to second. I was suitably impressed, both with the difficulty and with Steve for having led the pitch with no gloves. It is amazing how a good boost of adrenalin can warm the extremities.

It was now 5 p.m. and we were still over thirty metres from the col with only about one and a half hours of daylight left. The ground above looked steep. An initial thrash in a short overhanging corner convinced me that my sack was far too heavy for this type of action. I blamed the weight on Steve's propensity for bringing vast quantities of babyfood. He reckoned there was nothing wrong except for my being feeble and unable to control the sack.

Either way I felt a new man on leaving the sack hanging from a sling. Superb back-and-foot climbing and bridging on loose overhanging ground led to a capstone forming the final obstacle before the col. A direct ascent was out of the question but a tenuous line of holds up a gently overhanging wall to the right seemed to offer a possible solution. Efforts to emulate a Dover-style drive-in ice-screw placement by hammering one straight into the rock proved unhelpful. The rock merely disintegrated into thousands of granules. Steve looked concerned – a first – and encouraged me not to fall off. I didn't intend to and searched studiously for more protection. A Lost Arrow peg driven halfway into a more solid crack in the side wall was not bomb-proof but an awful lot better than nothing. From here the rock looked better out to the right and offered a traverse on some loose flaky holds. Then I needed somehow to surmount a gently overhanging section to reach what looked to be a good hold and possible resting place level with the capstone. Such plans rarely work out as imagined. The traverse of the flakes went well but the angle proved steeper than expected and I was badly in need of a rest by the time I reached the foot of the overhanging section. No problem, a good sky-hook placement presented itself. I reached down to pull it up from my harness-crutch karabiner.

'Shit.'

Steve looked worried. So was I. I had failed to make allowance for the incompetence factor. It is easy to remember things in retrospect but in a burst of organisation earlier on the route I had tied the sky-hook on to the back of my harness to stop it from getting tangled with other equipment. Now strength was fast draining from my naturally weedy arms as I fought to extricate it from its invisible position. Sod's Law dictates that tangles will occur in such situations and sure enough the knot on the sky-hook sling had somehow become inextricably tangled in my harness. An alternative course of action was called for. Up to my right a thin ice smear adorned the overhanging wall. A hopeful axe placement had surprisingly positive results. In such situations it is all too easy to ruin a good placement by trying for an even better one.

The axe had definitely 'twanged' in. Time was running out and failing strength meant that options were severely limited. Gently and unavoidably I clipped in and trusted my weight to the axe. So far so good. But although my new position reduced the physical strain it was hardly mentally relaxing. Less than a quarter of an inch of the pick was biting and any movement resulted in worrisome pivoting. Carefully I untangled the sky-hook and transferred to a hook placement over a solid edge on my left. A poor peg placement relieved the immediate tension but the darkness was almost total as I pulled across on to steep ice above the capstone and then floundered up bottomless powder to the col. It was snowing.

There was a much discussed possibility that this would be a good site for the tent – it looked to be the only one on the route – but the reality was an outrageous knife-edge of featherlight powder. In the last rays of light I swung up to a good peg belay. Two problems now presented themselves as I struggled to haul up my sack and belay Steve. First, in my panic I had put runners on both ropes and had no free rope with which I could haul the sack. Second, my head torch was in my sack. This latter point soon became a real problem. Steve could unclip the runners to enable me to haul but I was unable to pull the sack up in one go and had to keep tying it off to the belay. In the darkness though I dared not unclip anything and so the belay krabs rapidly grew impressive and totally confusing bunches of knots while I became worryingly cold.

It was 9 p.m. by the time the sack and Steve were safely at the col and 11 p.m. before we were able to struggle into sleeping-bags and begin to warm up again. I ended up hunched on a small step scooped out of the snow while Steve opted for slicing the top off the crest of the col and sleeping on the cornice suspended over the North-East Face. Steve was feeling talkative as we waited interminably for the stove to melt sufficient powder snow for a brew.

'Great climbing, isn't it? I'd say it's probably been the most enjoyable Himalayan route I've been on. And of course there looks to be lots of good action still to come. How does it compare with Spantik?'

I fought to avoid going to sleep. How could he possibly sound so perky after two such exhausting days' climbing? The man was clearly in his element. Personally I had a splitting headache and

could think of little else other than where I might have put the
painkillers. I tried to converse sensibly but somehow could do little
more than stay awake. How did it compare to Spantik anyway?
Certainly the last pitch to the col had been more difficult technically
than anything on Spantik but then Spantik was higher and arguably
more serious. I wasn't feeling very talkative, however, and avoided
the question.

'In retrospect I'm sure they will be equally enjoyable. How's the
babyfood coming on?'

By the time I hauled the forgettably bland evening meal of
babyfood and water up the length of rope connecting us I was all
but asleep. Comfort is irrelevant if the body is tired enough.

The next morning was our laziest start time – 8.30 a.m. Our
intended line moved round on to the North-East Face which we
had not been able to study closely before. We knew it to be largely
a snow and ice face but from the col it appeared to be set at a
distressingly steep angle. Also from this position it was obviously
guarded by a terrifying pitch of powder snow stuck on steep slabs.
Steve set off. By now I was beginning to appreciate that this sort of
ground is one of his fortes. Although the slabs were set at perhaps
sixty-five to seventy degrees, powder snow nearly a metre deep had
somehow accumulated. I had only ever seen such conditions in Peru.
Steve was persistent and methodical, sweeping away the snow and
then balancing up with his crampon points grating noisily on the
tiny rugosities on the granite slabs. Protection was very limited and
I think I must have been as relieved as he when after two hours of
continuous effort he reached a solid ice smear, belayed and brought
me across. More conventional but very steep ice ground followed
leading in 200 metres to a point beneath vertical walls rearing up
for the final 250 metres to the summit. A possibility of outflanking
these walls to the left presented itself but, having spotted areas of
very deep-looking powder snow set at a steep angle, a unanimous
decision was made to opt for a rising fault line leading back right
to the crest of the North Spur. Hard free and aid climbing were the
order of the day with my rucksack again being abandoned mid-pitch.
This time though, with sky-hook ready for action and Steve with his
étriers out, our progress was more efficient. Half an hour after sunset
we were hacking two single-person ledges out of a fortuitous small
snow slope. Placing the belay pegs my hammer head – which had
been loose for the last day and a half – finally parted company with

the main body of the tool. The soft alloy structure of the casting would suffice for a few peg removals but would not stand up to any prolonged heavy use. At least we had one hammer and one adze still in good working order.

One surprise remained for us before settling down to an evening's cooking. Just to one side of the bivi site was a blue sling. We knew that Andy Perkins and Brendan Murphy had reached a highpoint somewhere near here via the North-West Face in 1991 but to find one of their abseil slings gave us a better idea of our position and opened up the possibility of using their abseil points to facilitate our descent. This became increasingly appealing as we surveyed our equipment and contemplated the number of abseils necessary.

The summit was now only about 200 metres above us and we decided the time had come to leave our tent and sleeping-bags and go lightweight for the top. I must admit to being a little cautious about this. The ground ahead looked extremely difficult and the chances of yet another benightment seemed fairly good. Steve was persuasive though, pointing out that even if we failed to climb and abseil in the dark we could always sit it out and avert frostbite by wiggling our toes in each other's armpits. If it was good enough for Doug Scott and Dougal Haston near the summit of Everest, he felt sure it was good enough for us. What could I say? I was convinced. The lightweight push was on, with an added incentive to get back down to our bivouac site. An awkward snow-covered rock pitch with a challenging little wall led to another sling and what appeared to be the Perkins and Murphy highpoint. So close, yet so far. To fail so close to the summit must have been unbelievably frustrating. I even felt a little bit sad for them.

Above us reared a just-off vertical corner smeared with a thin coating of ice and leading to an ice-choked overhanging crack at fifty metres. Beyond this nothing could be seen other than that it was at least another fifty metres of very steep ground to the summit. Time was ticking by and I felt more and more that an uncomfortable night with Steve's toes was in store. The corner was my lead. The ice mainly formed an eggshell-like structure about three centimetres away from the rock. Frightening to climb on but just strong enough to take my weight and allow fast progress. As luck would have it protection turned out to be reasonable in those spots where I chipped the ice away. The final steep disintegrating bulge was avoided by aiding a crack in the right wall and I was belayed beneath Steve's pitch, a real nasty with no obvious protection and insufficient ice.

Steve looked worried. It was the first time on the route that I had seen him look properly worried. Most people who look this way start searching for alternatives, offer the lead to someone else or suggest going down. There were no alternatives and a very limited number of other people to whom he could offer the lead. I need not have worried – Steve is made of sterner stuff. He is after all the man who once insisted on taking his turn to swim out to an Irish Sea stack in a storm when he can't actually swim. What followed was an education for bumbly aid climbers such as myself: aid from tied-off ice-screws; an inverted peg behind a loose flake; Friends between rock and ice, and finally étriers on ice-axe placements. On the final move the thin ribbon of ice fractured with an audible crack but the pick held. To try again for a more secure placement would risk splitting the ice and releasing the lower axe. A calculated risk was called for.

'Watch me.'

I did. With a louder crack the ice around the top axe split away. The fall was only a metre and a half but the strain came directly on to the pick of the lower axe. It held. It could just as easily have given way, as could the runners below. Not a scenario to dwell upon. A further attempt was called for but with the ice strip only five centimetres wide care had to be taken not to demolish the whole formation. To do so would render the pitch virtually unclimbable. I need not have worried. A gentle central placement, some thrashing with the étriers, and Steve was up – on the seventy-five-degree ice plastered in thirty centimetres of powder which was, relatively speaking, no problem. My seconding efforts were less elegant. Two heavy-handed central placements split the ice longitudinally just as Steve was congratulating me on getting over the difficult section. I ended up dangling free and could just about reach the remains of the ice, and joined with Steve in a form of combined pull-and-hold technique which ultimately landed a very heavy-breathing Fowler on the stance.

Only twenty-five metres above a small cornice overhung the face. The deepest powder snow yet on very hard ice led to the final breakthrough and a release from the cold and inhospitable face. Warm sun filtered down and a magnificent new panoramic view was spread out before us. A short section of easy snow ridge led to the summit and that indescribable sense of elation that somehow makes even the most masochistic climbs seem worthwhile. We stood formally and shook hands – it seemed a suitably British thing to do, particularly for an American.

Including the 1989 fiasco, I'd spent ten weeks of my life trying to climb this mountain: ten weeks in India and only four days of upward climbing above the bergschrund. On this trip alone we had spent more time in Delhi dealing with the bureaucracy than on the face. Was it worth it? Strangely we concluded that it was. Mountaineering is like that.

Sitting down on the summit we took time to relax and admire the view. Inevitably the conversation turned to possibilities for the future. Before us spread unclimbed peaks in Kishtwar, unclimbed peaks in Ladakh, unclimbed peaks in Spiti. Further afield the peaks of Tibet glistened in the distance.

'Michael, there is a lot to do in the world.'

We sat silent for a few moments, each with his own thoughts. I contemplated beyond the horizon. Somewhere to the north-west were Spantik and Bojohagur; way away to the east was Taulliraju. Other areas that I had climbed in sprang to mind: Kilimanjaro in Africa; the arid wadis of Jordan in the Middle East; the extensive ranges in the ex-USSR, ranging from the Caucasus through the Turkestan ranges up to the Altai in Siberia. All these places were out there beyond the horizon and packed full of possibilities. And what about the places I had not been to? The Alaskan ranges, the Tien Shan, Antarctica, Patagonia, Baffin. The more I climb, the more I find there are more and more inspiring things to do. And of course, what about the possibilities in Britain? Unclimbed sea stacks and virgin sea cliffs still boast magnificent lines and cold winters bring into condition a whole host of worrying possibilities throughout Scotland, Wales and the Lake District.

'Time to start the bit we don't like.'

Steve brought me back to reality. Abseiling is not my favourite pastime. Some people make a sport of it and do it to the exclusion of all else. Not us though. We had spoken about this on the ascent and knew we shared a distaste for putting so much faith in one or two pieces of equipment. Stephen looked around as I placed the first abseil peg. He had clearly been lost deep in thoughts similar to mine.

'What about our next challenge, Michael?'

The single anchor peg was in a flared crack. I hammered it hard, keen to make life as safe as possible. With the final blow the whole head section of our remaining good hammer parted company from the shaft.

'Stephen, we have a challenge *now*.'

'Michael, without the challenge posed by uncertainty, life would be boring indeed.'

I pondered for a moment.

'Philosophical, Stephen – but true.'

Index

Abbreviations: MF = Mick Fowler; f.a. = first ascent;
map entries are in italic

224 Vertical Pleasure

Todd, Henry 93
Torridon 96, 99, 101
Tremadoc 27, 28–9, 31, 35
Troutdale Introductory (Black Crag) 17–18
Tsa, Aiguille de la 19
Tullis, Julie 22–3
Tullis, Terry 22
Tunbridge Wells 13, 22
Tunstall, Duncan 88, 195
Tusk Pinnacle (Swanage) 173
TV AM 101

Udaipur 202, 203
Ullapool 97, 99, 169
Umasi La 202, 206
Umbrella Fall (Liathach) f.a. 99
Under Rockes (Tunbridge Wells) 25
Ultar massif 128–9, 134, 135; nullah 136
Upper Girdle (Ben Eighe) f.a. 99

Valkyrie (The Roaches) 30
Vaynol Arms, Nant Peris 29
Vector (Tremadoc) 31
Vember (Clogwyn Du'r Arddu) 30, 31
Venables, Stephen 145, 207
Vietoris, Sonja 93

Walker Spur, Grandes Jorasses 107
Waterpipe Gully (Cuillin Ridge) 94
Watts, Chris
   at Dover 79–84; on Scottish weekends 85–9, 93,

97; f.a. Against All Odds 89–90; f.a. White
Wedding 96; f.a. Test Department 99; f.a.
Upper Girdle 99; f.a. Pipped at the Post 100;
f.a. St Pancras station drainpipe 101, 103–4;
on Taulliraju 109, 111, 116, 118, 119; f.a.
120–24; on Bojohagur 137; night plummet
140; 141–3; 147, 177
Wembley 22, 24, 27–8, 62, 66, 194
West Central Gully (Ben Eighe) f.a. 99
Whillans, Don 29
White Wedding (Cuillin Ridge) f.a. 96
Whiten Head (Sutherland) 170
Wick 187–8
Willa Park (Tintagel) 50
Willis, M. 178
Wine Bottle (Swanage), see Tusk Pinnacle
winter climbing
   in Scotland 87–97, 99–100; in N. Wales 91–2
Witch's Tit (Old Harry) 174–5
Wrecker's Slab (Cornakey Cliff) 44

Yakazina 157
Yarmouth (IOW) 177
Young, D. 178
Yungay 114, 115

Zangwill, John 109, 112, 116, 119
Zawa, Rajab (Spantik cook) 153–4
Zermatt 12, 19
Zmutt Ridge, Matterhorn 22
Zukator (Tremadoc) 31–2